THE BOY THROUGH THE AGES

LEAVING FOR SCHOOL.

B. Chardin

Photo Wolfrau

Fr.

THE BOY THROUGH THE AGES

BY

DOROTHY MARGARET STUART

AUTHOR OF

"BEASTS ROYAL" "HISTORICAL SONGS AND BALLADS"
"SWORD SONGS" "THE BOOK OF OTHER LANDS" ETC.

With Four Plates in Colours and 195 *Illustrations in the Text from
Museum Exhibits Manuscripts and other Contemporary Sources*

Fredonia Books
Amsterdam, The Netherlands

The Boy Through the Ages

by
Dorothy Margaret Stuart

ISBN: 1-58963-782-8

Copyright © 2002 by Fredonia Books

Fredonia Books
Amsterdam, The Netherlands
http://www.fredoniabooks.com

TO

MY FOUR BOY-FRIENDS

JOHN, PETER, RALPH, & ANTONY

PREFACE

THIS book has been written for the delight not only of child-readers, but of such of their elders as like and understand small boys. Its aim has been to present a vivid and faithful picture of the daily life of the average boy from the epoch of the cave-dwellers to the middle of Queen Victoria's reign, and to trace, by the way, the evolution of the modern attitude toward children from that of the earlier and less sympathetic periods in history. Some place has been given to the ideas of theorists such as Sir Thomas Elyot, Dean Colet, Roger Ascham, James I and VI, and Thomas Day, to say nothing of those arch-swishers, King Solomon and Orbilius : but for the most part the attention is focused upon the boys themselves, their studies, their sports, and the colour which their lives took from their surroundings.

To make the chronicle more real and convincing, illustrations have been gathered together from many sources—from museum exhibits, ancient manuscripts, and portraits in private collections and in public galleries. Each of these does, in good truth, 'illustrate' some point or some episode in the accompanying text.

Interspersed among the prose sections will be found twelve poems of which all but two (*i.e.*, " The Bison " and " The First Falcon ") appeared in the pages of *Punch* under the title of " Boy-Songs." For permission to reprint those ten here my best thanks are due to the Proprietors of that journal.

In the footnotes to Chapter III I have indicated the translators to whom I am indebted for the English versions of Greek poetry there quoted. All the translations from Latin, French, and German originals in other parts of the book are my own.

In conclusion, I should like to express my gratitude to all those who have so kindly authorized the reproduction in these pages of the works of art of which they are the owners, the custodians, or the holders of the copyright. In particular I am indebted to the Trustees of the British Museum in respect of the many items under which the name of the Museum appears.

D. M. S.

CONTENTS

THE BOY THROUGH
THE AGES

CHAPTER I

Dawn

IN a low cave on the face of a steep limestone cliff we catch one of our earliest glimpses of the human boy in Europe.

The cliff, shagged with tight-clinging trees, walnuts, maples, and elms, rises above the little river Orneau, which flows into the greater river Meuse. In the dim grey dawn of time, long before men had begun to invent letters or write history, that low cave was the home of a family whose rough tools of flint and bone were discovered there, among the ashes of their earthen hearth, only forty years ago.

What were the boys of this family like, and what sort of life did they lead ? It is not very difficult to imagine, though the world in which they lived was a strange, unfriendly world, and different in its forms and colours from the world we know. Where there are now great oceans there were then dreary wastes of land : the Irish Sea and the North Sea were deep valleys through which mighty rivers flowed, while the thirsty deserts of Arabia were then green and pleasant places. A cruel husk of ice covered huge tracts of what is now Northern Europe ; and through the ravines and wildernesses of the chill, forlorn, and almost form-less continent wandered the mammoth-elephant, the woolly rhinoceros, the reindeer, the bison, and the cave-bear.

Peering from his home in the side of the limestone cliff sixty feet above the Orneau, the cave-boy would have glimpses of a rain-swept world full of terror and mystery. Inside the cave there was warmth, even when the days were bitter and brief, for the boy's father knew how to make fire, and there was plenty of wood to keep the hearth glowing. And inside the cave there would always be something to do ; flints to chip, the hides of reindeer and bison to scrape and stretch, and tools and toys to fashion roughly out of wood and bone.

What sort of people were they who squatted round the flaming, fuming logs ? They were as wild and queer and uncouth as the world in which they lived. Short of stature—few were above five feet in height—they walked with their knees a little bent, and their chins always tilted up. Their foreheads were very broad and very low, and a shelving ridge of bone overhung their eyes. Their jaws were tremendously heavy and powerful, and their arms were longer in proportion to their legs than the arms of a modern man. A thick fluff of hair clothed their stunted limbs.

As the formation of his palate and jaw made speech exceedingly difficult for the cave-man of the Meuse valley, he cannot have spoken much. Such language as he had would consist of a few simple and unmusical sounds, expressing simple feelings and necessities—joy, sorrow, hunger, anger, and fear. There was no chatting round the cave-hearth, no singing of songs, no retelling of ancient tribal legends of gods or men.

When the odd-looking son of this family was quite a little fellow he remained in the cave with his mother while the father went out to seek for food. This was found in many places—in the hives of the wild bees, in the nests of the birds—by the river-bed where cool watercresses grew, and in the gleaming shallows where fish might be caught between the hands.

Sometimes there would be great rejoicings in the cave, and the family would utter all the grunts and growls that meant delight.

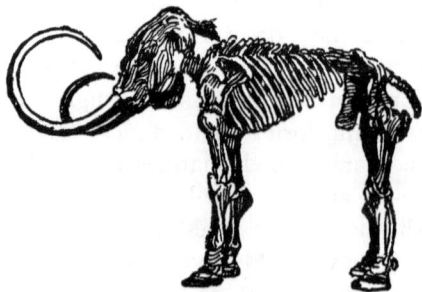

This happened when the hunters found some great beast, a mammoth, a bison, or a bear, caught in a trench they had dug, or in a bog where they could kill it with their stone axes, or else lying dead after a fight with some creature even stronger and fiercer than itself. Then there was much stirring and bustling in the cave. The flesh of the quarry would be roasted in the fire, and the boy would crack the bones to get at the marrow inside, splitting them lengthwise with a stone tool. The hide was scraped and smoked, and stretched out between stones, so that the family might have rugs and

SKELETON OF A MAMMOTH

cloaks of tough brown leather. The toys with which the boy
played, the tools which he learnt to use as he grew older, were all

A MAMMOTH
From a painting on a cave-wall

of wood or stone, for not till many thousands of years had passed
did the discovery of metals give new powers and new beauties to

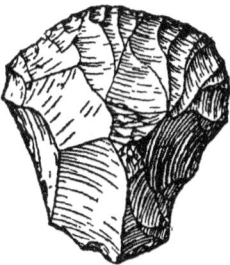

A FLINT SCRAPER

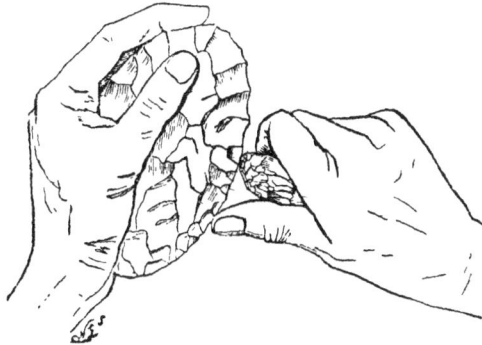

FLAKING FLINT BY PRESSURE
From *A Guide to the Antiquities of the Stone Age
in the British Museum*

the daily life of man. One of the first things he learnt was to
collect brushwood and fallen branches to keep the fire alive ; then
he would pick out from heaps of jagged blue-and-white flints

the sharpest and best-shaped, from which axe-heads and scrapers and javelin-tips could be made. He had tools of his own when he was strong enough to use them ; and they were laid beside him in the earth if he died before he grew from a cave boy to a cave-man.

His first great adventure befell when he went out with the men of the family in quest of the shaggy mammoth or the big brown bison which one of them had seen bogged or trapped somewhere within reach. Even a boy might help when they hurried to slay the monster with axe and battering-stone ; and he could also lend a hand when they hauled their prey back to the cave, where the hearth was piled up with spluttering faggots against their return. Reindeer were easier to kill, though harder to pursue.

(a) (b)

(a) FLINT TOOL RESEMBLING A
STONE AXE

(b) FLINT JAVELIN-HEAD IN
BRITISH MUSEUM

As the Fourth Ice Age closed down upon Europe, withering the tropical forests that had sprung up when the continent was moist and warm, the sun-loving animals turned to the sun and made for Africa, by way of the two great land-bridges—one where the straits of Gibraltar now lie, and one along the volcanic ridge of Sicily, which then linked the two continents. This dispersal and departure of the animal population continued for many years ; but at last only such shaggy beasts as could endure the cold remained, to be harried by man and by each other, while the sun grew fainter and more feeble in the cloud cumbered sky.

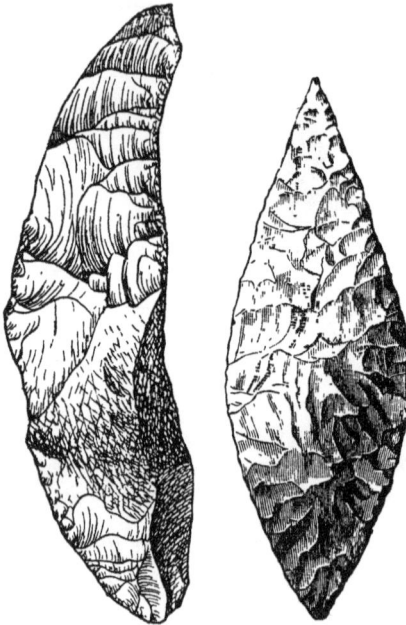

For the cave men it was a dreary existence, perilous and yet dull, with its circle of dim days and long nights, and its grinding,

14

spiritless struggle against seen and unseen foes.   For a long time
—perhaps as long as ten thousand years—this grey life lasted.
But slowly the great cloak of ice began to roll back toward the
North Pole during the last centuries of those ten thousand years,
and as the green grass followed the receding ice, another and
very different race of men came from some lost or forgotten
country in the south, following the green grass, and seeking

REINDEER
From the Cave of Font-de-Gaume, France

pasture for their flocks.   The day of the hunters was over when
the day of the herdsmen began.

Unlike the squat, heavy-jawed people of the caves by the
Meuse and the Rhine, the newcomers were tall and straight of
limb, and the form of their skulls was definitely human.   They
must have had a language—simple and limited, maybe, but still
a language worthy of the name ; one by which they could convey
to each other ideas more varied than the crude ideas of hunger,
anger, fear, and joy which the earlier cave-folk expressed by
hoarse grunting.

More interesting, and more varied too, would be the life led by the small boys of the race. Now, instead of lurking in the fumes of the cave or prowling furtively among the trees, these boys went out with the herds to pasture, and the many-coloured book of Nature, with all its quaint and beautiful pages, lay open before them.

Though these people were cave-dwellers, like the uncouth beings whom they blotted out, their homes in the cliff-side were not like the dark, rough lairs of the Orneau and the Rhine caves. At night they had a light other than the wavering firelight to keep out the terrors of the dark. In shallow stone bowls they burned the fat of the beasts they slew, and the flame of these rough lamps lit up pictures of those same beasts painted on their walls. The herdsmen were artists—the first artists in the history of the world. Not only did they paint pictures ; they cut outlines of bison and reindeer and horses on flat, smooth pieces of bone. The horse had not then been tamed, but in its savage state it was as valuable to the herdsmen for food and clothing as the mammoth and the other vanished beasts had been to the hunters.

A CHALK LAMP OF THE STONE AGE

British Museum

On the walls of caves in Spain and France the paintings of this time can still be seen in amazing vividness and vigour : paintings of wild horses galloping, bears blundering along, boars charging, bison halting, tail in air.

If the painter chanced to have a small son, his troughs of newly ground colours must have been a strong temptation to small

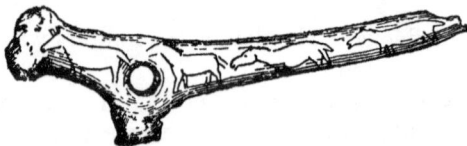

HORSES CARVED ON REINDEER-HORN

fingers. Sometimes a boy may have been allowed to help in grinding the oxides of iron and manganese ore from which the yellow, black, and red were obtained ; he could also scoop out a hollow bone, and stop it up at one end to hold the bright-hued powder. When the artist worked deep in the cave somebody

16

must have held the flaring stone lamp for him. That was the sort of thing a boy would love to do, not only because it would make him feel important, but also because he could then watch the painted beasts growing on the cave-wall under the artist's hand.

Whether the children of the herdsmen often wore clashing, glittering garments made of tiny shells pierced and threaded together we cannot be quite sure ; but it seems that they must have worn them sometimes in life, as such a garment was wrapped round more than one dead child before it was laid in the earth. A

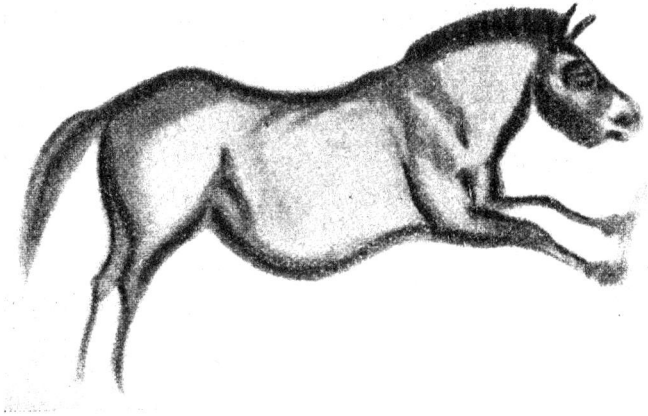

CAVE-PAINTING OF A HORSE

robe so brittle would hardly be appropriate for everyday wear ; but the herdsmen made up for their lack of woven attire by painting themselves with those same red and yellow pigments that their artists used to adorn the insides of their low-roofed homes in the steep flank of the cliff.

After another long lapse of time we can catch a glimpse of another prehistoric boy—a boy of the Stone Age still, but also of the Age of Bronze just beginning to dawn. Instead of living in a painted cave he had a most fascinating house raised on piles above the waters of a lake, and connected with the mainland only by a causeway. In appearance he was not unlike a modern European, except that his teeth met edge to edge, instead of the upper teeth overlapping the lower. He was tremendously far ahead of the first cave-boy, with the low forehead and the bent knees.

Our lake-boy happened to live in Switzerland, but about the same time other lake-boys were leading a life much like his in England and Ireland and Scotland—an amusing and adventurous life.

For several reasons this boy was far happier than even the later cave-children, with their painted walls and their robes of shells. His world was more interesting and less terrible, and his home

BISON
From the Cave of Font-de-Gaume, France
(See the poem at the end of this chapter)

was full of things that would have puzzled the cave-folk whose day was already remote in the mists of time. To live in a sort of nest above the rippling water was in itself delightful. When the boy began to observe what was happening round him he would sometimes see his father lift one of the planks of the flooring and let down a basket woven of twigs ; and then, presently, up would come the basket with a fish flopping and floundering inside. Meanwhile his mother would be busy plaiting another basket, or weaving a loose-meshed flaxen cloth, or grinding grain between two stones.

What were they like, his father and mother ? They were

quaint-looking, perhaps, but much more pleasant to behold than the relatives of the boy who dwelt by the Orneau. Their hair, which was thick and fuzzy. they wore fluffed up into big tufts, held in place by long pins of carved bone. Such of their garments as were not made of canvas were fashioned out of the hides of the red deer, the ox, and the goat. The great brown bison had not quite vanished from Europe then, but he was getting rare, and

RECONSTRUCTED VILLAGE OF LAKE-DWELLERS
From *Cave, Mound, and Lake Dwellers*, by Florence Holbrook (D C. Heath and Co)

the cave-bear did not often come down obligingly from his cave to the open ground by the lake where he could be more easily slain.

Round their necks the lake-people wore strings of coloured clay beads. Later, after men had discovered that tin and copper mixed together make a metal more useful than either, they had bracelets and rings of bronze as well. But for a long time their chief weapons and ornaments were of wood, horn, and stone.

When the lake-father went ashore he might take with him his flaxen net for snaring birds, his stone axe, and his bow with flint-tipped arrows. But, at certain seasons of the year, if he were not going a-hunting he took a wooden pole tipped with the horn of a red deer. By that sign the children knew that he was going to drive furrows in the earth by the lakeside, and that later he would sow seeds there, millet, barley, and wheat, so that later still there might be bread for them all.

When he was still a very little boy indeed the lake-boy's mother

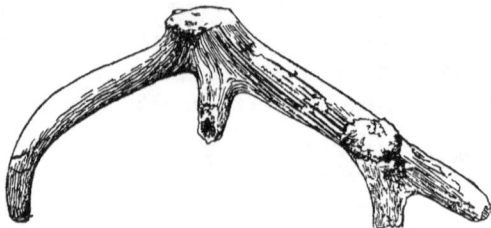

A STAGHORN USED FOR PLOUGHING
British Museum

kept him tethered by a cord round his ankle, in case he should tumble into the water while she was looking the other way. But there was plenty to amuse and interest him in the hut. At the farther end was the shed where the tame animals, oxen and goats, were stabled at night; round the wooden walls hung pottery jars and bowls, slung up by cords passed through the handles. If his tether allowed him to crawl far enough the boy would certainly try to get hold of the drum, made of leather stretched over an earthenware rim, or one of the bone whistles with which his father made music by the smoky light of the fire after darkness had crept down over the lake outside.

BRONZE AXE-HEAD FROM
SOUTH RUSSIA

From *A Guide to the Antiquities of the Bronze Age in the British Museum*

He had toys too, such as shapeless little birds moulded out of pink clay. After the discovery of metals he had tiny sickles and socketed axe-heads of bronze, formed just like the big ones that his elders used. The miniature bronze figures of men and women found in Italian tombs of the early Bronze Age may not have been intended for toys, but they look remarkably like them. With two such figures now in the British Museum any child could play games of make-believe. One is a little warrior with a club in his fist, the other a little lady with a high pointed cap, neither as much as three inches in height.

One of the reasons why the lake-boy was so much happier than the cave-boy may be found in the fact that animals, instead of being the dreaded foes or the stricken prey of man, might now be his servants and his friends. The curly-tusked mammoth, the two-horned rhinoceros, the sabre toothed tiger, had all disappeared, together with the people who had feared and yet pursued them. Bears and

A MOULD FOR A BRONZE AXE

bison still existed ; but, as we have seen, they were encountered less frequently. Great golden eagles that dwelt among the silver alpine peaks swooped down on a kid sometimes and bore it away ; but the kid was the companion of the human child now, as were the calf and the puppy. A change, and a happy change, from the old days of constant enmity between man and all the rest of creation !

As soon as the lake-boy was old enough he would be sent ashore with his elder brothers and sisters whenever the sun climbed above the white mountains beyond the lake : with them went the herds. The patient oxen and the restless goats would graze along the shore till sunset, watched by the chil-

TINY FIGURES OF A WARRIOR AND A LADY
From Italian tombs of the Stone Age
British Museum

dren, but never out of the sight of the elders in the huts.

So long as they did not allow the flocks to wander away the task of the little herdsmen was not a hard one, and left them plenty of time for play. There were blue flowers, cornflowers and flax, from which they could make garlands and posies. On the fringe of the woods above the grazing-ground there were crab-apple trees, whose fruit the lake-people loved to roast among the red ashes of the hearth.   Sometimes the bigger boys might be allowed to take a bone whistle or two with them, though the precious drum, heavy to carry and easy to break, might not be entrusted to any but ' grown-up ' arms.

If the father had a fancy to go fishing at the farther end of the

ANCIENT BRITISH DUG-OUT BOAT

lake he unmoored his canoe, scooped out of a tree-trunk with the rough bark left on, and paddled himself swiftly along.   It would be a wonderful day for the boy when he was allowed to climb aboard, and to take charge of the hooks and harpoons and the twig-woven basket. He must have glanced back with something like pity at the younger children left on shore to watch the nibbling flocks while he was borne along the lake before the dripping paddle-blade.   It was exciting too to help to drop the lines over the side of the canoe when it rocked at rest on the quiet water, and most exciting of all to pull them in when a bite was felt and put the catch into the twig basket.

Truly, he was a fortunate fellow compared with the cave-boy of the Meuse valley !   But as far beyond him as he was beyond the first cave-child stood the Bronze Age boy of Celtic Britain.

HARPOONS MADE OF BONE

The world into which the boy of the Bronze Age was born did not differ greatly from the world which we know now.   The island of Britain, where we will try to catch a glimpse of him, was much as it is to-day, except that masses of dense forest then covered what is now open country and there were beavers in the Thames, and bears and wolves lurked among the tangled growth of trees.

The Bronze Age boy of Britain was a Celt.   He belonged to a mysterious race whose way of thinking and living was far in advance of the ways of the original natives of Britain. Whence the Celts came neither they nor any man could tell. But now no longer did tribes and families drift about vaguely in search of pastures for their flocks, or herd together in blind ignorance of everything beyond the sky-line of their farthest march. This boy knew the seas that girdled his land on three sides did not mark the limits of the world, and that there were other lands and other seas far away. He had seen dark-haired merchants, chiefly Greeks from Marseilles, who came to trade with the dwellers on the western coasts of Britain, and to barter purple cloth and Sidonian glass for hides and tin ; he had heard of fierce, red-haired seamen beyond the mists of the North-east, who gave gold in exchange for British bronze. He had seen Gaulish traders too, and he may have had kinsmen fighting in the Gaulish ranks across the channel against the oncoming hosts of Rome. A Roman he had never seen ; but he knew that Rome was the name of a mighty power, and that the shadow of her might was moving slowly and surely westward toward the isle of Britain.

In the groups of people among whom our Celtic boy spent his

BRONZE DISC FOUND IN IRELAND
Probably used in connection with sun-worship
British Museum

GOLD ARMLET FROM
COUNTY CORK
British Museum

youth there were many different types and crafts and callings. The time was already long past when the father of each family was his own potter, carpenter, leather-dresser, herdsman, and fisherman. Men had now their separate tasks ; and with the coming of bronze came unimagined wonders of craftsmanship, new

23

splendours for the chiefs, and new outlets for the skill of the craftsman.

As yet there were no cities in Britain nor even towns. But large villages were springing up, formed of groups of beehive-

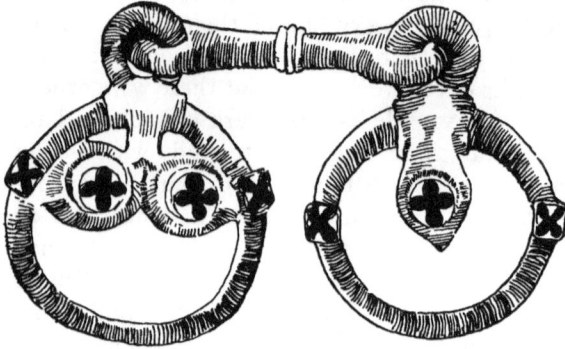

BRONZE AND ENAMEL BRIDLE BIT

shaped houses built for the most part of turf, though sometimes of wattles, wood, or stone. The Celtic boy opened the eyes of his mind on a world where religion and poetry illuminated the spiritual life of man, and where the instinct for beauty had touched his labours of every day. Then his pots and bowls,

STONEHENGE
Photo Frith

his swords, bracelets, and shields were all, in their own way, marvellously beautiful.

The great event of his childhood would be a journey with his father and mother to one of the mighty temples, of which the mightiest is still standing. Travellers approaching Stonehenge from the south came most of the way by water, along the river

Avon, then much deeper and wider, to the ford, whence a broad
straight road had been cut to the temple.   Other pilgrims came
by land, and when the day of a solemn festival drew near every
path and track was thronged with people, some plodding on
foot, some in chariots or on horseback.   A British chieftain was
a vision of splendour when he went forth to fight or to worship,
a torque of twisted gold about his throat, his leaf-shaped bronze
sword with its richly enamelled hilt swinging at his side, and the

RECONSTRUCTION OF STONEHENGE

collars of his horses laid over with thinly hammered plates of
pure gold.

Some of the wayfarers were piously inclined ; others were bent
on trading with the merchants who gathered under the very
shadow of the stone circle.   Others, again, were interested in
nothing more serious than the chariot-races which always took
place when the religious ceremonies were held.

The two great circles of upright stones with their cross-stones,
and the two inner horseshoe-shaped circles, formed not only the
most awe-inspiring place of worship in ancient Britain, but also
a sort of sacred ground where merchants might bring their wares
unafraid, and potters and flint-chippers might ply their craft
among the crowds of divers races drawn, as if by invisible cords,
to the wide plain where the temple arose.

Legend said that the inner circles, of a different colour from the
rest, had been brought by giants from some magic land beyond
the western foam.   The young Celt would be taught to look upon
a journey to such a spot as a high and holy adventure, and to

regard with almost breathless awe the white-robed priests who offered sacrifices there to the glory of the midsummer sun.

The most exciting festivals took place at intervals of four years, and were enlivened by chariot-races along the course, a mile and a half in length, that lay a little to the north-east of the temple itself. If the boy's father were a great man among the Britons it might be the boy's good fortune to stand on the raised mound at the eastern end of the track, where the judges and chieftains stood, and where he could see the start and the finish of each race. At the western end there was a loop which the chariots had to turn before they came hammering and swaying back to the starting-point. This may have been a more thrilling corner for the younger spectators, because the charioteers would all be trying to shorten the course by getting on the inside of the track at the turn, and there would be crashes and spills, and the chariot that leapt ahead on the straight would almost certainly prove victorious.

The less adventurously minded boys may have been more stirred by the sight of the white-robed druids, and the strange, unearthly sound of their chanting in the purple chill that comes before dawn. For ten boys who dreamed of being charioteers there might be one who dreamed of being a druid when he was old enough. To be a pupil of the priests, to enter one of their great training-schools, meant a long and arduous education, lasting, perhaps, for twenty years ; but at the end of the time a thoughtful youth might look forward to joining their learned and powerful priesthood, to penetrating the silent mysteries of the stars, and to learning the unwritten lore of the invisible forces that rule the visible world. We have Julius Cæsar's word for it that the priests of Britain were accounted the most wise of all the Celtic priests. Persevering and indomitable they must certainly have been in their young days, for all their sacred knowledge was committed to memory, and handed down in spoken, but never in written, chronicles.

A British boy of the Bronze Age who dreamed neither of steering a chariot to victory nor of cutting the mistletoe with a golden sickle might linger among the booths of the merchants under the shadows of Stonehenge, and listen to their harsh jangle of talk, and wonder at the gold coins glinting in their palms—coins whose image and superscription told of great men and great cities very far from Britain, of Tyre and Sidon, Rome and Carthage, Philip of Macedon and Lysimachus of Thrace. The wares they bought and sold and bartered would interest any boy : red amber from the Baltic ; coloured glass beads and bottles from Phœnicia ; bars of tin ; bronze harness-ornaments set with coral ; brooches and bracelets of bronze gay with discs of translucent enamel, red and yellow and green. There were living wares too : gaunt, grey hounds, trained for the chase of the wolf or the wild-boar ; sturdy, shaggy little horses ; and sometimes slaves, captured in some raid on a northern tribe.

Men from the north seemed quaint fellows in the eyes of a south-country Celt. To the boy whose father brought him to see the mid-summer sun rise behind the solemn triliths of Stonehenge there was

THE GOLD STATER OF PHILIP
OF MACEDON

The ancient Britons imitated these coins some 200 years B C.

nothing strange or ridiculous in the sight of a man stained with the intense colour crushed from the woad-plant, for certain seasons and certain ceremonies were marked by this stain-ing of the skin with blue. But the northern tribesmen had pricked the colour into their bodies in curving and twining patterns, so that when they walked unclad they seemed to be wearing wonderful close-fitting garments embroidered with fan-tastic art.

When the festival was over, when the feet that had trampled the grassy slopes bare had plodded back whence they came, when the voices died down, and the shadows of the stones fell at sunset on the grey ashes and the grim stains of the sacrifice, what would the boy remember most clearly ? His mind would be thronged with jostling memories. But if he were a true boy he rejoiced above all things that he had seen with his own eyes the famous temple races of Stonehenge. He knew that the skill of the British team-drivers was known beyond Britain. Now he knew for himself just how they handled their triple yoke of half-wild little horses, how well they could judge just when to tighten their hold on the reins and let the lash swing idle, just when to shout aloud and make the lash whistle in the rushing air.

It may be that some of the very charioteers whom our Celtic boy watched so eagerly were among those that gathered on the

Kentish cliffs when Cæsar's fleet of eighty galleys cast anchor in the straits between Britain and Gaul. Other boys in other countries of the ancient world had loved to watch chariots ever since men had taught horses to draw them. But the British chariots stand apart. They broke the first shock of the Roman onslaught.

On the summit of the stark white cliffs the men in the Roman transports saw the British chariots jolting above the mass of people that were come forth to meet the menace that had loomed out of the heavy August haze. The creeping shadow of Rome had then touched the shore of Britain at last. The island would lie now within the realm of recorded history. Cæsar and Rome so willed it. The two legions, the Seventh and the Tenth, chosen for the task were in readiness. Their ships lay at anchor in the straits, and Cæsar's own galley, with its purple awning, lay near them. But a sudden summer storm delayed the eighteen transports that were to follow with the cavalry. And so it befell that in the first brush between the invaders and the defensive forces great consternation and confusion were caused among the Roman ranks by the reckless valour of the British charioteers. Not for nothing had the Britons held races at their great religious festivals. Their charioteers, whose skill had so often made the green slope beyond Stonehenge clang with shouting, went forth against Rome, and in the first clash checked and daunted even the Romans. But not for long. A greater force and a finer intelligence met and overthrew them. The Celtic boy who lived in the last years of the Bronze Age in Britain saw the ending of a vast, vague, and barbaric story, not devoid of poetry and splendour, but rough and mysterious as the stones of the British temples. And as he saw the legions marching inland from the Kentish coast he saw the beginning of the march of English history.

BRONZE MODEL OF ROMAN GALLEY PROW
British Museum

THE BISON

20,000 B.C.

WITH little twigs and big twigs, and branches bent and dry,
We feed the hollow, hungry fire, for if it dies, we die.
    Then turn, branch, turn,
      Throw up a merry spark,
    Burn, you spluttering branches, burn—
      Outside it is dark.

My father goes a-hunting before the light begins,
And I, I chip the sharp grey stones that tip his javelins.
    Then clink, flint, clink,
      And clank, flint, clank,
    That when the bison stoops to drink
      You may pierce his flank !

When I saw the bison I did not stop to see
What the bison would do next, or whether *he* saw *me* ;
    It was run, feet, run,
      And climb, feet, climb—
    Or never had I seen the sun
      Rise up another time.

But when the bison stumbles in mud and cannot rise
We run with big stone axes then, and slay him where he lies
    Then, 'tis crack, arms, crack,
      And strain, wrists, strain—
    And so we haul the bison back,
      The bison we have slain.

We roast the mighty bison, we break his marrow-bone ;
My mother takes his thick brown hide and scrapes it with a stone.
    Then 'tis smoke, flame, smoke,
      Upon the thick brown hide,
    That we may have a rug and cloak
      When it is cold outside.

With straight twigs and bent twigs and clods of leafy earth
We feed that brother of the sun who dwells upon our hearth ;
    Then give, hearth, give
      Your flickering yellow light,
    For only if you live we live—
      And outside it is night.

CHAPTER II

In Ancient Egypt

AT the thrill of pipes and the throb of marching feet what town-born boy would not run to the nearest window? These sounds were heard often in the streets of Thebes, and the small Thebans would lay aside even their best-loved toys to listen. The city lay on the east bank of the Nile, on a broad plain at the foot of a range of gaunt, precipitous mountains; like a carpet of a thousand hues it lay, quivering with light and music and colour; but silence and shadow brooded over the cliffs and in the desolate ravine which cleft them—the Valley of the Tombs of the Kings.

The houses and temples of Thebes were painted gaily; and the

THE DOUBLE PIPES BEING PLAYED BY A FOX
From a papyrus in the British Museum

sun-smitten streets were seldom silent for long. But when a Theban boy caught the far-off voices of the double pipes he had no window to which he could run. His father's house was built round a courtyard, and its outer wall was blank. There was a door, however, cut in the painted wall, with a column at either side, and an oval tablet on each column bearing the owner's name, and a ledge at the top from which brilliant streamers were hung on days of rejoicing. All the doors of Thebes were flutter-ing when the priests bore the images of the gods through the city, or when the Pharaoh returned in triumph from some arduous pursuit of Hittites or Assyrians.

The Egyptian boy, in this shining, humming city under the shadow of the silent limestone cliffs, led a life rich in delights, while his undreamed-of brother-boys in the North and the West still dwelt in a meagre and perilous fashion in desolate wildernesses, among fierce beasts and vaguely wandering tribes of men almost as fierce as they. He was a lightly built boy, but his brown limbs were tough and supple, and few heavier boys could have beaten him at running or wrestling, or games needing endurance and skill. Except upon occasions of ceremony his only garments were a girdle of leather or thread and a necklace, from which swung a golden charm or a tightly rolled talisman of papyrus. His black hair was twisted into a plait which dangled over one ear. When King Tutankhamen's tomb was opened there was found, among the numberless treasures and marvels in the outer chamber, a casket containing one of these little plaits of black hair, inscribed : " The side-lock which his Majesty wore when he was a boy."

PAPYRUS OF THE BOOK OF THE DEAD
British Museum

If a sound of marching or music drew a small Theban from his play in the shady garden of his father's house he left behind him, forgotten for the moment, a host of fascinating toys : lions and crocodiles with movable jaws that wagged and snapped ; a wooden baker who kneaded a lump of wooden dough with tremendous energy when a string was pulled ; balls made of plaited rushes or of leather stuffed with husks ; and little clay models of beasts and fruits. But if the procession happened to pass the ' House of Books,' where he went every day to school, he might not hope to have even a glimpse of it ; for the master of the House of Books was a stern master, and thought that a small boy was better employed learning to know one from another those

TOY LION WITH MOVABLE JAW
British Museum

quaint characters, shaped like hawks and eagles and serpents and reeds, in which the sacred records of the Egyptians were written.

" A boy's ears," the master would say, " are in his back," and it was with his cane that he strove to make his pupils listen and remember. After he had learnt to puzzle out the meaning of the written words, and to make others like them, the boy was given sheets of silky brown papyrus from which to copy legends of the gods and words of wisdom—such words as those of the philosopher Im-Hotep, who said, " With a smiling face let thy days be happy, and rest not therein," and, " Be not haughty because of thy knowledge ; wisdom is harder to find than the emerald." Addition and subtraction and a rough sort of multiplication table were all the arithmetic with which the small Theban had to grapple. He may have found it rather good sport to learn how to guess the area of a field, or how much corn could be stored in a granary of a given size ; for these things also he was taught. Writing was his stiffest task. He had to write on the fragile

c   33 inner fibres of the papyrus-reed, squeezed together with gum to make them smooth ; his pens were also reeds, thin and fine, crushed at the tips so that they seemed more like brushes than pens. His ink, of two colours, he kept in hollows scooped in a wooden tray—this tray being often held on the thumb as a painter holds his palette.

The Theban boy must have thought wistfully, as he struggled with his lessons, of the garden at home, with its close-set palms and pomegranates and figs, its tank full of rippling water, where the fish flickered to and fro and the pink lotus-lilies floated at rest.

STRANGE GODS OF EGYPT
Thoth, Set, Sekhet, and Ra
From *British Museum Guide to the Third and Fourth Egyptian Rooms*

He must have grown bewildered sometimes at the enormous number of gods and goddesses whose names he had to write down and to try not to forget : strange gods in the form of hawks, crocodiles, cats, hippopotami, dogs, bulls, and apes ; gods who sat in council with Osiris (Amen-Ra) and Isis, the Sun god and Moon-goddess, the greatest of all ; and a huge family of lesser gods, some of whom possessed neither power nor dignity except in the town where they were worshipped, or by the river where that town had sprung up. Yet through all the many-coloured mists and shadows of legend and fable there ran one clear and definite belief which the Egyptian boy grasped firmly while he still played round the carved and padded footstools of his father and mother : the belief that in the life after death every man must answer for his deeds in this world, and that when his spirit should be borne in the boat of the dead along the unseen river his good and evil actions would be weighed on scales as carefully as

34

Pharaoh's scribes weighed the corn-sacks in the granaries of Egypt.

Not all the stories that the boy wrote down in the House of Books were stories of the gods : many were fairy-tales as simple as *Jack the Giant-killer*. There was a tale of a sailor shipwrecked on a magic island where a talking serpent dwelt, a tale of a turquoise coronet lost by one of the girl-rowers of the royal barge

THE JUDGMENT OF OSIRIS

Showing Osiris seated on a throne and, before him, the scales on which the hearts of the dead were weighed

From a papyrus in the British Museum

and rescued by magic from the depths of the lake, and another of a very ancient wizard called Dedi, to whom King Khufu, the builder of the Great Pyramid, ordered that a thousand loaves, a hundred jugs of beer, an ox, and a hundred bunches of onions should be given every day as a reward for the wonderful tricks he had performed before him. This Dedi was brought to the royal presence by one of the princes whose name was Hordadef, and who had told his father of the marvellous feats which, rumour said, the old fellow could perform. Hordadef went in one of the royal boats to fetch him, and when Dedi was led into the presence of Khufu, the King said to him, " Why is it that I have never seen

35

you till to-day, Dedi?" Dedi replied: "Life, health, and strength to your Majesty! A man cannot come until he is told to come." Then Khufu asked: "Is it true, Dedi, that you can take a head which has been cut off and fix it on again?" "It is true, O King." Khufu promptly gave orders that a prisoner should be brought from the prison and his head lopped off. But Dedi seems to have been a little alarmed by this energetic proceeding, and exclaimed: O King, live for ever! Do not let us try this trick on a man. Let us rather try it on an animal." So the King ordered that a goose should be brought and its head be cut off and laid on the eastern side of the palace-hall while its body lay on the west. Then Dedi stood up, and uttered magical words of might. And the body of the goose came waddling to meet the head, and the head came to meet the body.

It must have made the Egyptian boy quite hungry to read about the thousand loaves with which Khufu rewarded Dedi for this feat and for other tricks which he performed before him! But he was never left hungry very long, for toward midday the boys were allowed a brief rest, and then his mother brought him a flat loaf of wheaten bread sprinkled with sesame-seeds or caraways, or a round biscuit newly dinted by the four fingers of the baker; with these she would not forget to bring a bright blue pottery jar full of cool barley-beer. If many Egyptian ladies resembled the Queen of King Akhnaton, whose portrait-bust is now in the Berlin Museum, the boy was not far wrong, perhaps, if he thought his mother very beautiful indeed. This Queen, with the long, slim throat, the kind, smiling mouth, the deep, pensive eyes, must have wished sometimes that one of the small boys in the House of Books were hers, for though she had four daughters she never had a son, and not one of the many gods of Egypt listened when she prayed for one.

The Theban boys had the advantage of knowing the ends of the fairy-tales of which only broken fragments have survived to our days. We should give much to hear what happened to the young prince who was the hero of this half-told tale. It begins, as so many others have begun since: "Once upon a time"—there was a King of Egypt who was sorrowful because he had no son. At last the gods hearkened to him, and sent him a baby boy; but the Fates who came to the cradle to foretell the future said that the boy should die either by a crocodile, a serpent, or a dog. The anxious King thereupon built a little house far away in the desert and sent his son there, with faithful servants to watch over him. One day, when the young prince was looking from the roof of the house, he saw a man walking along, with a dog running at his heels. " What animal is that," he asked the page who was beside him, " What animal is that following the man as he comes along

PORTRAIT-BUST OF NEFERT-ITI, QUEEN OF KING AKHNATON
Berlin Museum
Photo Mansell

the road'? " " It is a dog, O Prince." " Then you must get me one just like him," commanded the Prince. The alarmed page went and told the King. And the King said, very reluctantly no doubt, " Lest his heart be sorrowful, get a little dog and take it to him." So they brought him a puppy, and it grew as he grew.

When at last the boy had grown into manhood he became weary of his beautiful house in the desert, and sought his father's leave to set forth on his travels and see something of the world. His father had not the heart to deny him. So he set forth, with his faithful dog, and journeyed till he came to the land of Naharaina.

There he found a great company of young princes encamped round a high rock, on the top of which was a beautiful house with no less than seventy windows. When he questioned them they explained that in the house dwelt the daughter of the King of the country, and that she was to be given in marriage to whichever of them could climb up the rock to her window. When they questioned *him* he did not reveal his rank, but answered that he was the son of an Egyptian officer. Then, of course, he determined to try to climb the rock. And, of course, he succeeded. When the King of Naharaina heard that the successful climber was not of royal rank, he wanted to kill him. But the Princess seized the youth's hand and said, " If he dies, I also shall die." So they were married, and after a time the Prince took his bride back with him to Egypt. When he told her that it had been prophesied that he should be killed either by a serpent, a crocodile, or a dog she was very anxious that he should get rid of his faithful dog. But this the Prince would not do. One evening he fell asleep, and the Princess brought a bowl of milk and put it beside him in case he should feel thirsty when he woke. And presently she saw a great serpent creep out of its hole and move toward the sleeping man. But instead of killing its victim, the serpent began to drink the milk, and when it had drunk so much that it could not move, she killed it with her dagger. When her husband woke, she said to him : " Lo, the gods have given one of thy three dooms into my hand ; they will give me the others also."

It befell one day that the Prince went out for a walk, taking his dog with him. They came to the river Nile, and the dog went into the water, and the Prince followed. And then suddenly a great crocodile rose out of the river. . . .

There the story stops. We do not know how the Prince escaped from the crocodile and whether he also escaped from the third doom, as the Princess said that he would. But the little Theban boys knew. Did they not read the whole story, a small piece at a time, spelling it out, word by word, on the smooth, tawny papyrus-rolls in the House of Books ?

When lessons were done, the scholars came running and skipping out of school with loud cries of delight, and scampered home to their toys—their snapping lions, their tiny fishes and hedgehogs and cats and cows modelled in brilliant purple and blue pottery, and their wooden horses which could be pulled along the paved path of the garden by cords threaded through their square-hewn wooden noses.   If he were in luck our Theban boy might meet on his homeward way one of the processions whose distant music had disturbed him at his books.   It might be a pious procession, bearing a little image of a god in a boat-shaped shrine.   Perhaps one of the priests who strode along so solemnly, in a robe of finely pleated linen and a leopard-skin cloak

WOODEN HORSE ON WHEELS
British Museum

with a clasp in the form of a golden lion's head, was his own father.

Pageants of gods and their priests, of captives and chariots, were often seen in Thebes.   More rare, and much more thrilling, was the spectacle when the Pharaoh himself passed through the city on his way to worship at some many-coloured, many-columned temple.

Then the boy would see the divine ruler of Egypt standing, erect and impassive, in a gorgeous chariot inlaid with lapis lazuli and cornelian and malachite, draped in a stiff, dazzling robe embroidered with turquoise and gold, wearing peaked and rosetted golden sandals on his feet, and many rings of brilliant blue on his tawny fingers.   If the occasion were one of very great solemnity the Pharaoh might be crowned with the towering red and white diadem of Upper and Lower Egypt.   His arms would be crossed, and he would carry in one hand the crook-shaped sceptre, and in the other hand the *ankh*, the looped T-cross which was the Egyptian symbol of everlasting life.

39

THE TEMPLE OF HORUS AT EDFÛ

Always the sacred golden asp would rear itself upon his dusky forehead, and always a pointed and perfumed beard was fastened to his chin—that beard which no Pharaoh ever grew for himself, but which every Pharaoh wore to proclaim his kinship with the bearded Sun-god Amen-Rā. Against the tilt of the chariot would lean his walking-sticks, marvels of craftsmanship, some overlaid with pure gold, others of ebony with golden handles modelled in the form of cowering captives from Asia.

EGYPTIAN BOAT WITH FIGURE OF RĀ HOLDING AN ANKH

Herodotus, far-wandering, wonder-loving Herodotus, says that in Egypt a son was expected to follow the same calling as his father. This may sometimes have been true of the eldest sons of the priests, who formed a privileged class apart, and also of the children of the poor folk who toiled in the fields and the quarries, but it seems that most youths had a certain freedom of choice, especially in the higher classes, and might, according to their tastes and opportunities, follow the career of priest, scribe, or soldier.

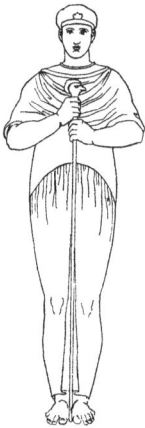

One of the most vivid fragments of Egyptian literature which have survived is a discourse written in the reign of Rameses II by a wise old Egyptian for the benefit of a boy-friend who had been dazzled by the splendour of Pharaoh's chariots, and dreamed of a military career. It was very natural that the boy should have been dazzled. The troops of the Egyptian army, whom he must have seen both when they were being trained in barracks and when they took part in triumphal pageants at the close of some arduous desert campaign, were a picturesque crowd. There were among them many men of other than Egyptian race—Sardinians, wearing horned helmets surmounted by globes; Etruscans, with high barrel-shaped headgear tilted queerly backward; dusky Nubians carrying clubs and bucklers; lighter-skinned Libyans who adorned their leather caps with gaily hued plumes. Each battalion had

A PRIEST OF EGYPT

41

its own standard, painted and gilt, and borne aloft on a pole. These standards were of many forms, and were tipped with images of boats, birds, wild beasts, human heads, and lotus-flowers. Like a forest of gilded saplings they swayed when the proud note of the military trumpet and the prolonged thunder of the drums called the troops of Pharaoh into the field.

But it was the chariotry that kindled the imagination of the boy. Pharaoh himself went forth to battle in a chariot. And the charioteer had most of the excitement of the fight, for he had not only to manage his two swift horses and manœuvre skilfully among the ranks of the foe; if the warrior, who stood

AN EGYPTIAN CHARIOT

with him in the chariot and shot with a great twanging bow, were hurt or hard pressed the charioteer could wind the reins round his waist and himself take a hand in the fray. The chariot was a thing of marvellous beauty, made of tough, shining wood strengthened with leather thongs and plates of metal, and decorated in gorgeous colours. It was so light that one man could carry it, and yet so strong that it would bear two men throughout the surge and stress of battle. At the side hung the bow-case and the quiver, the first pointing forward and the second back ; both were beautiful with figures of lions, and with fine inlaid work like a glorified draughtboard of black and scarlet, or blue and gold.

In the great battle at Kadesh between the Egyptians and the Hittites the Pharaoh owed his life to the courage and devotion of Menna, his charioteer. When the Hittites were scattered and broken the King called Menna before him, in the presence of all his captains, and taking the golden collar from his own neck he clasped it round the neck of his valiant charioteer.

Such stories did not reach our Theban boy through his ears only. On the walls of tombs and temples, on pillars and obelisks, on grim cliffs frowning above the desert, scenes of battle were painted and hewn—scenes where the Pharaoh and his chariot loomed huge and menacing over falling and fleeing enemies dwarfed to the proportions of sheep or hares. Then the boy had also seen trudging trails of captives, Hittites wearing thick-

ROCK SCULPTURE
Seti I returning with captives from Syria
From the Temple at Luxor

soled upturned boots, and carrying wicker shields ; Hebrews with hooked noses and shaggy beards ; Assyrians, broad-built with curled and oiled locks ; Bactrians, Scythians, and Syrians, all outlandish-looking, dejected, and branded with defeat. For a long time after such Egyptian victories men from the conquered territories would appear at intervals in the streets of Thebes, bearing tribute to the conqueror, staggering under jars of gold and baskets of silver, and bundles of lions' and leopards' hides, and stacks of elephants' tusks, or else leading on leashes half-tamed panthers and mischievous apes and frightened gazelles.

A stirring career, truly, to go forth in the low-hung, lightly bouncing chariot behind two almost wild horses decked with coloured linen cloths and nodding plumes, to grasp the quivering

reins and make the double lash on the whip flicker and snap, to
dash into the midst of Pharaoh's foes, those foes that always
looked so small, and foolish, and alarmed on the carven cliffs,
and then to steer so skilfully that the bowman at your side could
pierce an enemy with every whistling arrow that flew from his
five-foot bow !

So thought a certain boy in Thebes, more than three thousand
years ago. But his wise old friend, who had himself served in
the army and knew that battle-scenes in art are not always much
like battles in reality, counselled him to put aside his dream of

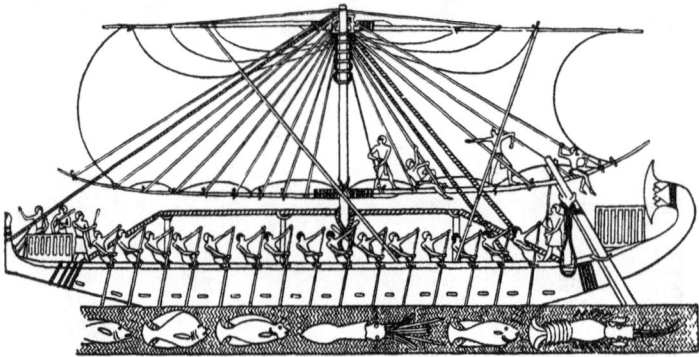

EGYPTIAN SHIP
From a bas-relief at Dêr-el-Bahari

entering the royal training-school for charioteers, and follow the
peaceful calling of a scribe instead. A scribe might remain
quietly at home, and wear his stiff linen kilt with its fringed sash
of gold, and carry his long staff to give sharp taps to any under-
lings who did not at once obey his lightest word. When ships
from Tyre and the Greek islands dropped anchor in the Nile the
scribe went on board, with his curled wig and his dangling pen-
case, to examine the cargo and collect Pharaoh's taxes. When
the great tombs and temples were being built it was he who
watched the progress of the work, saw that the blocks of stone
were truly numbered, and paid the workmen their wages. He
also went round, followed by an attendant with a pair of scales,
checking and noting down the weights of bushels of grain and
bales of flax, and making sure that the rings of gold and silver
used as currency instead of minted coins were pure metal and
not too light.

All records of law and commerce were kept by him. Often he rose to be a judge, or an officer in the household of the King. If he had wit and a touch of creative imagination he might write of matters less dull than grain-sacks ; he might—and very often did—write romances and poems and fairy-tales, and chronicles of the deeds of great men. When his hour came to pass in spirit to the Hall of Truth in the Temple of Osiris, he did not gasp out his life in some stark ravine or on some furrowed, thirsty stretch of desert, as all too many of the charioteers did. The scribe died

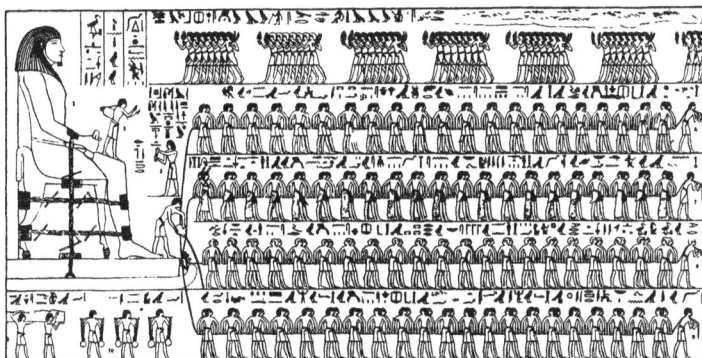

TRANSPORTING A HUGE STONE MONUMENT FROM THE QUARRY
From a wall-painting at El Bersheh. 172 men are employed in hauling the colossus, in addition to overseers and other workmen
From *Ancient Egypt*, by Sir J. G. Wilkinson

in his own house, on his bed of polished wood and netted cords, with its soft cushions covered with linen, purple, brown, or blue, and its crescent-shaped head-rest of blue-painted alabaster or shining sycamore.

Of all these things the Egyptian boy would be gravely reminded by his elders when his eyes turned wistfully to the chariots of Pharaoh. Whether he heeded such reminders depended very much upon his character. If he were a born fighter, with the ardour of battle in his blood, he would listen respectfully to his shaven and bewigged advisers, and stand before them with his head bent so low that his little plait fell forward and swung free ; but all the time the sound of the chariots would haunt his memory. A lazy boy, however, the sort of boy who liked better to fish with a line in the garden-tank than to go out fishing with nets and spears in a reed-woven boat, probably looked

45

forward quite cheerfully to being a priest or a scribe when he grew up, and was well content to leave the hardships and glories of military service to his more energetic playmates.

From his earliest childhood the young Theban had many opportunities of hearing the talk and studying the manners of his elders. When his father and mother invited their friends to a banquet the son of the house was often allowed to be present. Sometimes he sat at the feet of his mother, a beautiful figure in her dress of delicately tinted and pleated linen, her tightly curled, dark-brown wig, and her bracelets and necklaces of lapis and turquoise and gold. When he was quite a little fellow he was perched upon his father's knee. From that vantage-point he could watch the coming of the guests. Slaves ran to meet them, removed their long, peaked sandals, and flung wreaths of fresh lotus-lilies over their shoulders. A crown of these rose-coloured lilies was also placed on the head of each guest, carefully arranged so that either a full-blown lotus or a beautiful bud hung down a little in the centre of the forehead, like the sacred asp on the brow of the Pharaoh. When these crowns began to droop and fade watchful slaves removed them and brought fresh ones, either straight from the garden or from deep jars of cool water where the newly cut lilies were kept in readiness. Other slaves then came forward bearing alabaster caskets full of perfumed ointment with which the wigs of the company were anointed before the banquet began.

Two things the good-humoured Egyptians greatly loved— conversation and music. Occasionally they may have enjoyed both at the same time. But, as politeness was one of the graces they cultivated with most care, it seems more probable that the hum of talk and laughter would die down when the minstrels appeared. Harpers came, and players upon the lyre, the flute, the double pipe, and the tambourine. There were singers who sang kneeling on the ground, beating time with claps of their hands, and dancers who varied their graver dances by juggling deftly with balls and knives.

For the Theban boy, sitting so stiffly on his father's knee, the music and the dancing must have been the best part of the banquet. The long tales told by the guests may have made him a little drowsy, unless when they spoke of some stirring event, such as one of the crushing victories of Rameses II, or the explor-

ing expedition sent by the high-hearted Queen Hatshepsu to the
Land of Punt (Somaliland) to bring home the sweet, aromatic
trees from which the incense was crushed for the temples of
Amen-Rā. It would interest the boy to learn about the heroism
of Menna, and how the Pharaoh rewarded his charioteer, and
about the greyhounds and monkeys and peacocks which the
explorers brought home with their square-sailed, lily-prowed
galleys from the fragrant and mysterious Land of Punt. From
his point of view, perhaps, the day after the banquet was the best

A MINIATURE SHIP
Showing the ' look-out ' with lead in hand at the bow, the steersman at the stern, the captain
amidships, and the crew ready to obey orders

day. Politeness would not permit a little boy to stretch out
his hand for a grape or a fig in the august company of his elders,
but when all the guests were gone, and all the faded lotus-
garlands had been swept away, the children of the family must
have had their share of the relics of the feast, and helped to eat
up the drumsticks of the roasted geese, the half scooped-out
melons, the green noses of the cucumbers, the lingering carraway
cakes, and any tiny plump quail that had not disappeared during
the banquet. Quails were more seldom seen than geese. Roast
goose was an everyday dish in a Theban house, and geese were
often painted as part of the design running round its walls—
grave-looking geese, with plumage of silvery white and russet
brown, and flat golden feet. The walls of the house were like

the pages of a charmingly coloured picture-book; but more fascinating still were the wooden models of men and buildings which the boy's father was almost sure to possess, though we do not know whether his son was ever allowed to handle them.

One such model, about two feet square, was a miniature granary, with a little staircase leading to a loft above, and bins of grain, each with an inscription to show that it held seven measures. Other models showed men driving a plough drawn by two spotted oxen with long horns; or a set of six wooden soldiers about nine inches high, marching in step in single file, each with his knapsack on his back, a sword in one hand, and a spear in the other, and all looking very resolute and fierce. More beautiful were the miniature reproductions of the slender, graceful boats in which the mummies of the dead were fer-

A CAT DRIVING GEESE
From a papyrus in the British Museum

ried across the river from the shining, humming city to the dark and silent Valley of Tombs on the western shore. If—as seems likely—these exquisite models, with their tiny sails and ropes and oars, their lifelike little rowers and steersmen, were intended rather for grown-ups to admire than for small boys to play with, our Theban must have cast wistful glances in their direction, envying those fortunate elders who were not warned off if they drew too near.

He probably enjoyed himself best of all when he was playing out of doors with other Thebans not much bigger than himself. They played odd-and-even, using nuts, pebbles, bones, and beans; they played draughts and dice, and many games with balls. One rather attractive-looking game was played by two boys, each holding a crook, who had a hoop between them; the idea seems to have been that each player should try to catch the hoop with his crook, and whisk it away from the other.

Mock fights in which the boyish warriors rode on each others' shoulders would delight the boy when he grew old enough and strong enough to take part. And he must have been a proud fellow the first time he went fishing with his father in a lean, lightly woven boat among the high, bird-haunted reeds, or—an even more tremendous adventure —when they went out hunting in the desert, or fowling with slings. In this last sport cats were used instead of dogs to retrieve the game brought down by a well-directed pebble from the sling.

Pet animals were among the most interesting inhabitants of the typical Egyptian house. Cats were treated with the greatest regard, and honoured with elaborate mummification after death; grasshoppers were kept in cages of plaited rushes; monkeys were trained to pick grapes in the harvest-season ; gazelles pattered all over the house on their light, clicking hoofs. Some enterprising families even kept pet crocodiles, though it seems unlikely that these sulky, cumbersome reptiles ever learned any pleasing tricks. An even less strokable pet was the tame porcupine.

MUMMY OF A CAT
British Museum

The world was full of laughter for the little Theban boy when he quitted the House of Books and ran home, shouting with delight. The very walls of his room were painted so as to make him laugh when he looked at them—painted with whimsical pictures of cats driving flocks of geese, or hippopotami sitting up at table. The very names by which his father and mother called him were a constant reminder that they loved their merry-hearted little brown-skinned son. " Beautiful Morning," or " Young Wild Lion," they would call him ; sometimes, " Pretty Kitten," and sometimes, " I have wanted You."

PHARAOH'S CHARIOTS
1322 B.C.

GOLD-GIRT I see my father stride,
And clad in dappled leopard-hide ;
  The priest of Amen-Rā is he.
When I grow up it is his will
That *I* his basalt chair should fill,
  That *I* a priest of Rā should be.

My uncle is a scribe, you know.
With wig and wand I see him go
  Among the galleys and the bales.
It is *his* will when I grow big
That I should wear just such a wig,
  And write with reeds, and weigh with scales.

They know not that before mine eyes
Far other are the dreams that rise,
  Nor reck what sounds are in my ears :
The whirling wheel, the whip out-thrust,
The flash of plumes above the dust,
  The chariots—and the charioteers !

This morning, in the House of Books,
My master gave me fearsome looks
  When not one word could I repeat
Of old Im-Hotep's wisdom, for
Afar I heard the rush and roar
  Of Pharaoh's chariots down the street.

In a swift, gleaming multitude
They speed, those chariots many-hued,
  Swaying and leaping as they race.
The driver leans, and shakes the thong,
And loudly as he sweeps along
  The wind shrills past his eager face.

I will not wear the leopard-skin
To serve the Lord of Light within
  His mighty many-columned fane :
To be a scribe were little sport,
And stand bewigged in Pharaoh's Court
  Writing long lists of sacks of grain

Hear me, O Amen-Rā, thou whom
My father greets with incense-fume
And at the casting of the lots
Let mine be neither robe nor reed,
But let me follow where they lead,
The chariots—the chariots !

CHAPTER III

In Ancient Greece

WHEN a citizen of Athens, passing by the door of a friend's house, saw a wreath of olive-leaves hanging there, he knew that a son had been born within, and that the hearts of father and mother were glad.

The baby boy's nurse, after bathing him in a mixture of oil and water, had swaddled him in soft wool and had laid him in a cradle shaped like a small hammock or basket. Round his neck she had not forgotten to hang a cluster of little, dangling charms—swords, pigs, hands, and half-moons—which were believed to bring him good fortune. On his head she would place a queer little pointed cap.

A curious ceremony took place when the Athenian boy was five days old. In the low house of sun-baked pinkish-white bricks where he was born the most sacred spot was the hearth, set in the centre of the hall. Here were remembered and invoked the goddess Hestia and the kindly deities of the

A GREEK BOY EXTRACTING A THORN FROM HIS FOOT
Capitol, Rome
Photo Brogi

home, without whose favour the little fellow in the peaked cap could not go very far or very safely through his life. On the fifth day after his son's birth the Athenian father threw aside his *himation*, the loose cloak worn over the springy, crinkled linen *chiton* that was the characteristic garment of the ancient Greeks, and, taking the baby in his arms, ran swiftly with him

53

right round the hearth. This was done so that the hearth-gods might watch over the child while he was learning to walk, and help him to be steady and fleet of foot.

On the tenth day there was another ceremony, marked by a banquet and a sacrifice, and then a name was given to the hitherto nameless little Greek. The guests did not fail to bring him gifts,

YOUTH WEARING A CHITON   MAN WEARING A HIMATION

among which would be slippery cuttlefish, and curiously plaited garlands.

After that he was handed over to his nurse, usually a trusted and favoured woman-slave, who would watch over him throughout his childhood, and who, if he went on far journeys when he grew to man's estate, would still be found by the hearth when he returned. So did the storm-scarred Odysseus find his old nurse Eurycleia in the palace at Ithaca when he came back from his long wanderings in the dusty tatters of a beggar. It was Eurycleia to whom the sage Queen Penelope called to bring the settle with the soft fleece upon it, that the wayfarer might sit and tell his story. The story he told was not his, but he told it with such art that the Queen wept to hear. Yet she did not recognise the changed face and the feigned voice of her husband. Then Eurycleia, the faithful Eurycleia who had carried Odysseus as a babe in her arms, brought the shining cauldron to wash the feet of the stranger. She knelt down before him, and when her fingers touched the scar of the wild boar's tusk " she let the foot drop suddenly, . . . and the brazen vessel rang, being turned over on the other side, and behold, the water was spilled on the ground." Almost speechless with joy, she faltered forth : " Yea, verily, thou art Odysseus—my dear child ! "

It was in the arms of his nurse that little Astyanax, son of Hector of the glancing helm, was borne to the walls of the beleaguered city of Troy when his mother Andromache hastened thither to see how the Trojans were faring against the warlike Greeks. There Hector found them all when he came to bid his wife and child farewell before his great fight with Aias (Ajax). But when Hector stretched out his arms " the child shrank crying to the bosom of his fair-girdled nurse, dismayed at his dear father's aspect, and in dread at the bronze and horsehair crest that he beheld nodding fiercely from the helmet's top. Then his dear father laughed aloud, and his lady mother ; forthwith glorious Hector took the helmet from his head and laid it, all gleaming, upon the earth ; then kissed he his dear son, and dandled him in his arms, and spake in prayer to Zeus and all the gods : ' O Zeus, and all ye gods, vouchsafe ye that this my son may likewise prove even as I, pre-eminent amid the Trojans, and as valiant in might, and be a great king of Ilios . . . and may his mother be glad.' " [1]

So, like the far-wandering Odysseus and the little son of Hector before him, the Athenian baby was placed in the arms of a faithful nurse. She watched over him at night, and kept a boat-shaped flickering lamp of bronze or clay burning near him while he slept. If he awoke she sang him to sleep again with old, old songs. One of these songs was :

> Humpy tortoise, what do you here ?
> I'm weaving the wool and the thread, my dear.
> What of your grandson, and where went he ?
> White horses have carried him out to sea.[2]

If " Humpy Tortoise " did not make the wakeful baby drowsy again his nurse may have sung him this lullaby, first sung by Alcman of Sardis, and echoed down the ages till we catch its

[1] Translated by W. Leaf
[2] Translated by J. A. Pott.

last faint cadences in the familiar English hymn, " Now the day is over, night is drawing nigh."

> Sleep broods o'er the mountain crest
>   And the folds of the hill ;
> Hollow and headland rest
>   Silent and still.
> All things are slumbering,
>   Not a leaf is stirred ;
> Of insect or creeping thing
>   No rustle is heard.
>
> The beasts of the mountain sleep,
>   And the murmuring bees,
> And the monsters that haunt the deep
>   Of the purple seas.[1]

Every morning the small Athenian had a bath in lukewarm water, and he often had two or three more baths before night. After he was about a year old his nurse gave him a sort of broth, made of pulse sweetened with honey, barley-porridge, and goat's-milk cheese. No boy ever had more delightful honey, for it was brought either from Hymettus, the thyme-sweet, bee-haunted mountain to the south-west of Athens, or from the more distant mountain of Hybla in Sicily, where the flowers were so many and so marvellously fragrant that their honey was famed all over the antique world.

One of the first tales his nurse would tell him would be the main outline of the tale of Troy. Hector, the tamer of horses—glorious Hector of the glancing helm—proud Aias, sullen Achilles, Diomedes of the loud war-cry, and great-hearted Patroklos were the heroes of his boyish imagination, and to many a little warrior modelled in powdery pink clay must he have given their clanging and heroic-sounding names. The nurse would also enchant and appal him by turns with the legends of the Greek isles, and his dreams must have been disturbed sometimes by the Hydra's nodding heads and the Gorgon's glassy glare. But by daylight his walks in the low, shady woods of gnarled olives and stunted, wind-bowed oaks would be made more exciting by the sense that a hamadryad might peep at any moment from any tree, and that the reedy notes of the wind in the bowed branches might be the sound of the reed-pipes of Pan. Other tales of

[1] Translated by J. A. Pott.

wonder he would hear from his father's friends who had journeyed to the outermost isles of the Ægean, and who had fared as far as Sicily and Egypt, Carthage, and Etruria, and Tyre. His whole horizon was filled with visions and legends and wonderful stories many times told. But in the foreground were his pets and his toys. For pets he had dogs, tortoises, and ducks, and one of his less gentle amuse-ments was to tie a string to the leg of a cockchafer, and run after it as it tried to fly away. Of toys the children of ancient Greece had assuredly no lack. The first of these was an earthen-ware rattle, often in the form of a pig or an owl. A kindly old philosopher, Archytas of Tarentum, invented the rattle

CLAY HORSEMAN
British Museum

" in order that, having the use of this, children may not break any of the things in the house, for the little creatures cannot keep still." Then the small Athenian had chariots and horses stamped out of lead, and the most delightful models in clay, only a few inches high : models of rabbits, rams, birds, and dogs, of warriors on horseback or on swan-back, fish riding on mules and looking foolishly afraid of falling off, donkeys laden with loaves, and boys with broad-brimmed hats.

BOY WITH A TOY CART

Archytas was a wise as well as a kindly philosopher. There were all too many opportunities of breaking things in a Greek house. Shelves and cupboards seem to have been unknown, and though chests of polished wood were used to hold such

57

precious possessions as purple robes or golden vases, every corner of every room would be encumbered with tools, spears, sandals, baskets, distaffs, and jars. The chiton was sometimes hung on a peg fixed in the door, and a very great man like Odysseus would have a vaulted treasure-chamber underground ; but for the most part the belongings of the family were dumped down along the walls and in the corners, and no doubt the boy made the

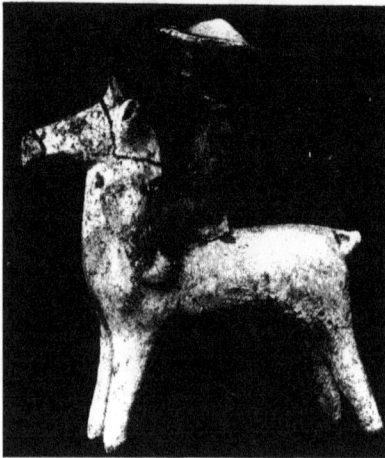 

(a)   (b)

CLAY TOYS

(a) Boy riding on a horse , (b) Man riding on a swan

British Museum   Photos Mansell

(See the poem at the end of this chapter)

general confusion worse confounded by leaving his toy-carts, his kites, tops, and hoops wherever they chanced to lie when he laid them down. In most Greek gardens would be found a swing with a cushioned seat, and perhaps a see-saw made with a plank and a big log as well ; but the garden was not cultivated with the same loving delight as were the gardens of ancient Egypt. It was either a paved courtyard or a small space, shaded by tamarisks and fig-trees, with plots where onions, parsley, radishes, and cress were grown for the table. A few flowers, such as the lily, the iris, and the peony, were sometimes grown for use in wreaths and garlands, though for that purpose the tightly curled, brightly hued little leaves of the parsley were often taken.

The Athenian boy dreamt of wearing the parsley-garland when

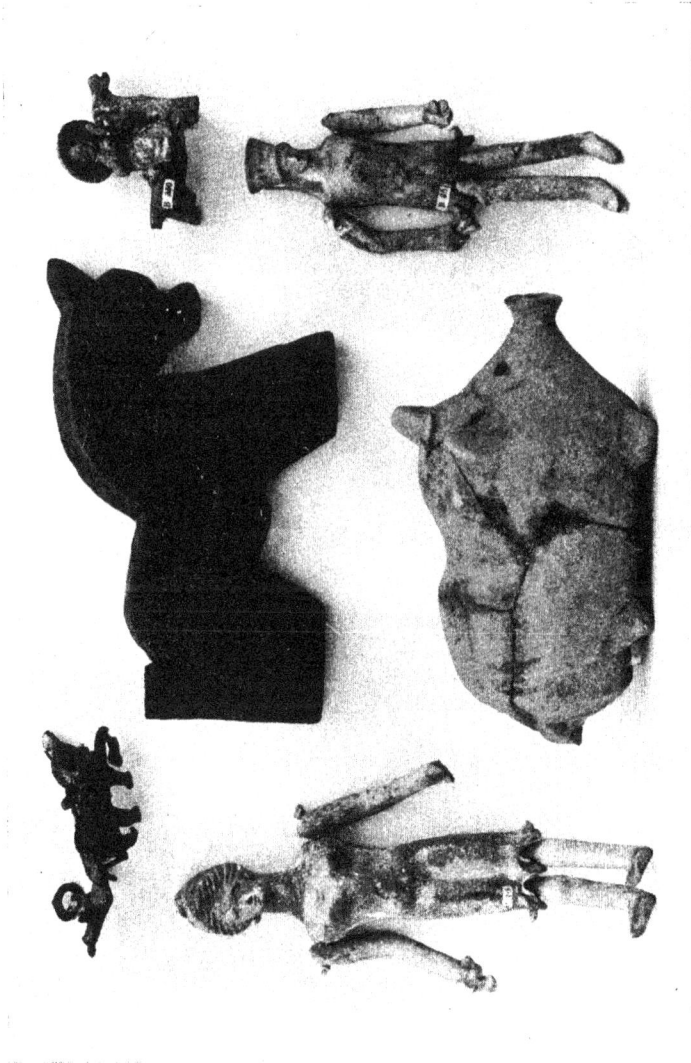

GREEK DOLLS AND TOYS   Fourth Century B.C.   In the British Museum
Photo Mansell

he should be old enough and strong enough to run or wrestle at the Panathenaic Festival or at the Olympic games. Running and wrestling formed a very important part of his later training, but while he was still in the charge of his nurse he had followed many pursuits which taught him to be swift of foot and of eye —blindman's-buff, and tug-of-war, and a quaint test of balance which consisted of jumping on an inflated wine-skin made slippery with grease. He played ball-games too. In one, called ' thanis,' the player threw the ball as high into the air as he could, and his opponent tried to catch it as it came down. In 'Apporaxis,' or bounce-ball, the bounces of the ball were counted till another player batted it back with his open hand.

When the young Athenian reached the age of seven his serious education began. He was removed from the indulgent hands of his nurse and placed in the charge of his *paidagogos*, an elderly slave whose duty it was to take the boy to school, to sit with a group of other *paidagogoi* and wait until the lessons were done, and then escort him home again. Plato, the greatest of the Greek philosophers, called a boy " the most unmanageable of all animals," and no doubt the teachers whose duty it was to train the small Athenian had their work cut out for them. With his jutting beard, his big stick, and his stern, watchful face the paidagogos is a familiar figure in Greek comedy and in Greek vase-paintings. Poor fellow, he *had* to be stern and watchful, for it was his part to make sure that his young charge used his left hand for bread and his right hand for other eatables,

THE WRESTLERS
Uffizi Gallery, Florence
Photo Alinari

60

that he did not sit cross-legged, or prop his chin on his hand, or speak pertly to his elders, or break any of the chief rules of conduct.

The Greeks attached great importance to the quality which they called *kalos kagathos* and which we should call 'good manners.' If the paidagogos did his duty faithfully and the boy

AN ATHENIAN GRAMMAR-SCHOOL
Sixth century B C.
From a *kylix* (bowl) in the Berlin Museum

did not forget what he had learned in the days when the big stick still had terrors for him, he would not, when he grew up, bring discredit on himself and his teachers by bustling along too quickly, or walking with a slow, pompous stride, by rolling his eyes about, or fixing them sulkily on the ground, by talking too loud, or by jostling roughly against passers-by. Even in the matter of adjusting his himation there were certain rules which *kalos kagathos* imposed. If it were too short, he would look like a country lout ; if too long, like a fop. On a certain occasion the great orator Demosthenes described his opponent scornfully as a man who " marches through the *Agora* (market-place) with his cloak touching his ankles, stalking along, and puffing out his cheeks."

To return now to our seven-year-old Athenian, just about to begin his education. The beginning did not seem very serious or alarming ; much time was given to what would now be classed as gymnastics, and one of the very first ' lessons ' would be a wrestling-bout with another boy of his own age and weight. The two would be stripped, anointed with oil, and sprinkled with

61

sand. After they had finished, a bath was exceedingly necessary, and if the sea or some river were anywhere near, a plunge and a swim soon made them pink and cool and clean. Running was another important lesson, along a 200-yards' course; and high and long jumps, with and without a run, and throwing spears and quoits at targets, helped to make a good athlete of the young Greek. In the Olympic games and at the great Panathenaic festivals there were special races for boys only.

BOY RUNNING

From a *kylix* in the British Museum

Through all these exercises can be traced the Greek idea that the discipline and development of the body should be not only the first aim of education but the main purpose of life. Yet these people, the most keenly intellectual people that have ever been, were in no danger of neglecting the mind. Those earnest, eager youths who flocked to hear the philosophic discourses of Socrates and Plato, and whose earnest eagerness amused and annoyed the comic poet Aristophanes, had been carefully trained in reading, writing, simple arithmetic, drawing, music, and the first rules of geometry. The memory of those youths would be haunted by " the surge and thunder of the *Odyssey*."

In learning to write, the small Athenian would use either a wooden wax-coated tablet upon which the letters were scratched with a metal stylus, or he might write with a pen upon brown papyrus from Egypt and fair parchment from Pergamum. In the British Museum may be seen one such tablet, filmed with dark-coloured wax on which the stylus of some Greek boy has scratched, in unsteady white scratches, the multiplication table as far as " three times ten."

Probably he was not allowed to handle the more costly and

elaborate writing materials until he was a skilful penman, and even then not unless he were going to follow some career, such as that of a teacher, law-giver, philosopher, or poet, in which the art of writing would fill a great place.   When it was a really serious piece of work which he was going to attempt, he had to surround himself with an almost bewildering array of objects : a disc of lead with which to rule lines ; a sponge to blot out mis-takes ; a piece of pumice to smooth the parchment ; a little

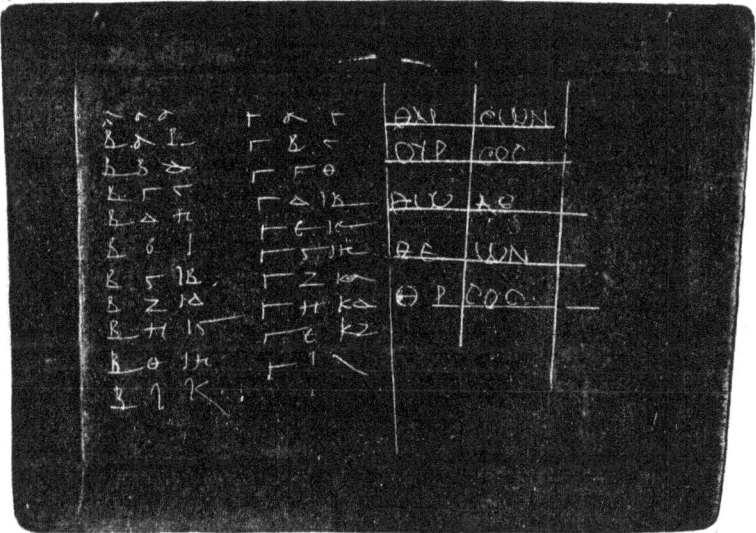

WAX TABLET WITH MULTIPLICATION TABLE
The numerals run up to 3 times 10   On the right is a list of words
divided to show stems and terminations
British Museum

knife to keep the pen-point sharp ; the pen itself, made of a stiff reed or a bird's quill ; and a pot full of ink, either real cuttle-fish ink, or a fluid crushed from oak-galls.

In the golden age of Athens, the fourth century B.C., the wisdom and wonder of books were not held in pages between flat covers as they began to be in Egypt some seven hundred years later, and as they are to-day.   The papyrus-sheets, or the parchment-skins, were cut into long strips and wound round a wooden roller which the reader held, by a projecting foot, in his right hand while with his left hand he gradually unwound

63

the scroll. After his eyes had travelled down the first two or three columns he began to make a fresh roll in his left hand, so that all the time he was reading he was encumbered with two heavy, shifting rolls, of which one grew fat as the other grew thin. There was a Greek saying which may be roughly translated, " The larger the book, the greater the evil." It is easy to understand how this idea arose if we remember that the remark was first uttered by a Greek—Callimachus—who had charge of the great library at Alexandria, and had to spend many dusty hours wrestling with huge rolls and rollers in the hot and heavy air of Egypt.

A lesson which interested the boy if he had a good ear and wearied him if he had not was the inevitable music - lesson. He had not only to learn to sing, alone or in chorus, but also to play passably well on the seven-stringed lyre. After the wars with Persia the music of the double pipe became suddenly fashionable in Athens, but it was soon abandoned, as it was impossible to play it and sing at the same time, and also because the Greek sense of symmetry was affronted by the puffing and twisting of the pipe-player's face.

BOYS WITH LYRE

When our Athenian boy reached the age of sixteen he made a drink-offering to the lion-clad god Herakles, and cut short the hair which he had hitherto worn in long locks on the nape of his neck. Two years later his name was enrolled in the list of the " city-tribe " to which he belonged. Then he became one of the *Ephebi*, a body of youths trained and equipped by the state to defend harbours and frontiers against any possible invasion. First he was presented to the citizens assembled in the great open-air theatre, armed with a shield and a leaf-shaped bronze sword, and then led to the sanctuary of Agraulos, at the foot of the rock-built citadel, where he took a solemn oath to defend his country with his life.

It is very probable that when he was still struggling with his wax tablets under the fierce eye of the paidagogos the Athenian boy looked forward almost wistfully to the time when he should wear the broad-brimmed hat and the jaunty short cloak which all the Ephebi wore. The last years of their military service were spent on the more remote and perilous boundaries of Greece ; but their first duty was the pleasant one of going to garrison one of the three fortified ports of Athens, the Piræus, Munychia, and Phalerus.

At Munychia, the little, deeply-indented harbour between the other two, there was a great temple sacred to the goddess Artemis,

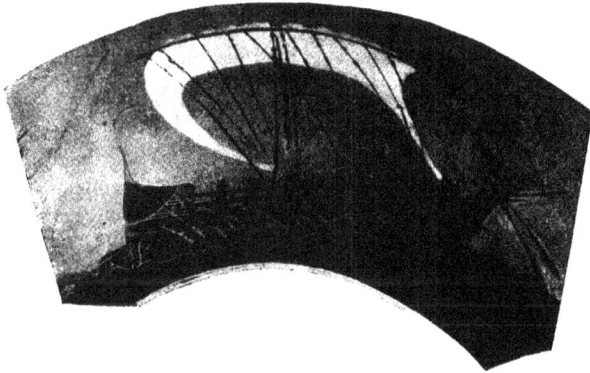

A GREEK GALLEY
From a *kylix* in the British Museum
[The prow has been added from a second galley on the same *kylix*]
Photo Mansell

where at festivals little cakes set round with nodding, flickering lights were offered to the " fair silver-shafted Queen forever chaste." In the Piræus sometimes as many as three hundred ships would be lying at anchor. These ships were of so many different forms and colours that to watch them must have been an unfailing source of amusement to the Ephebi, as it was to the younger boys walking on the tremendously long sea-walls with which Athens was girt. Most common were the single-masted ships, built of long, tough planks, oak-, pine-, alder-, or poplar-wood, their hulls painted blue or crimson, their sterns ornamented with a trophy like a fish's head, or a bird's, or, if the vessel came from Egypt, a lotus-flower. In sea-fights it was always the aim of the pursuer to lop off and bear away this trophy from the

E

stern of a fleeing foe. The Greeks could not put their whole
trust in their solitary linen sail hung from a cross-beam of fir
and lashed with ox-hide ropes, so each ship had a crew of rowers,
twenty, fifty, or even a hundred and fifty, who plied the shovel-
shaped oars fastened to the gunwale with leathern loops. Some
of the broader and deeper vessels had wooden bulwarks and
projecting turrets as a defence against pirates. Beside the lank,
swift war-galleys such vessels looked oddly heavy and cumbersome. For neighbours they might have fantastic Etruscan ships
built in the forms of boars or birds or sharks, and in and out
among these big fellows lying majestically at anchor dozens of
smaller craft, of many quaint shapes and gay colours, were in
continuous movement, dodging almost under the beating oars of
the great ships as they entered and left the harbour.

The sight of all these beautiful vessels, beautiful even when
tempest-battered and salt-stained, must have made many a
young Athenian long to go forth across the wine-dark sea to the
perilous and marvellous lands of which returning seafarers
brought home such astonishing tales. But every young Athenian
firmly believed that no city of the world was worthy to be named
in the same breath with his own. It mattered little to him that
the streets of the city were narrow and ill-paved, that the close-
huddling houses were built of brick so brittle that it crumbled
almost at a touch ; Athens was not that straggling tangle of mean
byways—it was the sacred city of Athene, the grey-eyed, wise,
and unforgetting Athene, whose colossal image, wrought in ivory
and gold and facing the sunrise, stood in the pillared shadows of
that great temple—the Parthenon—which Athens had raised to
its divine patroness. This was not the only temple on the rugged
Acropolis hill, where Artemis also had her shrine, and wingless
Victory hers, and where Poseidon, the sea-god, shared a little
red temple with Athene herself, despite their many differences of
opinion during the Trojan war. But the Parthenon was the
glory of Athens and of Greece, famous throughout the antique
world, and a thing of wonder even now, in its gaunt and scarred
decay.

On the south-east flank of the craggy, temple-crowned Acropolis lay the great theatre of Dionysus, where twice a year
dramatic performances were given in honour of the " monarch
of the vine," whose worship held so much that was barbarous

and so much that was beautiful in the beliefs and customs of the early Greek tribes.

The greater of these two festivals was given toward the end of March, and then the terraced slopes of rock, out of which the

INTERIOR OF THE PARTHENON

seats of the audience were hewn, seethed and swayed with a crowd of twenty thousand eager citizens and not less eager strangers. At each festival twelve plays were acted, four by each of the three poets chosen from among the many who competed for the annual prizes in the Dionyseia.

Wearing ivy-garlands and bearing cushions and refreshments,

67

THE ACROPOLIS

Photo English Photographic C

the crowd began to arrive almost before the first rays of the spring sunlight gilded the peaks of Hymettus, and there they sat till the red light waned and sank beyond Mount Ægeleas. Whenever the Greek boy was old enough to endure all this excitement and fatigue his father took him with him to the theatre of Dionysus, and he saw the incomparable tragedies and comedies of the greatest of the Greek poets unfolded before the people of Athens. O most happy boy, to hear the frogs of Aristophanes croak their unmusical chorus for the first time ! When he went home, did he not hasten to mimic those frogs for the amusement of the younger children, and hop about singing, " *Brek-ek-eks, ko-ax, ko-ax, ko-ax* " ? He was happy, too, when he saw the reconciliation between the rash Theseus and his noble son Hippolytus, the recognition of Orestes by Electra, and the passionate despair of the Trojan women in the cool, translucent spring air under the pillared slope of the Acropolis. If the audience were not keenly interested they would munch and chatter and gape, and think about something else ; but if the play or the players seriously displeased them they would cluck, stamp, whistle, and even pelt the performers with pebbles, figs, and nuts. Of an unpopular actor it was said that he could start a fruiterer's shop with the fruit that had been thrown at him ; while another who borrowed some stones to mend the wall of his house promised to repay the loan after the next performance with the stones which would certainly descend upon his unlucky head.

Sometimes the long speeches of the characters and the arguments of the chorus may have wearied the boy a little when he was first taken to the theatre of Dionysus. But, being a Greek, he had no lack of natural wit. Often he already knew the plot of the play now being unwound in gorgeous poetry, thrilling with music and colour, by the queerly arrayed actors and the well-drilled groups of the chorus. Very quaint did the actors look, wearing buskins with wooden soles six inches thick, their chests padded to twice their real size, and their faces hidden by huge, gaping masks of stiffened linen. When a tragedy was being played the open mouths of these masks were bent dolefully downward at each corner, and their eyebrows were given a distressed upward tilt ; but in comedies the lips were drawn apart in a merry grin, and creases of laughter were made round the holes for the eyes.

A boy who was not used to the idea that this was just how the characters in a play ought to look might have felt inclined to laugh, even at the most tragic moments of the tragedies. But the Athenian boy felt no such inclination. He saved all *his* laughter for the comic plays, and even then he must sometimes have laughed because his father laughed, and not because he could thoroughly understand all the jokes. The comic poet poked fun at all sorts of grave and solemn people—judges, and generals, and philosophers, and tragic poets. To understand his mockery it was necessary to understand exactly what it was that he found wrong, or foolish, or absurd in the lives and doings of these people.

Some of the jokes were simple enough, however. For instance, in Aristophanes' *Clouds*, where fun is made of Socrates' "Thinking Shop" and of Socrates himself, who is shown seriously experimenting and philosophizing to discover how far a flea can jump, and whether a gnat buzzes through its head or its tail.

AN ACTOR WITH MASK
From *Costume of the Ancients,*
by Thomas Hope

On his way through the streets of Athens the boy had probably seen the butt of the poet's chaff—a broadly built man, who went barefoot even when it was cold, a terribly ugly man, with a broad, flat nose, bulging cheeks, an overhanging brow, and a face that seemed to be all knobs—a man at whom some men glanced with awe, and others, again, with mocking or angry eyes as they murmured his name among themselves, and whispered: " There goes Socrates ! "

CLAY WARRIORS

399 B.C.

THIS little man of clay
Was Hector yesterday,
Hector, the tamer of horses, the swift in pursuit :
Along the marble path
I made him run in wrath,
But I made him run too hard, and he chipped his foot.

Poor little smiling man,
I liked him better than
Warriors whose arms won't wag, but are stiff like those.
He still wags *his*, I know,
But how could Hector go
Forth to fight the Achaians with broken toes ?

No more he is Hector : yet
A parchment tent I'll set
Here by the side of the place where he tumbled down.
I wish he would not smile
For just a little while ;
He is Achilles now, and should stand and frown.

But now what shall I do ?
I have not got a new
Warrior to take his place on the wall of Troy.
Myself I built that wall
So well, it will not fall—
Unless it be pushed down by some other boy.

Who will be Hector now ?
I have a goose, a cow,
And a man that rides on a swan instead of a horse,
Two rabbits and a ram ;
A luckless boy I am !
Lacking a Hector, what is my Trojan force ?

The swan-man I must take,
But gently, lest he break :
Better a warrior that rides on a swan than none !
Since better may not be,
Hearken, swan-man, to me—
You are Hector, the tamer of horses, the valiant one.

CHAPTER IV

In Ancient Rome

THE gods of Rome were very ancient gods. Before Rome was, they were. When the hills of Rome were lonely wooded steeps those gods were worshipped there by the simple herdsmen—the gods of the light and darkness, the flocks

HEAD OF A ROMAN YOUTH
From an ancient Etruscan bronze
Photo F. Bruckmann

and the trees. Invaders came, Sabines, Albans, and Etruscans, who threw up earthworks and built walls on the Palatine Mount and the Quirinal. They had bowed down to divinities of their own in their old homes. But after the scattered farms had grown into a city, the gods of the seven hills, who had never been frightened away or forgotten, came back into the minds of men, and were honoured in the old way, though not always under the old names.

Dearest to the hearts of the early Romans were the household spirits, the *Lares* and *Penates*, whose images were set in little shrines in every Roman house. The settlement grew into a city, the city into an empire, but the kindly Lares and Penates were not neglected or laid aside. Only, many lesser gods, more like the elves and fairies of nursery legends, crowded unseen round the hearth, flitted about the woods and meadows, and peeped in at the door. Many of these lesser gods were especially interested in children. There was Levana, who presided over the ceremonial act by which the father, lifting up a baby in his arms, accepted it as his; Cunina, who guarded the cradle; Nundina, who graced the festival at which the little Roman received his name; Fabulina, who taught him to utter his first word; Ossipago, who made his bones grow straight and strong; Interduca, who kept an eye on him as he trotted to school. At Nundina's festival a circular pendant of gold or gilded bronze containing an amulet or charm was hung round his neck, never to be taken off until he donned the *toga virilis*, the garb of a full-grown man. Sometimes—though not very often—a day came in the life of a Roman when he *did* wear again the pendant charm which he had put away with other childish things; if that day came, it was when he was drawn in triumph up the slope of the Capitol, and had gained the highest point of glory to which any son of Rome might aspire.

A ROMAN CITIZEN IN
HIS TOGA
From *Costume of the Ancients*
by Thomas Hope

The choice of first names for Nundina's festival was very narrow; there were only seventeen from which to choose. But almost every noble Roman had two others. The middle one was his family name; the last, the *cognomen*, either marked to what branch of the family he belonged or was conferred on him—as the name ' Africanus ' was conferred on Scipio—as a token of honour.

A Roman boy's earliest impressions would be of the *atrium*, the central hall of his father's house—the centre not only of the house itself but of family life and family religion. It was an oblong room, with an outer roof which slanted inward and downward. In this roof was an opening, the *compluvium*, through which the rain fell when it rained and the smoke of the hearth rose when the fire fumed; beneath was a basin, something like the basin of a fountain, called an *impluvium*, to catch

ATRIUM OF THE HOUSE OF THE SILVER WEDDING, POMPEII
Showing the compluvium, the impluvium, and base of the altar of the Lares
Photo Anderson

the rain. On its edge sometimes stood the altar of the Lares. For the boy, as he began to look round and patter about, the atrium was a most interesting place. There were patterns traced in little square stones of various colours across the tessellated floor, and it was good sport to follow these patterns with your finger and crawl after your finger wherever it went, before Ossipago had made your legs so straight and strong that you could walk without holding on to anybody or anything. At either end of the atrium was a recess where he would see hanging the wax portrait-masks of his ancestors, very lifelike and gruesome to behold when the dusk was creeping down, or when a sudden flicker from the fire lit up the glass eyes or the jutting nose of some stern-looking grandparent. On festal occasions these masks were crowned with flowers, and when there was a funeral in the family they were fastened to the faces of slaves who walked in the funeral procession. To the youngest of their

ROMAN TESSELLATED PAVEMENT
Discovered in Leadenhall Street, London
From *England,* by Gilbert Stone

descendants these waxen ancestors must have been something between a terror and a delight.

In little, recessed shrines, or even in a chapel all to themselves, stood the household gods, the Lares and Penates, in the form of youths wearing short tunics, and bearing drinking-horns and libation-bowls. These were among the oldest of the old gods that were before Rome was. Their statues were kept brightly polished with wax, and libations of wine were poured forth in their honour at the end of every meal. It was important to keep them in a good humour, for the Penates took care that there should be no dearth of food in the house, and that the granaries and larders and store-shelves should always be full, while the Lar was the guardian of the fields where the flocks pastured and the corn grew. The Lar was originally an outdoor divinity, and his mission was to mark the boundaries between one farm and another; but after the houses multiplied on the hills by the swift, tawny Tiber the Lares joined the Penates indoors and helped them to take care of the household, though they still had open-air duty as the guardians of streets, landmarks, and high roads.

ALTAR OF THE LARES CAPITALES

It would amuse the Roman boy to see his mother making offerings before the shrines of the little gods, crowning them with myrtle and rosemary, offering them tiny cakes, and scattering salt upon the flames that crackled and turned blue as it fell. When he was old enough to understand that he must not laugh or sneeze or interrupt during the more solemn ceremonies, he would act as *camillus* (acolyte) to his father. Every Roman was a head-priest in his own house, and in every Roman house the primitive religion of the race was kept alive, even when, in the days of the later Emperors, Persian and Greek and Egyptian gods came and thrust themselves in among the ancient gods of Rome, and when the public worship of the imperial city-state was in the hands of the *flamens* and *augurs* of the great priestly caste.

BRONZE STATUETTE
OF A LAR
British Museum
(See the poem at the end
of this chapter)

The garment worn by all free-born children, both boys and girls, was a purple-edged cloak known as the *toga prætexta*; and it is interesting to realize that the only grown-up

people who had the right to wear this garment were the priests
and the magistrates chosen to offer sacrifices to the gods on behalf
of the state. From this it is clear that the toga prætexta had a

(a)   BRONZE TOYS   (b)

(a) Goat, found in the Thames (*British Museum*) ; (b) Dog (*Guildhall Museum*)

religious significance, and that it was given to children not only
because they served as camilli before the shrines of the household
gods, but also as a symbol of unsullied holiness and innocence.

BRONZE BOAR AND BULL

Found in Britain

British Museum

How important this purple-edged toga was as a sign of free
birth may be seen from an anecdote which a famous teacher of
law told his students, and bade them discuss and consider as a
legal problem. A company of slave-merchants were landing a
boatload of slaves at Brundusium. Among the slaves was an

unusually beautiful and intelligent boy, for whom the slavers hoped to get a very large sum of money. But they were a little nervous lest the customs-house officers should seize him. So before they took the boy ashore they hung a golden amulet round his neck and wrapped him in the toga prætexta of the free-born child. When afterward they brought him to Rome to be sold it was declared that by giving him these recognised tokens of freedom they had made him free, and that they had no further rights over him according to the laws of Rome.

(*a*)   (*b*)

(*a*) TINY BRONZE FIGURE OF MARS
(The spear which he once held in his right hand is missing)
Guildhall Museum

(*b*) IVORY STATUETTE OF A GLADIATOR
Found near Colchester
British Museum

Our small Roman had many delightful toys. Besides the tops and marbles and balls which boys seem always to have had everywhere, he had tiny bronze animals—bulls, boars, geese, and goats—and figures of gladiators in carved bone, and chariots of bronze or ivory with wheels that really turned. His balls were stuffed with feathers, hair, or fig-seeds, and covered with cloth or hide of divers colours. He played so many games with nuts that the phrase *nuces relinquere*—to give up nuts—came to mean, "to put away childish things." In the British Museum there is a carved tomb raised by a Roman lady to her "sweetest son Lucius Æmilius Daphnus," aged four years; winged gryphons

79

uphold the stone coffin at each end, but along the centre panel fourteen chubby little boys are playing with clusters of nuts. It was not only the children of Rome, however, who took delight in such sport. If the Emperor Augustus caught sight of a group of boys playing with nuts or marbles when he was out for an airing in his litter he would sometimes descend and join them.

Rather an overwhelming experience for the boys if they recognized in the fair-haired, keen-eyed personage, with the big nose and the small, tight mouth, none other than the divine Cæsar Augustus himself !

A favourite game of the young Romans was 'soldiers.' Most of them had friends or kinsmen serving with the army, and could have told you the names and numbers and badges of the legions—the Valeria Victrix, the Parthica, Gallica, and Augusta, the famous Tenth, the stubborn Nineteenth, the triumphant Twentieth —with their boars and bears, their minotaurs and lions and winged horses on their *signa* (standards)

Few of the legions were recruited in Rome. Many of the legionaries came from far lands, from Gaul and Scythia, Nubia, and Spain, serving at distant outposts as far apart as the Jordan and the Clyde, and never beholding with their own eyes the imperial city whose soldiers they were. But that city, never

ROMAN STANDARD-BEARER (SIGNIFER)

From *Costume of the Ancients*, by Thomas Hope

seen by them, thrilled at the tale of their victories, and the small boys of Rome refought their battles, fought first amongst burning sands or blinding snows, on the polished pavement of many an atrium. Other soldiers there were whom the Roman boy saw from time to time : the Prætorian guard, whose duty it was to watch over the Emperor ; the troops who came to march in triumphal pageants ; and now and then some battered, war-stained legionary on leave from his remote outpost, and dazed by the noise of the noisiest city in the antique world. The clink of their hob-nailed sandals, the jingle of their metal surcoats, the clash of their two-edged bronze swords as they moved through the thronged streets would always make a boy turn his head to have one more look at them. All too soon came the day when the young Roman had other things to do than playing with nuts and watching the many coloured life of Rome. When he was seven or eight years old his education began, and he had to devote all his attention to the tasks before him if he wished to escape a frequent whack from his teacher's rod.

Like the Greek boy, he had a watchful pædagogus to take him to and from school. Indeed the Romans imitated the Greek

RELIEFS ON TRAJAN'S COLUMN

These two spirals are at the base of the column   On the lower band Roman soldiers are seen issuing from the gate of a city and crossing the Danube, while ' Father Danube,' from his cave, views the proceedings with interest   On the upper band Romans are constructing fortifications.

Photo Alinari

system very closely, though not always with the same end in view. While the Greeks taught music and gymnastics in order to create balance, harmony, and grace, the aim of the more practical Romans was vigour of body and mind. Music they thought a somewhat girlish accomplishment, and they admired the qualities of toughness and hardness to which so many of their finest achievements were due. The poet Horace, indeed, lamented that Roman youths were becoming too soft to hunt, and preferred to trundle hoops instead !

Our boy's first lessons were writing and counting. Later came the study of Greek, which was to the Romans what French was

F

to the English during the Plantagenet period—the one language of elegance, refinement, and charm. As in ancient Greece, writing was done with a sharp stylus on a wooden tablet filmed with wax. The pupils sat in rows on benches, and the master sat in his high chair with a birch-rod, a cane, or a cleft strap within easy reach of his hand. Sometimes, so forcibly were the lessons of the day impressed upon the boy's memory, he would pause on his homeward way to scratch upon some blank wall the Greek letters he had just learnt to make.

In calculating, the fingers of the left hand were used for numbers below a hundred, those of the right hand for numbers above. The sums given were severely practical, and often consisted of addition and subtraction with *denarii*. Æsop's fables were given as dictations, and the scholar soon found himself deep in the resounding waves of Virgil's *Æneid*, or struggling with a Latin translation of Homer.

One of the most celebrated of Roman schoolmasters was a certain Orbilius, who had had a quaintly varied career. Born in Beneventum, he spent his youth in the army as a military trumpeter—an odd beginning, unless by making him long-winded and teaching him the value of discipline it had something to do with his success in a very different calling. When Cicero was Consul, this enterprising trumpeter arrived in Rome and started a school. Among his pupils was a boy who afterward became one of the most admired of Roman poets—Quintus Horatius Flaccus, better known as Horace. It was Horace who applied to his teacher the adjective *plagosus*—giving stripes or weals—which has stuck to him ever since.

It seems that the parents of some of Orbilius' pupils found him either too expensive or too severe, for he wrote a book to prove that parents are, on the whole, stingy and ungrateful people. But neither the slowness of his boys nor the ingratitude of their families shortened the life of the whacking teacher. He lived to be nearly a hundred years old, and before he died he saw his own statue set up at Beneventum, his native town. In this statue the marble Orbilius was seen seated in a marble chair with two marble writing-desks beside him. We are not told whether he had a marble rod in his hand ; if he had not, the sculptor missed the most characteristic touch of all.

The Roman boy's learning-day began betimes, and at certain

seasons of the year the pædagogus had to carry a lighted lantern as he and his charge made their way through the grey streets ere sunrise. On his way to school the boy might buy a loaf of hot, new bread from an early-rising baker, but he returned home for the *prandium*, the midday meal, which consisted usually of cold meats left over from the previous night's supper and was almost certain to include some sort of salad. The Romans were especially fond of salad, and strings of slaves were to be seen hurrying through the streets of Rome with baskets on their heads, full of green-fringed leeks, pearly young onions, sleek cucumbers, aromatic marjoram, and cool, dark cress.

Despite the drubbings which he received in school-hours, the Roman boy had much to make life pleasant. If his father possessed a villa in the country the days spent there must have been days of enchantment for the children. Living for part of the year in the crowded, clamorous city, the whole family must have rejoiced when the time came to betake themselves to the cool shadows of the Sabine hills, or the gleaming blue foam of Puteoli, Baiæ, and Sorrento.

WRITING-TABLET AND STYLE
In the Guildhall Museum

There the boy forgot the sting of the supple, whistling rod ; but, unless his master had failed most dismally in his effort to make him love and remember the poetry of Virgil, there must have been moments when, almost before he realized it, lines from the *Georgics* or the *Æneid* would come suddenly into his mind.

If he was watching the sky to see if rain or fair weather were coming he may have thought how Virgil sang of the signs of coming rain :

> Aut argutâ lacus circumvolitavit hirundo,
> et veterem in limo ranæ cecinere querellam ;
> sæpius et tectis penetralibus extulit ova

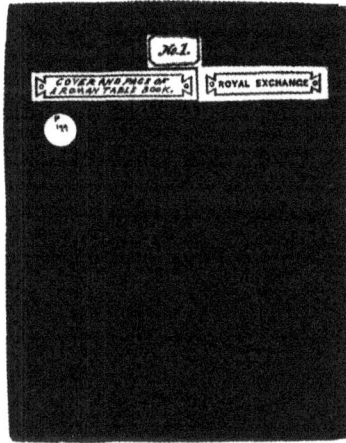

83

angustum formıca terens ıter, et bıbit ıngens
arcus et e pastu decedens agmıne magno
corvorum increpuıt densıs exercıtus alıs.

(Twittering round the pools flıts the swallow. the frogs ın
the mıre croak their ancıent plaint ; often, also, the ant brıngs
forth her eggs from her hıdden abode, treadıng out a tıny path;
a great raınbow drinks ; and a host of rooks, quıttıng theır
feedıng-ground ın a long-drawn lıne, comes wıth a rush of fast-
followıng wings.)

Horace, indeed, confessed that the swishings he received from
the too-energetic Orbilius had left with him an enduring prejudıce
against the poems thus painfully acquıred, but other gifted boys
either got off more lightly or had less terrible teachers.

In the year 106, after the Emperor Trajan had dealt a smashing
blow to the rebellious Dacians, a wreath called the "Capitoline wreath" was offered to him who could best celebrate the victory. One of the competitors, who made up Greek verses as he went along, was an eleven-year-old boy, Quintus Sulpicius Maximus ; and the prize-winner, Lucius Valerius Pudens, was only two years older. Another boy, Lucan, famous afterward as the author of the *Pharsalia*, was so stirred by the tale of Troy that he made a tremendously long poem all about Trojans before he reached his fifteenth birthday.

These were not ordinary boys, however, and it is the ordinary boy whose life and ideas are most interesting.

THE ORATOR
Archæological Museum, Florence
Photo F. Bruckmann

Apart from his lessons and his games, the young Roman had
plenty to think about and to do. He went to many places with
his father : to the circus, to the theatre, to the assemblies at
which famous orators spoke. At one time boys were allowed
to attend the meetings of the Senate, but when it occurred to the

Senators that their secret plans and schemes might be revealed by some light-hearted schoolboy and carried all over Rome, they passed a law that no one should be admitted to the Senate until he had donned the toga virilis.

When that time came, the time to ' relinquere nuces,' the boy left the tasks and the joys of boyhood behind him, and shouldered the responsibilities of a Roman citizen.   If he aspired to enter the service of the State he had to study oratory and rhetoric ; to learn, not only to think swiftly and clearly, and put his thoughts readily into words, but also to use his voice and his hands, and

LE PONT DU GARD
A Roman aqueduct near Nîmes
Photo Giraudon

to choose phrases whose very sound would sway his hearers like the sound of music.   Many youths went far afield to study this art—as far as Rhodes and Tarsus, Smyrna and Mitylene.

If it were as the governor of a colony or a province that he dreamed of serving Rome the youth had to be willing to go and mete out her laws to foreign people, in far, strange lands : to the tribes of the rain-swept isle of Britain, to fierce Teutons, talkative Gauls, or, perhaps, to meek Jews and turbulent Dacians—indeed, to any of the many peoples who became subject to Rome when the creeping line of roads and bridges spread into their lands, when Roman viaducts flung mighty arches across their deep valleys, and the image of a Roman Emperor was set up in their market-places to be honoured by all who passed that way.

The Roman boy, even if he were not borne off by his father to some grey or golden outpost of the Empire, must have been far

85

ROMAN BRIDGE AT EL KANTARA, ALGERIA
By permission of Messrs Thos Cook and Sons

more conscious of the wonder and vastness of the world than any
boy that had lived before him. In the amphitheatre he would
see beasts of many types, and men of many breeds. There must
have been glee among the children of Rome when Julius Cæsar
brought back from his African campaign the first giraffe they
had ever seen, and when the bewildered creature, with its
dappled coat and its astonishing neck, was led in triumphant
procession through the roaring streets.

From his babyhood the boy had taken a lively interest in the
rival charioteers of the Four Colours, white, green, red, and blue,

CHARIOTEER DRIVING IN THE CIRCUS
From *Costume of the Ancients*, by Thomas Hope

whose contests were followed breathlessly by the whole population of Rome. In the reign of that very eccentric Emperor,
Caligula, the Greens were the favourites, and the satirist Juvenal
wrote on one occasion : " All Rome has flocked to the circus
to-day, and the uproar of the crowd can be heard miles away.
I understand from this that the Greens have, as usual, been
the victors ; otherwise I should see the city in deep mourning,
just as if the Consuls had been slain a second time at the battle
of Cannæ." This seems a little hard on the White, Red, and
Blue teams ; but no doubt their turn came, when the fickle
favour of the crowd deserted the Greens. The names of the
successful charioteers, and even of their horses, have come down
to us through being recorded on bronze and marble tablets, on
walls and monuments, stamped on red pottery bowls, and carved
on knife-handles and on children's toys.

One of the most popular charioteers was a young fellow called

Crescens, a native of Africa. We do not know whether his hair was woolly or smooth, or what was the colour of his skin, but we *do* know that he had earned 1,558,346 sesterces by the time he was twenty-two.

Like Diocles and Scorpus, he was the idol of the citizens. His name, and the names of his horses, were in every mouth. The boy must have listened eagerly when he heard his elders discussing the skill of the rival charioteers, and the speed and beauty of their chariot-teams, their fleet horses which bore such names as ' Victor,' ' Palm-bearer,' ' Ocean,' ' Greek,' ' He-who-goes-round,' ' Charming One.' He may himself have been the owner of a toy chariot, not unlike the one preserved in the Capitoline Museum, round whose wheels were written the names of well-known horses, or he may have had a knife with a bone handle ornamented with a horse's head and the cap and whip of a charioteer. In his childhood Nero had just such a chariot, carved out of ivory, and he had to be constantly called to order by his tutors for talking ' horse-talk ' during lesson-hours.

The boy probably listened with less attention when his father's friends talked politics, or growled against the treachery of the Carthaginians and the blunders of the Senate ; but anything like a victory or a public funeral interested him, for that always meant the chance of a gorgeous procession. These processions were not simply long lines of marching people. In the triumphs captives walked chained to the chariots of the victors ; in the funerals there might be images of dead heroes moved by machinery, or masked actors mimicking the gestures and bearing of the departed. At the games held to celebrate Trajan's defeat of the Dacian Decebalus—it was on the same occasion that young Lucius Valerius Pudens won the Capitoline wreath— eight hundred ostriches with crimson-stained plumes were let loose in the arena, and eleven hundred wild beasts were slain.

These *Ludi*, or public games, became so frequent and lasted so long that in the days of the later Cæsars they went on practically all the time. How any work got done in Rome, and why the streets should always have been so crowded, when the greater part of the inhabitants sat almost incessantly watching circuses, it is a little difficult to understand.

The games were held for various reasons ; sometimes to commemorate events in Roman history, or to mark the funeral ceremonies of some mighty Roman ; sometimes to please the gods, often to please the people. From the 17th of January to the 22nd each year games took place within the walls of the imperial palace itself, and the less dignified Emperors, such as Caligula, Nero, and Caracalla, descended into the arena. The *plebs*, the great mass of the Roman populace, was, however, more interested in the shows which it was able to see with its own eager eyes. The crowds that seethed up the steep terraces of the Flavian amphitheatre and the Circus Maximus became so hardened that they saw nothing cruel or brutal in fights to the death between gladiators, and those wholesale massacres of bewildered wild animals which made the sanded space reek with blood.

When Pompey the Great celebrated his last triumph the people were so stirred by the quaintness and intelligence of the elephants driven to be slaughtered for their amusement that, Pliny tells us, " the whole multitude rose in tears, and called down upon Pompey the curses which soon descended on his head." But a century or two later no Roman crowd would have shown so much good feeling. Their sense of pity had been dulled, and the noble Romans were not a whit more compassionate than the stony-hearted and horny-handed *plebs*. The same Emperor who set guards round the stable of his favourite horse, lest the animal's rest should be broken, loved to see blameless, elderly Romans flung to the lions.

Apart from the brutality of these sports in the arena, there was certainly an element in them that appealed to a boy's natural love of excitement, contest, and danger. That quite small boys followed the gladiatorial duels with interest is clear from the number of toy gladiators, complete with sword, helmet, trident, or net, carved out of bone or ivory, some with movable arms, which have been found from time to time in Rome itself and on the sites of Roman settlements in other countries. But there were various thrills which one might hope to have in the amphitheatre. Freakish Cæsars, Caligula and Nero among them, sometimes let gaily hued birds loose over the crowd, or scattered sweetmeats upon the serried mass of human heads. It was even more exciting when, instead of sweetmeats, little discs were thrown which entitled those who caught them to claim some magnificent or embarrassing gift—it might be a golden cup, or it might be a live lion.

This whimsical way of giving presents appealed to the more frivolous Cæsars. A boy whose father had gone to dine with Heliogabalus would wait impatiently to find what lots had been drawn at the vast banquet of that Emperor of greedy memory ; would the *paterfamilias* bring home ten camels or ten flies, ten pounds of gold or as many pounds of lead ?

Frequenters of the Circus Maximus, the headquarters of the Greens, were sometimes rewarded with an even more remarkable experience in the days of Nero. It occurred to that wild-witted

THE COLOSSEUM
Photo Anderson

Emperor that his feats as a charioteer ought to be witnessed by the people at large instead of only by slaves, freedmen, and courtiers in his private circus on the Palatine hill. As the Greens were his favourite team he decided to give exhibitions of his skill at the Circus Maximus ; he wore a green tunic, and had the track strewn with copperas to give it a greenish tint. The imperial charioteer, with his dumpy, fat legs, his wobbling cheeks, and his scowling face, must have been anything but an impressive sight. But he dashed home ahead of all the other charioteers in every race for which he entered. His light-hearted habit of ordering the immediate execution of anyone who happened to annoy him deterred even the keenest competitor from drawing level with the imperial chariot. On the day when his chin was shaved for the first time Nero appointed a

new festival, the *Juvenalia*, and had five theatres erected for
the performances which he himself supervised. The boys of
Rome must have thought Nero a model Emperor. What were
victories in Dacia compared to circuses at home ? Five thousand
Roman youths had reason to take a very real interest in Nero's
pranks. He assigned to them the duty of applauding his
efforts as a singer when the whim seized him to sing in public,
and he rewarded them generously for their applause. When the
Emperor appeared, in the tunic of a Greek minstrel, and puffed

A TRIUMPHAL CAR
Photo Anderson

and panted in his efforts to produce his naturally weak and
husky voice, the faithful five thousand shouted in chorus : " O
incomparable Cæsar ! Apollo to a hair ! Augustus, and yet
surely the Pythian god ! On our oath, Cæsar, no man could
excel thee ! "

Certainly it was much more amusing to be one of Nero's pages
than to quail under the rod of some imitator of Orbilius !

On the north side of the imperial palace there was a large
house called the *Domus Gelotiana*, used, after the death of
Caligula, as a sort of training-school for the Court pages. These
lucky boys, released from the severe discipline of the pædagogus,
could not resist the temptation to scratch joyful remarks on the
walls of their new home. Their inscriptions are still to be seen.
Most of them tell the same tale in the same words, the name of

the boy only varying: *Corinthus exit de pædagogio, Marianus Afer exit de pædagogio*. But one page, more inventive than his fellows, added a little sketch, and explained his idea in eight words scribbled below. The sketch represented a donkey turning a mill, the eight words were: *Labora, aselle, quomodo ego laboravi et proderit tibi !* (Work, O little donkey, even as I have worked, and it shall go well with thee !)

The boy who had drudged at his books as hard as the little donkey at its mill-wheel would be all too eager to forget everything he had learnt when he escaped from the thra dom of the cane, and when he found himself among other boys as madcap as himself in the ample but unacademic walls of the Domus Gelotiana. There would be much talk among them of gladiators and charioteers, and little of Homer and Virgil. With the aid of ivory chariots and tiny warriors of wood, the Imperial pages must have re-run many a glorious race, and re-fought many a fierce battle. One would swear that there was no fighter so good to watch as the *retiarius*, the net-thrower ; another would be all for the *mirmillo*, who came forth in a gilded casque in the form of a dolphin's head, and yet another would raise *his* voice for the *Thrax*, for him who fought without breastplate or helm and met the bronze blade of the mirmillo with no more formidable weapon than a sickle. Then some enthusiast would be sure to invoke on behalf of *his* favourite branch of gladiatorial strife no less a divinity than Capitoline Jove himself, the patron of the city, whose image on the Capitoline hill was painted bright red by each Censor who entered on his office in Rome. Æneas would fade from the memory of Cæsar's pages, and the glancing helm of Hector himself might wax dim, but there were some chapters in Roman history that no Roman boy, having once heard them, could well forget. Would not that boy thrill as he stood upon the Sublician bridge ? It was a stone bridge in the time of Caligula, and long before his time ; yet it had not always been of stone. The name means ' wooden,' and this, the first bridge ever thrown across the tawny Tiber, had been wrought of wood once, clamped with great bolts of bronze. It was the bridge defended by Horatio Cocles against Lars Porsena of Clusium, " in the brave days of old."

WAX ANCESTORS

A.D. 30

By day the atrium fire burns low,
And in a shadowy, dusty row
    The waxen masks hang on the wall.

Then in the *impluvium* I can float
A dove's quill, like a little boat,
    And never mind those masks at all.

And o'er the shining pavement grey
I make my chariots run by day,
    Forgetful of my drowsy kin ;

Because they almost seem asleep
When no bright golden flickers leap
    To touch them on the nose or chin.

But after dusk the shadows shake,
And then my waxen forbears wake
    And wink at me with glassy eyes.

I do not *think* I am afraid
When the faint lights of sunset fade,
    And from the logs the red flames rise.

For, if I were, how could I stand
Alone before that ghostly band
    And watch them by those wavering flames ?

I have no fear. I know them well ;
One from another I can tell,
    And all they did, and all their names

The first, whose nose is cracked in twain,
He followed Cæsar into Spain ;
    And Quæstor was that crookèd one.

I whisper to the mask between
What chariot-races I have seen
    Because *he* loved to see them run.

The last is very old and dim ;
I never try to talk to *him*
    Or to pretend he talks to *me* ;

Though when the logs flare on the stone
I'm not afraid to be alone—
    A Roman boy should never be.

But then—somehow—though I've no fear
I'm glad the Little Gods are near,
    Each watchful in his little shrine.

And when dusk deepens in the street
I'm glad they have no hands or feet,
    Those waxen ancestors of mine.

CHAPTER V
The Norse Boy

IN the dark, troubled times that lay between the fall of Imperial Rome and the rise of the Christian civilization of the West a special prayer was added to the Litany which the Western priests chanted in their churches every Sunday: " *A furore Normannorum, libera nos !* " (" Deliver us from the fury of the Norsemen ! ") People shuddered when they heard that prayer. Boys who were old enough to understand what it meant wished passionately that they were old enough to go forth and defend their homes from those red-haired, braceleted barbarians who surged mysteriously out of the sea, and left a trail of smoking belfries and ruined villages behind them when they set sail again.

It was in the year 515 that a fleet of long, narrow Viking ships, with their high-peaked prows, their golden dragon figureheads, their painted bucklers slung along the bulwarks, first loomed out of the grey northern mists to the terror of western Europe. They came up the river Meuse

VIKING SHIPS
Morris Meredith Williams

and plundered the rich lands then ruled by a Frankish prince called Theoderic. This prince sent his son Theodebert to cut off

95

the retreat of the raiders, and their leader, Hughelik, was surprised and overwhelmed just as he was directing the re-embarkation of his men with their booty.

Perhaps the pirates were discouraged by this unexpected ending to their first adventure. At any rate they were in no hurry to come forth again from their cold northern homelands— the lands now called Norway, Sweden, and Denmark. In those days there were no clear frontiers dividing the fierce peoples, who wielded the same weapons, worshipped the same gods, and dreamed the same dreams of sea-wanderings. There, for nearly three hundred years after Hughelik's escapade, the Vikings, the men of the creeks or *viks*, remained, and the Christian communities of the West were left in peace.

Under Charlemagne, the mighty Emperor of the Franks, the hammer of the heathen, the conqueror of the Slavs, the Saracens, and the Saxons, a powerful Christian state had begun to grow up on the continent of Europe, and the various foes of Christendom, the fierce, fair foes and the terrible dark foes, had been held at bay. But when Charlemagne died in the year 814 his Empire crumbled into fragments, and there was no longer a powerful barrier between the scattered Christian princes of the West and the forces that menaced them from north and south.

The Norsemen must have had ways of hearing what came to pass in the lands of which they dreamed. They were allied in blood and friendship with the pagan Saxons whom Charlemagne harried so heartily, though they tried to hold aloof from the influence of the new faith long after Saxonia had accepted it. They must have heard much, these restless, hungry Norsemen,

THE PROW OF A VIKING SHIP
From the Oseberg ship
Oslo University
(See the poem at the end of this chapter)

96

of the splendours of the churches of Ireland and Northumbria, the golden candlesticks, the jewelled chalices, the embroidered vestments ; rumours reached them of the wealth of the Frankish princes and the Saracen lords of Spain.

But it was not upon the shores of Spain or Gaul, Ireland or Northumbria, that the second Viking raid took place, nearly three hundred years after the pirate Hughelik was slain on the brink of the Meuse. One fine morning word was brought to Beaduheard, the portreeve of the Anglo-Saxon King of Wessex, that three strange ships had cast anchor off the Wessex coast. Down rode the portreeve in haste, to demand the dues which must be paid by all vessels using that anchorage. But a sharp shock awaited the poor man. These were no peaceful merchants, coming to trade with the King's lieges ! Never had Beaduheard seen such odd-looking craft, so long and narrow and high-prowed, all hung with gaily painted shields, and thronged with mighty fair-haired giants clamouring in a strange tongue. The strangers, the sons of the Golden Dragons, were pirates from Denmark. They promptly slew the luckless portreeve, seized what plunder lay nearest to their hands, and sailed away into the dim distances from which they had come.

A stirring tale, this, for the small boys of Wessex—a tale of gigantic raiders with winged helmets, of glittering shields, and dragon-headed ships ! It may be that some of those boys, un-mindful of the hard fate of the worthy portreeve, watched the waves eagerly for many days after to see if a golden dragon's snout would peer suddenly above the foam.

So great was the terror inspired everywhere by these grinning, golden monsters, the Vikings themselves sometimes removed them from the prows of their homeward-bound ships lest the guardian spirits of their own shores should be alarmed !

The dash upon the Wessex coast was a small matter enough. The Norsemen soon had heavier work in hand. And ere long a whole fleet of golden dragons appeared off the holy isle of Lindisfarne, where the learned and gentle Aidan had founded a brotherhood of devout and unselfish monks. The pirates flung themselves upon Lindisfarne, pillaged and then burnt the monas-tery church, and slew such monks as were not able to flee in time. A cry of indignation rose from the whole of Christendom. But men did not yet realize the greatness of this peril looming out of the northern mist and foam. A year later the pirates returned, and the beat of their oars was heard in the Wear and the Tyne. Jarrow, the home of the Venerable Bede, the first and not the least of English historians, was laid in smouldering ruins. Then the raiders pushed on to Wearmouth. But a storm sprang up suddenly and drove their long, glittering boats on to the crags. So for a time they harried Northumbria no more.

Deliver us from the fury of the Norsemen!

That fury fell, like flame and tempest, upon Ireland and Wales a year after the sack of Jarrow. And in the years that followed the golden dragons clove the waves of many seas, and the ripples of many rivers were golden with the reflection of them. The Scheldt and the Seine, the Loire, the Garonne, and the Rhine were cleft by Viking prows. The Saracens of Spain and the Greeks of Constantinople gazed in wonder, as poor Beaduheard of Wessex had gazed, at the queer, peaked ships and the gleaming winged or horned helmets of the Norse rovers.

HORNED HELMET
From a bronze plate with raised figures found in Öland

Thrice in sixteen years the Vikings sacked the city of Paris. They ravaged the Etruscan city of Luna, on the gulf of Genoa, under the mistaken impression that it was a far mightier city— none other and none less than Rome! The Anglo-Saxon kings and kinglets, Alfred the Great among them, waged a desperate and not always successful defensive war against the dreaded seafarers, who sailed up the Thames and dug a deep trench, of which the line can still be traced in the Bishop of London's garden at Fulham. But while one fleet was in the Thames, other fleets were plundering the coasts of Mauretania and Majorca.

"From the fury of the Norsemen——" When the small boys of France and England heard the priest pray for deliverance from that consuming fury did they ever wonder what it might be like to be a small boy among the Norsemen? They could guess only dimly what sort of life the children of the Vikings led, in their home beyond the perilous North Sea, and they could not guess how closely the games and playthings of the small Norsemen resembled their own.

Instead of the kindly fairies that watched over the cradle of the tiny Roman, the Norse boy had for his guardians three stern spirits called Norns. They were sisters, and they dwelt at the foot of the mystic ash-tree Yggdrasil, whose roots they watered every day. They came to the house of the father and mother the night after a baby was born : at least, nobody dreamt of doubting that they came merely because nobody happened to see them come ! The father or, if he were away on some Viking voyage, his nearest kinsman, lifted up the child in the folds of his cloak, and looked at it keenly to see if it were strong and well-formed. If, for one reason or another, the parents did not feel inclined to welcome the new arrival it was given to some herdsman to take out into the forest. There he would lay it down, at the foot of a tree or in a sort of cradle of stones, and leave it to its fate. Sometimes a compassionate passer-by would find and adopt the baby. It must have been on the chance that this might happen that a piece of salt pork was often put in its tiny fist for it to suck, until either some human hand rescued it or the Norns came and bore off its spirit to the land of the dead.

When, as more often was the case, the boy was welcomed by his family a ceremony much resembling Christian baptism took place. Water was sprinkled upon the baby, and a name was chosen for him. It was believed that some of the good qualities and some of the good luck of a famous hero or a doughty kinsman might pass to the child who received his name. So the choosing of that name was a very important matter. Thus we read, in one of the ancient Sagas or epic-poems of the Norsemen, that when a son was born to Ragnar Lodbrok, the son of Sigurd Hring, the mother bade the maidservants carry the child to the hall of the long, rambling, smoky wooden house. There Ragnar took his little son in his arms, folded his cloak round him, and, when he was asked what name should be given, said :

> " Sigurd shall the boy be named ;
> He will fight battles,
> And be much like his mother,
> And be called his father's son ;
> He will be called foremost
> Of Odin's line."

Sometimes the baby had a whole string of names. Thus Helgi, the son of King Sigmund, was called 'Sun-mountain,' 'Snow-mountain,' 'High Town,' and 'Heaven-fields.' It was considered lucky to have more than one name; so Sigmund was

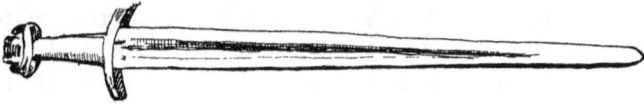

NORSE SWORD

evidently determined to do all that he could to bring good luck to little Helgi.

Gifts, known as 'name-fastenings,' were made to the baby when he received his name: rings, bracelets, pendants, and

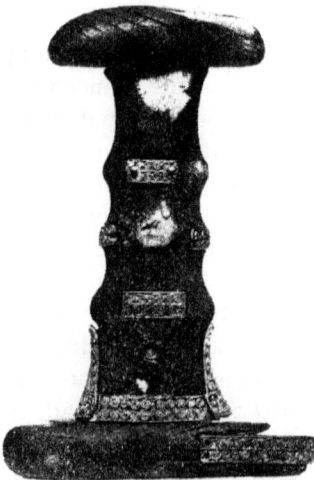

neck-rings of gold, silver, or bronze; ornaments wrought in the form of a serpent or of the hammer of Thor; drinking-horns; strange spoils from sea-raids, gold coins from Bokhara or blue glass bowls from Tyre. Among these gifts there would certainly be warlike weapons of various kinds, fit for the son of a warlike race. The sword was the chief weapon of the Norsemen, though they had axes, javelins, spears, and bows as well. They called the sword the " Blood Serpent," the " Fire of the Sea-Kings," the " Gleam of the Battle," and they loved to adorn its hilt and scabbard with elaborate designs wrought in iron, ivory, and silver, set with deep

HORN SWORD-HANDLE WITH GOLD
FILIGREE AND GARNETS
Found in Cumberland
British Museum

red garnets or inlaid with pale yellow gold. Legends gathered round the more ancient and famous blades. Some were said to have been made by no mortal hands but forged and tempered by Wayland, the smith of the gods, and wielded by divine warriors in unearthly battles.

The little Norseman might also, if his father were a great man

100

among the sea-kings, receive the gift of a little colt, born about the same time as himself, or even the gift of a bondsman as small as he. Thus we are told of Earl Haco (otherwise Haakon Jarl), a hero whom we shall meet again, that a youth named Kack, born on the same night as himself, had been given to him for a bondsman.

The young Viking seldom spent the whole of his childhood in the one-storied wooden house where he was born. It was a custom among the Norsemen to hand over their children to friends or kinsfolk of slightly lower rank than themselves to be brought up and trained and taught all the accomplishments necessary for the son of so hardy and venturesome a race. Very often the foster-parents grew to love the adopted son as well as if he had been their own ; but by allowing the son of another man to be formally confided to him and set upon his knee a Norseman acknowledged that he regarded himself as of less account and lower degree than the child's own father. This is shown in a curious old tale of which one of the ' heroes ' is King Athelstane of England.

Athelstane, whom the teller of the tale calls ' the Good,' but who would seem also to have deserved to be called ' the Sly,' thought of a ruse by which he might entrap Harald Fair-hair of Norway into owning him as his overlord. So he sent a messenger to the Norseman bearing a beautiful sword wrought with silver and gold and precious gems. The messenger held out the hilt toward the Norse King, saying : " Here is a sword which Athelstane of England sends you as a gift." Harald, not unnaturally, stretched out his hand and grasped the hilt. Whereupon the messenger calmly remarked : " Now, even as our King willed, you have taken hold of his sword. Henceforth are you his vassal and his sword-taker."

Harald was exceedingly wroth, and his first impulse was to slay the audacious messenger. But older and wiser men reminded him that it would ill become one king to lay violent hands upon the envoy of another ; and they added that the best way to answer a trick of this sort is to play a better one. So the messenger was allowed to go in peace.

But the following summer Harald sent his greatest friend, Hauk Habrok, on a journey to England, and before Hauk steered west in his dragon-boat the King laid in his arms a baby boy called Haakon, a child of the blood-royal, though his mother was but a bondwoman, and explained the little surprise he had planned for the King of England.

Hauk found Athelstane in London, and when the tables had been cleared in the great hall of the palace he went in, followed by thirty of his men, and saluted the Anglo-Saxon King. Little Haakon, hidden in the folds of Hauk's cloak, was probably fast asleep, otherwise by beginning to cry at an awkward moment he might have brought Harald's plot to nought.

The King welcomed the Norseman courteously. And then Hauk said : " Lord King, Harald, the King of the Norsemen, greets you well. He sends you as a gift a white bird, well-trained, which he prays you to train even better hereafter."

Therewith he flung back his cloak, and, before Athelstane could prevent him, set the baby Haakon upon the royal knee. The King gazed at Hauk with mingled astonishment and rage, but the tall Norseman was nothing daunted, for he had a great Viking blade swinging on his left side, and he knew that there were thirty more such blades behind him.

Then Athelstane asked sternly : " Whose child is this ? "

Hauk answered : " The child of a Norse bondwoman, whom King Harald bids you rear."

Athelstane looked at the boy, and said : " This child has not the eyes of a thrall."

" Though the mother be a bondwoman," returned Hauk, " there is royal blood in the veins of the child, and now that he has been set upon your knee you owe the same duty to him that you would to your own son."

Then Athelstane asked wrathfully, holding the boy with one hand and his sword with the other : " Why should I rear this babe, though he were the son of Harald and his queen ? "

Then Hauk made answer : " You have had this child upon your knee ; you are therefore his foster-father. You may kill him if you will, but with him you cannot kill *all* the sons of Harald, and it will be said hereafter, as it hath ever been said, that he who fosters the child of another is the lesser man."

Then, before the astonished Athelstane had the presence of mind to continue the argument, away marched Hauk Habrok, his cloak under his left arm, his sword in his right hand, and his thirty men following him in single file.

It is pleasant to know that instead of killing little Haakon King Athelstane had him brought up at his own Court, and that he and his brother-king of the North played no more tricks on each other to prove which was the mightier king.

Though the young Norseman had none of the difficult lessons to learn which took up so much of the time and energy of the boys in Athens, Thebes, and Rome, his education was a serious and strenuous one. He did not learn to write on tablets or on parchment, but he had to learn something about the mysterious characters called ' runes ' which the Norsemen were wont to inscribe upon slabs of stone, upon their weapons and drinking-horns, and the rudders of their ships. Of these holy letters, which legend said had been first taught to the Norsemen by Odin himself, the greatest of their gods, the boy had to gain some knowledge, even though he should never carve them upon wood or ivory or stone. He had also to remember the names and the deeds of the fierce, far-wandering heroes of his race,

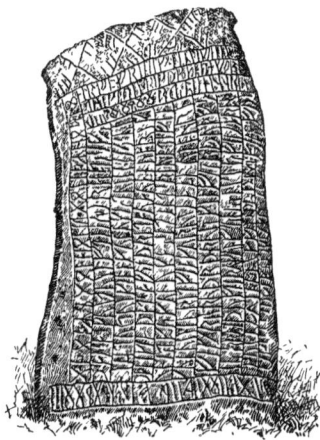

RUNES ON SLAB OF STONE

From *Mediæval and Early Modern Times* by Professor Hutton Webster (Heath)

and the names and attributes of its not less fierce divinities. In order to remember well he studied the art of the skalds, or bards, who handed down the legends of gods and men in interminable, unrhyming songs, whose rhythm is like the rush and clash of the waves against a craggy coast. Another study was the *Hávamál*, " The Song of the High," a tremendously long code of laws, also said to have been given by Odin himself to his faithful Norsemen. These laws are curiously humdrum and practical to have been the chief laws of so warlike a people. Early rising, temperance, hospitality, prudence, silence, fidelity in friendship, are among the virtues praised in the *Hávamál* ; but pity for the weak, chivalry to a fallen foe, clemency, and forgiveness had no place there.

Other branches of the Norse boy's mental training were the games of chess and draughts, the art of working in woods and metals, playing the harp, and speaking one or more of the strange tongues which the Vikings picked up in the course of their travels.

So much for his intellectual accomplishments. Far more important was bodily prowess. He was no worthy son of the sea-kings who could not wield a sword with either hand, throw two spears at once, draw the bow, row, swim, wrestle, ride bare-backed, run upon skis, and train hawks and hounds for the chase. A more unusual feat, which sounds both difficult and dangerous, was to leap from one oar to another while a galley was in motion. A certain Kali, son of Kol, thus modestly described his acquirements :

> " I am ready to play chess ;
> I have nine accomplishments.
> I am not like to forget the runes,
> I can read, I can work as a smith,
> I can slide on snowshoes ;
> Well can I shoot with the bow and ply the oar ;
> I know also
> Both harp-playing and verse-laws."

That a knowledge of these verse-laws might come in very useful is shown by this anecdote : King Olaf was annoyed with a bard called Hallfred, and said to him : " Thou art a *vandræd-skald* [a troublesome bard], yet shalt thou be my man." Hallfred, thinking of the gifts bestowed on a boy when he receives his name, replied : " What wilt thou give me, O King, as a name-fastening, if I am to be dubbed Vandrædskald ? "

The King, probably amused, gave the bard a sword without a scabbard, and commanded him to make a song, introducing the word ' sword ' in every line. So Hallfred sang :

> " There is one Sword of Swords (*i.e.*, the King)
> Who has made me sword-rich ;
> Now the wielder of swords
> Will have swords enough.
> I shall not lack swords ;
> I deserve three swords ;
> If only there were
> A scabbard to this sword ! "

Olaf gave him the scabbard. " But," he remarked, " there is

not a sword in *every* line." " Nay," retorted Hallfred, " in one line there are three." " That is true," agreed the King.

Though the *Hávamál* strongly urges the importance of being strictly moderate both in eating and drinking, it is to be feared that the Norsemen did not always bear these excel-
lent counsels in mind; and the greatest heroes seem to have been the most given to quaffing the sweet, heady mead out of the huge drinking-horns which

DRINKING-HORN

it was considered impolite not to empty at one draught.

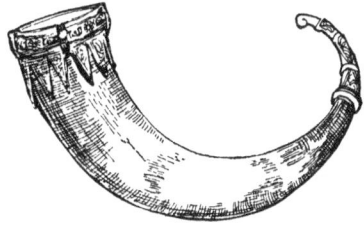

Feasting was, indeed, one of the principal pastimes of the sea-
kings when they were on shore. Great would be the excitement of the boys of the family when they saw the preparations for the feast begun, the fresh holm branches strewn on the earthen

WOODEN WAGON FOUND ON THE OSEBERG SHIP
By permission of the authorities of Oslo University

floor, the weapons that hung on the rough walls newly burnished, and the great joints of swine's flesh sizzling before the open fire. Greater still would be the excitement when the guests began to arrive, some on horseback and some in jolting, bronze-plated chariots. The guests would be most gorgeous to see, in their fur-lined cloaks clasped with jewelled brooches, their tunics of red, brown, or blue sewn down the seams with glinting threads of gold. On their legs they wore long woollen trousers, often cross-gartered with silk ribbons from the ankle to the knee, and round their waists were massive gold or silver belts wrought in discs and bosses of intricate goldsmith's work. The hair was worn very long, and neatly parted down the middle. One might imagine that these fierce sea-fighters would be sternly indifferent to their personal appearance. On the contrary, a Viking who possessed fine auburn hair, not too curly, was quite inordinately pleased with himself! His cherished locks were held in place by a fine circlet of gold ; over this he would pull a woollen cap or hat of black, grey, or white when he was out of doors. His long boots were of reindeer-skin, and in cold weather he kept his fingers warm with mitten-like gloves of the same leather ; upon the Norseman's breast swung a magnificent pendant of some rare metal, richly chased or embossed with figures of men and horses, or with runic words ; round his neck he might wear, as well, a neck-ring of twisted gold, or a string of amber beads. The rings on his powerful hands often reached from the roots of the fingers to the middle joints. After their mighty feasts of pork and mead the Vikings whiled the winter nights away by asking riddles—an amusement in which the boys of the household would early be allowed to share, as it was part of a Norseman's education to learn to ask and answer riddles wittily. Not every man was, or even believed himself to be, as clever as Heidrek, King of Reidgotaland, who had claimed to be able to solve any puzzle put before him. This Heidrek once indulged in a contest with a blind man named Gest, but he does not seem to have had a sporting chance as Gest called upon Odin to aid him, and Odin, somewhat unfairly, granted his prayer. Some of the riddles which Heidrek *did* succeed in guessing were handed down in one of the Sagas, and must have been repeated round many a banquet-board by simple-minded Vikings.

GILT BROOCH

There are runes on the reverse side

British Museum

" What wonder was this," asked Gest, " that I saw outside ? It had eight feet, and its knees were higher than its stomach." " The King of Webs," replied Heidrek, meaning a spider. " What wonder was this," Gest then demanded, " that I saw outside? It turns its head to the Underworld and its feet to the sun." " A leek," returned the King. " What kind of drink did I drink yesterday? " asked the blind man. " It was neither water nor wine, ale nor mead, yet it quenched my thirst." " Thou didst drink the night-dew," answered the King.

Considering that Gest had the advantage of Odin's aid his riddles might have been a little better !

Other means which the Norsemen used to make the interminable winter nights less tedious were tugs-of-war, with strips of walrus-hide for ropes, and ball-games, played with wooden bats and balls in high, barn-like sheds built for that purpose. Sometimes a match would go on for a fortnight. At other times ball-games were played upon the ice, and played with such energy that thumbs were dislocated and noses broken.

When the Norse boy had learnt all that he could learn at home the most interesting part of his education began. This was the Viking voyage. Until he had gone forth on one of these perilous pirate raids, and learnt all the lore and the craft of the sea, he counted for nothing, he was as much a child as the two children whom St Olaf found swimming wood-chips in a pond and pretending that they were war-galleys. But when he had returned from his first voyage he would be a man among men, with marvellous gifts to bestow and marvellous tales to tell.

Eirik, son of the famous hero Haakon Jarl, was only ten or eleven years old when he went on his first far journey with his father, and it is recorded that " when they went at night into harbour Eirik was not pleased unless his ship lay next that of the Jarl." He probably felt safer when his redoubtable father was near at hand.

The ship on which the young Viking sailed might be one of a brave fleet setting forth to assail some neighbouring country, or she might be one of a little dauntless company bound for some hitherto unknown shore. She would bear some beautiful name, such as ' Raven of the Wind,' ' Gull of the Fjord,' ' Deer of the Surf.' She was steered from the starboard, as whalers are to this day, and the steersman stood on a little raised deck beneath which was the sleeping-cabin of the chief of the crew. That crew consisted usually of about sixty men, all of whom would be ready to take their turns at rowing (two or three of them to each oar), watching, and the various tasks of seamanship, and all of whom would be eager to gird on their war-harness and fight when the hour for fighting came. Each ship had her weapon-chest, well stored with swords, axes, spears, and helmets, and it is certain that ample space would be left for the booty which the pirates hoped to collect when they dropped their anchor (quaintly nicknamed ' the Cold-nosed One ') in some harbour far away. It was a thrilling moment for the Norse boy bound on his first sea roving when the lean ship, glittering with the burnished shields slung along her sides, was pushed down the wooden rollers into the sea, when the oars began to beat the frothing water, and the square sail, woven in broad stripes of gay colour, filled with a friendly breeze.

If on their outward journey the adventurers caught sight of a flock of wild swans swooping and flashing against the clouds they believed that they had had a glimpse of the doomful Valkyries, the shield-maidens of Odin.

It was not always quite clear beforehand why a boy was sent on a Viking raid, nor whether he would turn out well from the Viking point of view. Sometimes a great Jarl, not over-serupulous, would pack off a youth of his own blood who happened to be in his way, hoping that the 'prentice pirate might never return. Legend tells that this was the case with two sea-roving celebrities, Ragnar Lodbrok and Rolf, who, however, survived to win riches and renown. Or sometimes, when there was dearth in the bleak northern lands, a number of men and youths would be chosen by lot, and sent off in a ship to seek their fortune somewhere, anywhere, beyond the Path of the Sea Birds, the Necklace of the Earth.

A boy who had shown neither spirit nor courage in his childhood might then develop, quite unexpectedly, all the Viking virtues. Such a boy was Thorstein Thorgyngsson, a sort of boy-Cinderella, who had been wont to lie on the floor among the ashes, as close as he could to the fire, so that people going to and fro tripped over his legs. Every one was astonished when this lazy fellow asked leave to go with his brother on a Viking expedition ; but from the moment that he rose from the ashes and washed and armed himself he seemed a different boy, and in after-years he was famed among the sea-kings.

For fair winds the rovers prayed to Thor, for quiet waves, clear skies, and swift victory. Even after they had become more or less Christianized on the surface they could hardly refrain, in moments of peril, from calling to their old friend the hammer-wielder, the thunderer, to come to their aid. When the ship drove her golden prow into the foam the pirates had not always decided whither to steer their course. Sometimes they tossed up a lance to help them to decide, sometimes they blew a feather into the air and watched which way it would float. But as a rule they knew beforehand to what point they would bend the grinning golden prows ; it might be to the bubble-shaped domes of Mikkelgaard (Constantinople), it might be to the misty coast that lay beyond Greenland, that coast where Leif the Lucky found grapes growing wild, and which is now part of what we call North America.

Upon many far shores their ships must have been shattered ; in the depths of many dark seas their golden dragons must have been strewn. But when a sea-rover failed to return it did not always mean that he had perished. Some of them settled in the lands they had ravaged. And there to this day fragments of their language remain embedded in the common speech of men. The names by which the days of the week are known in all English-speaking countries are the names of Viking gods, and wherever on the map of England there are place-names ending in ' wick,' ' ness,' ' thwaite,' ' toft,' or ' garth ' it is more than likely that those places were once inhabited by the northern warriors who, abandoning the terror and splendour of the sea, planted themselves on the island where many of their blue-eyed descendants dwell to this day.

Others, following Rolf, most dauntless of leaders, overwhelmed that part of France still called Normandy and induced King Charles the Simple to conclude the Treaty of St Clair-sur-Epte Others, again, enrolled themselves in the bodyguard of the Byzantine Emperor at Constantinople—a force still recruited from the Norse countries when, five hundred years later, the Turks crushed the gorgeous Christian Empire of the East. And others, many others, when their wanderings were done, returned to their Norse homelands to die.

Yet even in death the sea-kings were not forgetful of the sea. When one of those fierce and fearless rovers died he was clad in his war-gear and laid in his own ship. His goodly sword was girt about him, his axe and spear were put near his nerveless hand. Near him also were the draughtboard and draughtsmen that had gone with him over many leagues of wild water, his great bossed shield, his drinking-horn, and the richly decorated bridle of his horse. Then the ship would be drawn up on the shore, her sail hoisted, her golden prow pointed toward the sea, and there she would be burned, till nothing but a few charred timbers and some half-molten fragments of bronze and gold were left. Or it might be that instead of burning the brave ship the Vikings would pile great stones about her, till a solemn cairn rose to the sky.

STIRRUP INLAID WITH BRASS
Found in the Thames at Battersea
British Museum

There was yet another way in which the dead sea-rover might be laid to rest. Then, instead of burning his ship on land or heaping a cairn of rocks above her, his kinsmen would push her down the beach into the sea, and then let the flames devour her as she vaguely drifted at the will of the waves and the wind. So went many a battle-scarred warrior, lying in his armour with his sword beside him, and borne in his flaming sepulchre along the " Path of the Sea Birds," that mysterious path which he had followed long years before, an eager boy setting forth on his first voyage to the unknown lands beyond the grey verge of the sea.

TERMINAL OF DRINKING-HORN
British Museum

GOLDEN DRAGON

A D 980

THE sail, the great square sail is furled,
　　Not yet we grip the oar ;
Our ship, that seeks the brink o' the world,
　　Still lies upon the shore ;
With clashing spear and wingèd helm
　　They fill the armour-chest ;
Then forth, o'er Ægir's silver realm,
　　Forth, forth unto the west !

My runes are learnt ; I have laid by
　　My balls of wood and bone ;
Now I must con the runes o' the sky
　　And leave all toys alone.
The golden dragon on the prow
　　Stares fiercely out to sea ;
He feels the salt wind's kiss and now
　　He longs to go, like me.

Our golden dragons of the north,
　　Our grinning beasts of fear,
Cleaving the cold grey waves go forth
　　And toward the sunset steer.
And till a boy has sailed away
　　To sunset and beyond
A babe he is, and best had play
　　With wood-chips on a pond.

Soon down into the frothing blue
　　The lean, long ship will slide,
With all the bucklers of the crew
　　Swung gleaming on her side ;
Soon will the dragon's golden scales
　　Be flecked with silver foam,
When all our red and purple sails
　　Fill with strong winds from home.

Now whither will our dragon swim,
　　When land dips down astern ?
Although he looks so wise, from *him*
　　I cannot hope to learn :

Only our leader knows, who stands
  Behind the dragon's wing,
Shading his fierce brows with his han
  And softly muttering.

It may be wise, it may be well
  To fill the ship with stores
Of ham that has a sharp salt smell
  And mead that speeds the oars ;
But I, I would our sails were out
  To catch the humming breeze,
And that our dragon's golden snout
  Were thrusting through the seas.

Whither ?   I care not—or not much–
  And I can wait to learn
What far, strange shores our keel sha
  What far walls we shall burn ;
Nor hams nor mead our casks shall h
  As back to port we speed,
For they seek gold and they find gold
  The Golden Dragon's breed.

CHAPTER VI
The Anglo-Saxon Boy

AGAINST the advance of the Christian missionaries in England the fierce gods of the Norsemen put up a stubborn fight. The last to yield was Odin, who fought with the rearguard, and retreated very slowly. In the year 683 he was still being adored in the Isle of Wight. Southern England clung to the Norse deities long after Celtic and Saxon teachers had made Northern England a stronghold of Christian culture, and even after the Italian Augustine had converted Kent, and the Northumbrian Wilfrid, Sussex.

About this time, when Odin was making his last stand off the Hampshire coast, it chanced that a great pestilence fell upon the monastery of Jarrow. In the beautiful church, the pride and joy of the Abbot and the monks, the chants became fainter and more ghostly until they almost died away altogether. And at last only the Abbot remained unsmitten—the Abbot and one small boy.

With a heavy heart the poor old Abbot betook himself to the deserted church at those hours of the day and night when it used formerly to thrill with the deep voices of the monks and the clear trebles of their little scholars. Some of those scholars were very little indeed. The one who, like himself, escaped the pestilence had been sent to the monastery-school when he was only seven years old.

It was disheartening for the Abbot to utter the noble words of the psalter in the echoing church from which no chanted responses came back to him, and he knew that it might be many days ere the sick brethren were healed and ere new scholars, coming to fill the places of them that had died, could learn the words and music of the chants. Yet, after all, the good Abbot was not absolutely alone. He had that one small boy to help him. And very proud that small boy must have felt when he lifted up his high, fluting boy's voice and sang the responses to the strong, sonorous intoning of the old man. Between them

H   113 those two kept the monastery rule unbroken, and went through as many services as it demanded. These were eight in each day. *Mattins*, sung at midnight or soon after, and followed immediately by *lauds*; *prime*, sung at six o'clock in the morning; *terce*, at nine o'clock; *sext*, at noon; *none*, at three p.m.; *vespers*, toward sunset; *compline*, before retiring to rest. Until we realize that from the Church's point of view six o'clock in the morning is the *first* hour it seems strange that it should be called ' prime ' and that midday should be ' sext.'

So from the dark hours before dawn until the dusk that follows sunset the Abbot and the little boy left none of the offices of the day unsung, and continued to wend their way sturdily to the deserted church until, one by one, the surviving monks crept back to their stalls.

The name of that boy, whose young voice once lost itself among the massive Saxon pillars of Jarrow, was Bede. After his death he came to be known as the Venerable Bede. He will be remembered always as one of the gentlest, kindliest, and most learned of Anglo-Saxons, and as the first Englishman to write English history or to translate the Gospels into the language of the simple people.

Bede was destined from his childhood to a life of study and seclusion, but not every Anglo-Saxon boy who spent part of his boyhood in a monastery spent the rest of his days there. A great and noble enthusiasm for learning sprang up among the hard-riding, deep-drinking earls and thanes. Few of their more promising sons were denied an opportunity to sharpen their young wits upon the ponderous volumes of grammar, rhetoric, and theology which then formed the be-all and the end-all of higher education. They were an open-air people, these Anglo-Saxons of the seventh to the eleventh centuries. Unlike the Romans, who gathered themselves together in towns which soon spread into cities, they tended to disperse, and to build isolated homesteads among their woods and fields. Groups of houses formed themselves into villages in course of time, but a Saxon town was seldom larger than a village that had overgrown itself. The Anglo-Saxons were bluff and sturdy in body, and, for the most part, simple in mind, yet capable of admiring—and even of creating—what was beautiful. From this race of husbandmen and hunters were born cunning craftsmen, brilliant scholars, and

unforgotten saints. And this stalwart race responded eagerly
to the influence of the great men it brought forth—men like
Alfred, Alcuin, and Bede, Dunstan, Wilfrid, and John of Beverley.
Some of the handiwork of the Anglo-Saxon craftsmen endures to
bear witness to their skill, and to
fill us with admiration for the
scribes who wrote out the Latin
gospels at the behest of King
Athelstane, the goldsmith who
wrought the golden cross of St
Cuthbert, the masons who built the
tower of Earls Barton. Still, the
scattered communities of Anglo-
Saxon England were open - air
people. The Anglo-Saxon boy's
earliest impressions would be all
of country life, of the fields and
farms round his home, and the
different labours and rewards of

THE GOLD CROSS OF ST CUTHBERT
In Durham Cathedral Library

the farmer's year. In the meadows great herds of swine roamed,
often under the care of boys no bigger than himself. Another boy
would trudge beside the slow-moving oxen that drew the plough,
shouting encouragement to them till he was quite hoarse.

As soon as a child was old enough to be useful it was not
allowed to spend many idle hours, and nobody thought then that
reading and writing, those deep and difficult arts, should be imparted to any but the most intelligent children. A certain Ælfric,
Abbot of Eynsham, who had translated Priscian's famous grammar and other grave works into Anglo-Saxon, bethought him of
writing a series of dialogues for the use of schoolboys, and we
learn from him that the boys of the early eleventh century went
out and worked in many ways while they were still young enough
to go to school. Ælfric represents a group of youths coming to
a schoolmaster, telling him that they are ignorant, and praying
him to teach them to speak Latin. They include a young monk,
a ploughboy, a shepherd, a cowherd, a huntsman, a fisherman, a
fowler, a merchant, a seaman, a cobbler, a salter, a cook, and a
baker. The master asks these boys if they are willing to be
flogged. One of them replies, " We would rather be flogged than
remain ignorant." The master then proceeds to ask each pupil

questions about his daily life, and he hears how the ploughboy has to go out and yoke his oxen at dawn ; how the shepherd, with his trusty dog, guards his sheep from wolves, and makes cheese from their milk. The next boy is one of the King's hunts-men, who lays snares for wild beasts and chases stags, wild boars, and hares with his hounds ; he is rewarded by his royal master with the gift of a horse or a bracelet when he has done well. He and the fowler, who catches birds with nets or lime, lures them with whistling, or hunts them with his hawk, chat to each other and agree to exchange a large hawk for a swift hound. The schoolmaster then questions the fisherman's boy, and learns that he fishes chiefly in the river and sells eels and min-nows, pike and trout to the people of the nearest town. " Why don't you fish in the sea ? " inquires the teacher. " I do sometimes, but it is a long way off." " Are you anxious to catch a whale ? "

TOWER OF EARLS BARTON CHURCH
NORTHANTS
From *England*, by Gilbert Stone

" I am *not*." " Why is that ? " " Because," replies the unenter-prising fisherman, " whale-catching is a dangerous business." The teacher reminds him that many of his craft catch whales, and gain much money, but the boy returns : " You say true, but I dare not ; I am too lazy ! " The answers of the merchant's apprentice call up visions of an eleventh-century Dick Whitting-ton, sailing to regions beyond the sea, and bringing home rich cargoes of purple and gold, ivory, silk, and wine. The cobbler's boy can do many useful things as well as making and mending shoes ; he has learnt how to make bottles of leather, purses, spur-straps, and bridles. The salter claims that without his aid butter and cheese and herbs would perish. The baker declares that no man could live very long or very well without *him*, that his bread strengthens the hearts of men, and that little children cannot pass him by.   The cook's boy then speaks up, and says that lacking his art meat would be eaten raw, and there would be no good sauce for it.   A blacksmith then points out that without *his* aid not only would the ploughboy have no plough-share and the fisherman no hook, but the tailor would lack a needle, the cobbler an awl—from which it would seem that the Anglo-Saxon blacksmith was a resourceful fellow.   And it is clear that food was always uppermost in the Anglo-Saxon mind !

ANGLO-SAXONS AT DINNER
From a manuscript in the British Museum

In the house of an earl or thane the whole household would sit down together to the principal meal, the family and the guests of honour above the great saltcellar, the servants, farm labourers, swine-herds, and chance wayfarers, below.   The scene at an Anglo-Saxon repast of this kind, with its barbaric hospitality and rough abundance, is vividly painted in *Ivanhoe*.

At other times the boy might dine with his father and mother and their friends at a smaller oblong table covered with a linen cloth.   There were no forks, but at each place lay a sharp, broad-bladed knife.   Ale or wine they quaffed from polished cow-horns rimmed with silver.   On the table itself would be several massive dishes, one containing small dome-shaped loaves, another a whole fish staring up at the rafters of the oak roof with its glassy eye, another such fruits as were in season.   Hot joints were brought crackling from the kitchen-fire on long iron spits, so that the diners could help themselves, and hack off as much as they pleased with their own broad knives. A boy who had been sent to one of the great monastic schools at Canterbury, Jarrow, Malmesbury, or York must have thought wistfully sometimes of the cheerful table at home—the smoking golden-brown j o i n t s, the shining s i l v e r fishes, the songs of the gleemen—when he sat at the frugal board of the monks, plodding through his bowl of very solid barley-porridge, and listening to the grave voice of one of the brethren reading aloud from a big, solid book. What a contrast, too, between the rows of silent monks with their shaven heads, their dark, rough gowns, and the people who sat round the long, noisy table at home ! Then the boy's own dress

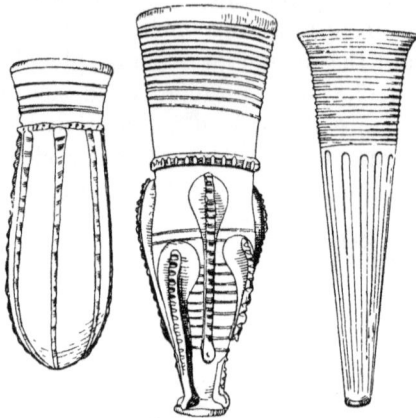

ANGLO-SAXON GLASS
British Museum

had been much like his father's—a tunic of well-spun woollen cloth, dyed some deep, rich colour, and embroidered at the hem with beautiful flowing and curving designs in threads of many hues mingled with threads of gold. Out of doors this tunic would be almost covered by a very full cloak, reaching to about the middle of the leg, clasped by a flat brooch or gathered up on the shoulder through a large ring of some precious metal. These rings and brooches were often exceedingly beautiful, both in craftsmanship and design. Many still exist, finely chased or embossed, set with crystal or enamelled with luminous colours. The craftsman was seldom at a loss for an idea.

DRESS OF A SAXON BOY
From a manuscript in the British Museum

On one such brooch there are two queer little peacocks; on another an amazingly angular Daniel is seen standing between two stiff, square lions. Round his neck the noble Anglo-Saxon sometimes wore a pendant jewel, similar to the famous 'Alfred jewel' discovered at Athelney. That this oval pendant of gold, crystal, and enamel really belonged to the greatest of all Anglo-Saxons

GOLD RINGS
British Museum

seems beyond doubt, for the inscription running round the crude little figure of a man grasping two flowers is, " Alfred had me made."

Such ornaments, together with the not less costly jewellery of the ladies of the family, would be kept in caskets of wood or of whalebone elaborately carved with scenes from the Norse Sagas and from the Bible—the Biblical characters bearing a strong resemblance, both in face and costume, to the heathen heroes in the adjacent panels. Bone and wood were used to make many beautiful things of daily use. The comb with which the boy and his father and mother kept their long locks in order was often an elaborate piece of carving, adorned with fierce-looking

lions' heads and curling, flowing scroll-work. The carver was
sometimes so charmed with what he had
done that he signed it, as an artist would
sign a picture. On the case of one such
comb in the British Museum is written, in
old Saxon script : " Thorfast made a good
comb." Thorfast certainly did.

The boy's father would need Thorfast's
comb even more than the boy did, for he
had not only very long locks to keep tidy,
but also a flowing beard which hung down
from the chin in two peaks. Edward the
Confessor had just such a beard, so fair a
flaxen as to be almost white. But by the

KING ALFRED'S JEWEL time of the Norman invasion the younger
Anglo-Saxons had taken to shaving their
chins and cultivating moustaches with two long, drooping ends,

GOLD NECKLACE WITH GARNETS AND THE CHRISTIAN EMBLEM
Found at Desborough
British Museum

ANGLO-SAXON JEWELLERY IN THE BRITISH MUSEUM

Buckles and pendants found in the King's Field, Faversham

as did Harold and his brother Tostig. On his legs the boy wore close-woven woollen hose, usually cross-gartered after the fashion of the Norsemen from ankle to knee, and on his feet were peaked

BEADS OF AMBER, GLASS, AMETHYST, AND CRYSTAL
From cemetery at Kempston, Beds
British Museum

shoes of neat's leather with an oval opening on the instep and curving slightly upward at the toe. Hats were not often seen, but pointed woollen caps were worn in cold or rainy weather.

Hawking and hunting were sports which the Saxons, like their Norman conquerors, loved most passionately. When he was old enough to ride after his elders with his own pet hawk on his gloved wrist and

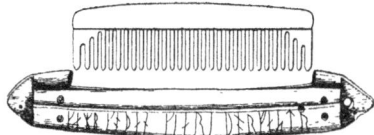

BONE COMB-CASE
The runic characters state that " Thorfast made a good comb " The comb is indicated above the case
British Museum

his own hound barking and leaping beside him the Anglo-Saxon boy must have been as happy as a boy could well be. Under the high, wooden saddle his horse had housings of bright-coloured cloth cut into streamers which flapped and flew as

121

they galloped along. A collar hung with tassels and bells, and beautiful iron stirrups inlaid with bronze scrolls often added to the picturesque appearance of the Anglo-Saxon steed, which, for the rest, was an animal more remarkable for solidity and staying-power than for grace or spirit.

Shooting with bow and arrow was another sport at which the English youths would be anxious to excel ; but they had indoor games as well, draughts, chess, and tests of skill with long wooden bats and wooden balls about the size of tennis-balls. Back-hand strokes seem to have been admired, and, if we may judge from the pictures of the players which have come down to

A SAXON NOBLEMAN HAWKING
From a manuscript in the British Museum

us, it was necessary to lunge with one knee bent, or else elegantly point one toe, before either serving or hitting back a ball.

As Alfred the Great did in his boyhood, the boy would pick up, almost without knowing it, the songs of the wandering harpers, and fragments of the interminable old tales retold in rambling but not unmusical rhythm by the gleemen who sang round the smoky hearth on winter nights, when the wild geese honked weirdly over the roof, and it was dark and windy outside.

Life was rough and hard and simple, yet pleasant in many ways. A small boy must have been sad to leave all these delights behind him and submit to the bleak discipline of a monastery school, however well he loved his monkish teachers, and however much he wanted to learn all that they could teach him. Yet many boys—among them little Bede, who chanted the responses to the Abbot of Jarrow—grew to love that severe and secluded existence so well that they cared for no other and remained in the cloister, imparting what they had learnt there to another generation of little boys, who were sometimes attentive and sometimes unruly, as they themselves had been.

ANGLO-SAXON GLEEMAN
From *The Sports and Pastimes of the People of England,* by Joseph Strutt

It was not always in some great monastery-school such as those at Canterbury or York that a Saxon scholar first conned his lessons.

ANGLO-SAXON DANCE
From an illumination of the eighth century in the British Museum

Aldhelm, one of the most learned men of the age before the Conquest, was, according to tradition, once a pupil in a school very unlike the lofty building with polished pillars and painted

123

windows which Wilfred reared on the banks of the northern Ouse. The facts of Aldhelm's life are a little vague and misty, with the vagueness and mistiness of far-off, hardly visible things, but, according to the old chroniclers, he was a pupil of that Adrian of Africa who with his dark face astonished the flaxen-haired children of Kent to whom he taught the tongue of the ancient Greeks at Canterbury. Before, indeed long before, he went to study there Aldhelm is said to have betaken himself to a quaint sort of school kept by an Irish (or, perhaps, a Scottish) hermit called Maidulf. This man, seeking a spot where he might meditate in peace, halted on the edge of a great forest near the borderline between Wessex and Mercia. A Roman-British township had once stood there, but Saxon or Viking invaders had overwhelmed it, leaving only one fragment of wall upright. Under the shelter of this broken wall Maidulf built himself a hut of tree-trunks. As his aim was solitude and tranquillity it seems a little curious that when his wooden dwelling was finished Maidulf should have started a school ! Yet that is what he did. And, so intense was the enthusiasm for learning which had sprung up in southern England, pupils came to him from far and near.

Aldhelm was all his life an ardent scholar. When, in later years, his friend Bishop Hedde invited him to spend Christmas at Winchester he wrote excusing himself on the ground that his studies would make it impossible for him to pass the festive season dancing [*tripudians*] in the company of the brethren there. This allusion proves that life in a monastery was not one weary round of prayers and vigils and lessons from year's end to year's end. Christmas was a time when severity was laid aside, when small boys dressed up as bishops, and bishops played ball with their clerks.

In Maidulf's school on the edge of the greenwood, where the songs of the birds must have distracted the attention of the scholars sometimes, the course of study would not be so full or so varied as that which the boys at York pursued under Ethelbert and Alcuin. " There Ethelbert moistened thirsty hearts with divers streams of teaching and dews of study, imparting to some the science of grammar, pouring into others rivers of rhetoric. Some he taught to play the flute of Castaly, some to rove, lyre in hand, upon the Parnassian hill." Alcuin, who was Ethelbert's pupil and then his successor, wrote thus of his old master, and he added that the harmony of the planets, the laws of the sun and stars, the characteristics of men, birds and beasts, and the mysteries of holy writ were also among the subjects pursued by the boys at York.

There is an anecdote of the boyhood of Alcuin which, it has been suggested, may indicate that some of his teachers ' dressed up ' one dark night, and came to his bedside in the guise of

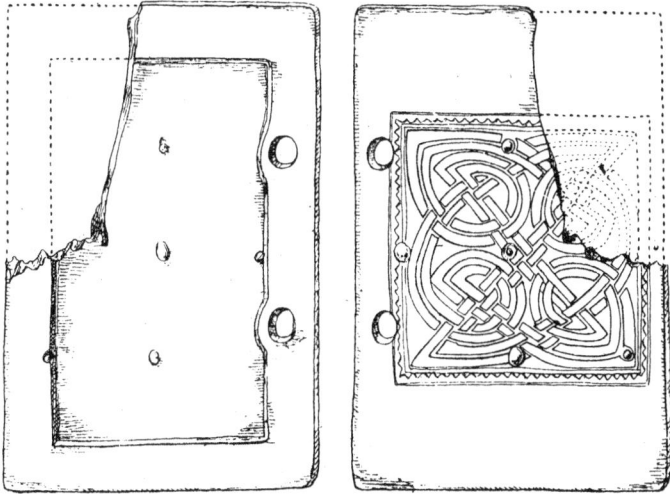

BONE WRITING-TABLET
(Inside and out)
Found at Blythburgh, Suffolk
This was no doubt fastened by two thongs to its twin, as in Roman times. Wax was spread on the sunk panel inside to be written on with a stylus
British Museum

visitants from another world. Alcuin himself, with his knees knocking together and his heart thumping wildly, believed them to be the spirits they declared they were, and was deeply impressed when they warned him against indolence, against reluctance to rise at midnight in winter to sing mattins and lauds in the dark, freezing church, and against taking more delight in the sweet verse of Virgil than in the sterner songs of King David.

Alcuin is in many ways one of the most interesting of the Anglo-Saxon scholars whose careers we can trace, though sometimes indistinctly, from the time when they began to learn their letters in the raftered hall of some monastic school. He became head-master of York, where he had been such an inattentive small

boy, and the fame of his learning went abroad till it reached the
ears of Charlemagne, the Emperor of the Franks, who invited
him to come and act as tutor to his sons and to the noble youths
of his court. Alcuin went. And the tall, golden-bearded Emperor himself loved to sit and listen when the witty monk of
York was explaining to the Frankish princes the movements of
the stars, the rules of rhetoric, and the marvels of unknown
countries far away. Theodore of Orleans, one of Alcuin's friends,
thus describes the scene :

> He brings forth pious lessons from Holy Writ,
> And solves the puzzles of numbers with favouring jest.
> Now he puts an easy question, now a hard ;
> Of this world now, now of the world above.
> The King alone of many that fain would
> Can solve the skilful puzzles Alcuin sets.

Fortunate pupils, whose master could enliven even an arithmetic lesson with a " favouring jest " ! But all the lessons they
learnt from Alcuin cannot have been quite so easy. He made
his royal pupils plod through the grammatical treatises of
Priscian and Donatus, and in the works of neither is the ' going '
otherwise than heavy. Grammar, that is, of course, Latin
grammar, was one of the most important studies that a boy had
to approach. He had also to try to understand what his teacher
told him about geography and astronomy, and music and rhetoric
were never omitted from the list of his lessons. The cheerfulness
with which these eighth-century dominies expounded to their
pupils the movements of the stars, which they believed to circle
meekly round the world, and the form of the world, which they
believed to be more or less flat and square, is rather astonishing,
and can only be explained by the suggestion that the worthy
fellows had no idea how little they really knew about it all.

Confronted by a modern map, Alcuin and his boys would be
exceedingly disconcerted. According to the monkish geographers
of the tenth century the countries and continents had the oddest
shapes, and were dispersed over the world in the oddest manner.
At the extreme west of the map stood—or were believed to
stand—the Pillars of Hercules, named after the muscular hero
who was said to have planted them there to mark the boundary
of the habitable world. It has been supposed that the ancients
gave these names to the rocks Calpé and Abyla, at Gibraltar and

Ceuta ; but it is always easier to imagine what the ancients *may* have done than to make sure what they really *did*. There is little attempt, in this old map, to divide the continents in an

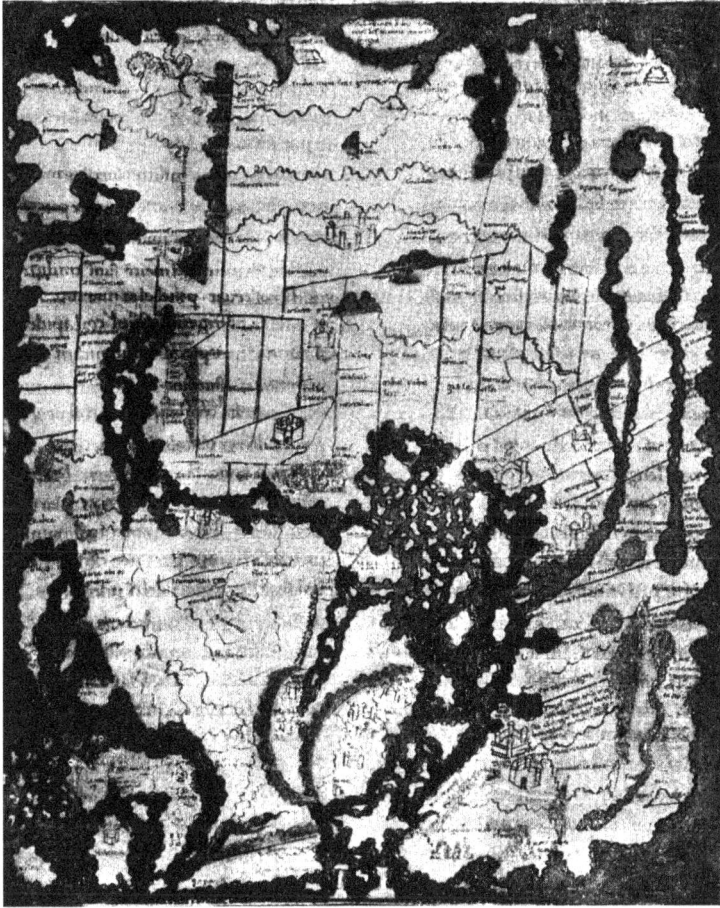

A TENTH-CENTURY MAP

(Note that the west is at the foot and the east at the top of this map, and the north and south left and right respectively)

From a manuscript in the British Museum

intelligible way ; but the monk who drew it realized that England was somewhere up in the north-western corner, and that Egypt, Arabia, Chaldea, and Medea were more or less in the south-east. But he had not a glimmering notion of the outline of the various

127

countries. He draws Britain as an irregular crescent with its two horns pointing due west. Spain he makes like a dunce's cap with the tip toward the North Pole, while the Danube, due south from Constantinople, flows into a nameless sea almost opposite the plain of Troy.

What this ancient geographer lacked in knowledge he made up in imagination. Never at a loss, he plants mountains, rivers, and cities freely on the jagged masses of dry land between which the nameless seas appear in the most unexpected places. Of the cities he does tiny sketches, showing them with walls and towers. At the north-eastern summit of the world he puts a four-legged beast, curly-maned and snub-nosed, and writes above : " Here lions abound." Sometimes he is more cautious, as when he notes : " Here there is *said* to be a burning mountain." Of an oval-shaped island which he calls " Tabrobanea " he tells us that it has ten cities and that the fruit-harvest is gathered twice in the year.

Alcuin's humour must have lit up even the dull pages of Priscian and Donatus, and it was not only arithmetic lessons which he enlivened with jests. He amused himself—and his pupils—with riddles. On one occasion a friend had sent him the gift of an ivory comb with a lion's head carved at each end. To the giver he wrote : " I send you as many thanks as I have counted teeth on your gift. I am not terrified by the fearsomeness of this beast, but charmed with the looks of it. I have no fear of its biting me with its gnashing teeth. I am delighted with its fawning caresses, which smooth my hair." And then he proceeded to compose a riddle, which his royal pupils cannot have found very hard to guess :

> " A beast has suddenly come into my house,
> A wondrous beast with two heads.
> Two heads it has, but one jaw-bone only.
> Twice three times ten are its terrible teeth,
> Yet it does not eat with its teeth,
> Which are fed with a crop which grows on my head .
> Tell me—what beast is this ? "

Surely this cannot have been one of the " skilful puzzles " which no one but Charlemagne had wit enough to solve !

The Anglo-Saxon idea of education was well summed up by the greatest of Anglo-Saxons, King Alfred. " No man," he wrote,

FROM AN ANGLO-SAXON BOOK

An illuminated page of a Gospel written early in the eleventh century

British Museum

" can govern unless he has fit tools—men of prayer, men of war, and men of work." In order to provide himself with these tools he, like Charlemagne, established a school at his own Court where both Latin and Saxon books were studied, especially Saxon narrative-poems and the psalms of David. To these studies the boys applied themselves until they were old enough and strong enough to learn " hunting and other arts befitting well-born men." In the King's own words, it was his wish " that all the free-born youth of England should be set to learning . . . until such time as they have mastered English writing. Let those be taught Latin whom it is proposed to educate further and to promote to higher office."

Alfred himself had few opportunities, in an arduous and often anxious life, to devote his mind to the quiet and leisurely pursuit of learning ; but that he, man of action though he was, realized

> . . . what a world of profit and delight
> Of honour, glory, and omnipotence
> Is promised to the studious,

STATUE OF ALFRED AT
WINCHESTER

Hamo Thorneycroft, R A.
Photo Woodbury

his own deeds and words from his earliest youth bear witness.

The story of how he was inspired by his mother's promise that whichever of her sons should first learn its contents by heart should be the owner of a beautifully illuminated book she showed them is almost as familiar as the story of the charred cakes. And it was Alfred's eagerness to be able to work at his books, reading, writing, translating, that led him to devise a little funnel of horn to shield his lamp from the draughts which blew through the unglazed windows and ill-hung doors of his palace, and made the feeble flame waver and bend.

Alfred's idea was, after all, not very remote from the ancient Greek idea : cultivation of mind and body, so that each is truly and justly balanced by the other. Not only in the Court-schools

founded by the Frankish Emperor and the Anglo-Saxon King was that sane and splendid aim pursued.   There were monkish teachers who had no desire to keep their pupils stooping all the time over the knotty pages of Priscian in the quiet shadow of the cloister : such a teacher was St John of Beverley, Bishop first of Hexham and afterward of York.

When John of Beverley was visiting the scattered parishes of his far-stretched see he would take some of his boys with him, both those who were dedicated to a monastic life and those who were to return to their families and to the world outside the monastery-walls when their education was completed.   The boys,

AN ANGLO-SAXON SCHOOL
From *Domestic Manners and Sentiments,* by Thomas Wright

released from their lessons, joyfully followed the good Bishop on horseback over the Yorkshire wolds.   When they saw an expanse of smooth turf before them they used to ride races against each other.   One of these boys, Heribald by name, who afterwards became Abbot of Tynemouth, related to the Venerable Bede how in a race of this kind he had nearly lost his life.   He told how, on one of these episcopal journeyings, they had found themselves on the edge of a wide and level ground, well suited to racing. Immediately they gathered round Bishop John, imploring him to allow them to have a race.   At first the Bishop hesitated ; but they pleaded so hard, he relented, and said that they might do as they wished, on condition that his favourite pupil, the teller of the tale, remained at his side and took no part in the contest.   So off galloped the others, leaving the future Abbot of Tynemouth behind.   But not for long !   The vision of the receding horses, the thud of the flying hooves, were too much for the boy. Before he realized what he was doing, before the startled Bishop could stop him, he too was off, spurring wildly to overtake those who had got the start of him. Behind him he heard a voice exclaiming dolefully : " Alas, what sorrow this horse-racing brings upon me ! "

But the horse, urged thus impetuously forward, stumbled and fell, pitching the disobedient scholar upon his head. Years afterward he told Bede how the Bishop had knelt all night in prayer by the bed where he lay unconscious, and how his was the first face that he saw bending over him when consciousness returned ; and he told how, when he opened his eyes, he exclaimed : " Is it indeed thou, beloved master ? "

DRAUGHTSMEN OR GAMING-PIECES MADE FROM
HORSE-TEETH
British Museum

BIRDS' LATIN

A.D. 1020

IF he would have our memory filled
  With all the dusty lore of Rome,
Why did our master choose to build
  His home so near the small birds' home?
      While we with rhetoric strive
        And over grammar pore,
      It seems that all the birds alive
        Are singing round the door.

Sometimes the wisest of the birds
  Perch on the ledge—though not for long;
So have they learnt two Latin words
  And mix them sometimes with their song.
      Beyond the log-built wall,
        From leafy gleams of sky,
      Venite, pueri ! they call,
        Venite, pueri !

Is it not hard to twist one's brows
  O'er Priscian—would he had ne'er been born !—
When birds are singing in the boughs
  From the first glimpses of the morn?
      I would their new-learnt lay
        Were not so clear to me;
      Venite, pueri ! they say
        As plainly as can be.

I and the other boys are sure
  That we have rightly understood
The words with which they try to lure
  Our thoughts away into the wood.
      Before our master grew
        So old and grave and grim,
      Did never a bird when skies were blue
        Call *Veni, puer !* to him?

CHAPTER VII

The Norman Boy

THE principal and most plain duties of a hero of chivalry were two : firstly, to go forth to battle on horseback ; secondly, to live in a castle. Among the foremost to fulfil these two duties with anything like thoroughness and enthusiasm were the Normans, the French-born descendants of

CONISBOROUGH CASTLE
Reconstructed by C H. Ashdown, F R G S.

the Norsemen who had settled in the lower Seine valley at the end of the ninth century. Wherever they tarried the Normans built castles, not in Normandy alone, but in Sicily and Calabria and Apulia. Where the Anglo-Saxons had dwelt magnificently or miserably in rambling houses and huts of ill-jointed wood, their conquerors dug moats and reared keeps, and made towering strongholds of tight-knit masonry. Long before any Norman wore a crown many a Norman was ' king of the castle,' lord of the tower, looking down, as an eagle does from its dizzy nest, upon the woods and waters spread out mapwise far below.

135

THE BOY THROUGH THE AGES

Our first acquaintances among the Norman boys must be the grandsons and great-grandsons of those Vikings to whom King Charles the Simple had given leave to take and to hold that pleasant land of orchards and rivers and green hills thenceforward known as Normandy. These men, sea-rovers and Woden-worshippers no more, but still a keen-eyed, sturdy, and venturesome folk, learnt many of the arts of peace while forgetting none of the arts of war. They mastered the crafts of the land without losing the lore of the sea. When they turned their backs on Woden and all his works and opened their arms to the saints

HAWKING

From a manuscript of the thirteenth century in the Bibliothèque Nationale, Paris

From *Mediæval and Early Modern Times*, by Professor Hutton Webster (Heath)

and heroes of the new faith the Normans did not forget their own old leaders, and the boys who grew up in the castles of Normandy, stout-hearted boys who learnt early how to let slip a hound, how to call a hawk home to the wrist, had heroic figures of various kinds and colours to kindle their boyish enthusiasm. One of the most picturesque

of these was Rolf the Ganger, son of Rognwäld Jarl. This tremendously tall and tremendously doughty pirate owed his nickname to the length of his legs. He was too tall for the little Norwegian horses, and so, perforce, wherever he went he had to 'gang' on foot. Those long legs of Rolf's bore him, after brief incursions into the Orkneys and the Netherlands, to the pleasant land of France. A king whose nickname was ' the Simple ' could hardly be the sort of man to hold his own against the gigantic Norseman and his fierce followers. The French barons made a desperate effort to drive out the strangers ; but Rolf and his men would not return whence they had come.

From their headquarters at Rouen the Vikings made raids on the prosperous cities of the surrounding country. From Bayeux their leader brought back not only rich spoils, but a fair French bride, the daughter of Berenger, Count of Bayeux. Their son,

136

William Longsword, and their grandson, Richard the Fearless, are among the famous Normans of whose boyhood we catch vivid glimpses. After a time Charles the Simple performed the one wise action of his otherwise feeble reign. He made a treaty with Rolf, and granted him as a dukedom the goodly lands thenceforward called Normandy. Rolf agreed to be baptized, but the name of 'Robert,' then bestowed upon him, never seemed to stick. He agreed to do homage to the witless King, but when the moment came the proud sea-rover flinched. One of his followers had to undergo the ordeal in his place, and even this simple fellow could not bring himself to kneel and kiss the foot of Charles. Instead, he seized it and raised it to his lips with such energy that the luckless King toppled backward, and lay prone. Norman boys who laughed at the tale of the Viking's homage did not pause, one fears, to pity the Viking's victim.

The tall figure of Rolf would be among the most memorable in the mind of

A NORMAN NOBLE WITH HIS HAWK
E. M. Robinson

these boys, by whom, after his death, he would be given the French form of his name—Rollo or Rou. And then came his son, William of the Long Sword, whose upbringing was very different from that of his father. To do his duty and follow where fate led, the Ganger had little need of bookish learning; but he was determined that his son should learn other arts than those of warfare and the chase. He may, indeed, have feared that he had carried the experiment too far when young William developed a quite unexpected ardour for his lessons, and declared that he would rather be a monk than Duke of Normandy. But

this pious humour passed, and when the great sea-rover was laid to rest in the cathedral of Rouen, his son, instead of disappearing into the shadows of the cloister, came forward as a wise and warlike leader of the people. They dubbed him ' Longsword,' and he was, in truth, the first of the mighty Normans, for the blood of the French Berenger ran in his veins with the blood of the Viking Rognwald Jarl. He, in his turn, was anxious that nothing should be left undone to make his little son worthy to fill his place. The boy gave early promise of quick wit, high courage, and good looks, and William, fearing or foreseeing that he might not live to watch him grow to manhood, handed him over to his own old tutor, Botho. " My son, Richard," said Longsword, " must be noble among nobles, scholarly among scholars, steady in the saddle, swift in the field ; he must know all the lore of the countryside, the bends of the rivers, the boundaries of meadow and woodland ; he must know how to fly his falcon, how to cast a net, how to throw a javelin, let slip a hound, and slay a deer." And in the generation that followed all these things were part of the training of all the boys who were born and grew up in the castles of Normandy.

A Norman boy learnt early to be self-reliant and resourceful, and to bear his part modestly and yet fearlessly among men. It happened more than once that some little fellow would be chosen, for family or political reasons, to fill a bishop's throne. The tiny prelate would go through the ceremony of installation with as much dignity as he could muster ; often, if the stern and warning eyes of his elders had not been fixed upon him, he might have felt inclined to laugh or to yawn, or to gather up his trailing vestments in both hands and run for his life.

No boy had ever more desperate need of fortitude than Richard, the son of Longsword. Before he was as tall as the famous blade from which his father's nickname grew, Arnoulf, Count of Flanders, had ambushed William of Normandy, and had compassed his death.

When the fatherless Richard was solemnly crowned in the Cathedral of Rouen the ducal diadem was too heavy for his head, and had to be held up by two of the fierce Norman barons, and the great crimson mantle lined with ermine trailed on the cathe-dral pavement far behind him. Richard let the barons ease the weight of the overwhelming crown, but when others wanted to help him to carry his father's sword he stoutly rejected their aid, and carried it alone, swaying and stumbling a little on the way, from the high altar to the ducal chair. A good beginning for the boy who was to earn the nickname of ' the Fearless ' before he had left boyhood long behind him !

He soon had even greater need of all his courage. The King of France at that time was Louis the Fourth, called, because he had been brought up at the Anglo-Saxon Court across the Channel, Louis d'Outremer. This King, when he heard how Arnoulf of Flanders had brought about the death of William Longsword, bethought him that the dukedom of Normandy, with its orchards, its thriving towns, and its lordly castles, might be a fief for his bandy-legged younger son, Lothair. The dead Duke had stood godfather to Lothair, and, according to the old way of thinking, the link between a godfather and the kinsfolk of his godchild was as strong as though they were allied in blood. What could be more natural, then, more simple, or more praiseworthy, than for the French King to ride to Rouen and offer to take charge of young Richard of Normandy ?

The Norman barons were anything but pleased when Louis d'Outremer appeared, with a large force of men-at-arms, before the walls of Rouen. They knew only too well that the King was in league with the traitor Arnoulf of Flanders, the betrayer of Longsword, and they must have wished bitterly and vainly that they could defy him to wrest the boy-Duke from their keeping; but they dared not. The barons had neither the provisions to stand a siege nor the men to risk in a sally, so they had, perforce, to deliver Richard over to his royal ' friend.' Great hopes had been centred in this brave-hearted Norman boy. In the eastern and more cultured districts of the dukedom he was loved for his French blood and his skill in bookish learning ; in the west it was remembered that he was the grandson of Rolf the Ganger, and that he could speak the vigorous speech of his Norse ancestors as well as the courtly French and the solemn Latin. Love without power could not rescue Richard. The anxious Normans saw him carried off to Laon, the French King's fortress on the crest of a half-moon hill, and their only consolation was that the boy's tutor, Osmond de Centeville, had been allowed to go with him. But what could Osmond do, alone against so many foes ? Gerberga, the Queen, was among the most powerful

of these. And there was Arnoulf of Flanders, who did not like
the idea that the son of the tall Norman whom he had betrayed
might grow to manhood and avenge his father, and who never
ceased to urge his friend Louis d'Outremer to make young
Richard's captivity as strict as possible. Arnoulf did not forget
to remind Louis that if Richard were kept out of the way—or,
better still, *put* out of the way—the Norman barons could soon
be dispersed and overcome, and Normandy would once more be
a fief of the French Crown. Clearly, the first thing to do was to
get rid of the watchful and devoted Osmond. But, for some
reason or other, Louis put off this most necessary proceeding
from day to day, and contented himself with keeping tutor and
pupil in stifling and irksome bondage. How could the son of
Longsword learn how to fly his falcon and let slip his hound
within the stern towers of Laon ?

On a certain sunny autumn day Louis had to remain within
doors, judging the various claims and disputes laid before him
by his subjects. Then it occurred to Osmond—or perhaps first
of all to Richard—that this would be a glorious chance for them
to escape and have a day's hawking in the meadows below the
castle-hill. So while Louis sat frowning and nodding in his
chair of state his two prisoners were off and away, flying their
fleet falcons, and spurring eagerly in pursuit when the birds
swooped suddenly to earth. So far did the falcons range, so
far did Osmond and young Richard follow them, dusk had fallen
and the King's ordeal was over before they returned to the castle.
Then the storm broke ! Louis' sickly terror changed to wild
wrath when Rolf's grandson was in his clutches once more. He
swore that he would have him maimed and crippled for life, and
that he cared not a jot who knew it ; he threatened to put out
Osmond's eyes ; and he poured forth cruel words against Longsword and all his breed.

Woeful tidings these, for the barons and the people of Normandy ! The story of the King's wrath was not slow in reaching
their ears, and then a solemn fast was proclaimed throughout the
land, and through all the Norman towns walked processions of
priests chanting the penitential psalms, and imploring the help
of Heaven for their beloved Duke. The next news they had of
him must have made them fear that their prayers had been vain.
Richard had fallen sick. Every one who saw him serving the

King and Queen at table—as high-born children were taught to serve their elders in those days—was painfully struck by his altered looks. He would neither eat nor sleep. The French Court soon decided that he was fretting himself to death, and that Lothair would not be kept waiting long for his dukedom.

Louis and Gerberga, and all their well-wishers, rejoiced greatly. They were to get rid of Richard without shedding innocent blood ! Bandy-legged Lothair would succeed to the broad domains that Rolf and Longsword had made strong, and prosperous, and proud.

The sentinels grew careless. Why should they spend wakeful nights and watchful days when death was coming so soon to set their prisoner free ? And soon it seemed that death was very near. The King proclaimed a banquet in the great hall of the castle, and there, in the smoky, flickering gleam of the torches, deep tankards were quaffed to the health of Lothair, the future Duke of Normandy.

When the revelry was at its height Osmond suddenly remembered that he had not given his horse fresh litter and a feed of oats that evening. It casts an interesting sidelight both on the affection of the Normans for their horses and the rough simplicity of Norman manners that he should have undertaken this task himself, instead of entrusting it to a groom.

While the tankards were being filled and emptied and filled again in the clamorous hall Osmond slipped quietly down to the stables with a big bundle of straw across his shoulders.

Many hours later, when the torches were dripping stumps and the first pale streaks of dawn were creeping through the narrow windows, the revellers began to rub their eyes and to bethink themselves that it might be well to find out if the boy whose death they had been toasting were really dead yet. Those who first climbed up the tower to have a peep at Osmond's pupil came stumbling down with blank faces of dismay. Osmond was gone —and the boy too ! Then a hurried search of the stables showed that Osmond's horse—the brave beast for whose comfort he had been so anxious the night before—had vanished also. By the time that their enemies at Laon had discovered their flight Osmond and Richard were safe within the high walls of the Château de Coucy and in their own *Terra Normannorum* once more.

Solemn historians have paused to wonder how this Richard won his nickname of ' the Fearless ' without having shared in any famous exploit of war, and without giving any greater proofs of courage than every knight was expected to give—and almost invariably gave—in those perilous and stirring old days. It surely seems not unlikely that it was his proud fortitude during captivity that gained him that noble name, and that it was given to him by the Normans when they heard how their little Duke, not then twelve years old, had borne himself with unflinching valour, alone among his father's foes ; how, though the long ordeal came near breaking his spirit, he never wavered or bent before crafty Louis, or cruel Gerberga, or any of their false, fierce friends.

That was the part of Richard's history that would stir the blood of the Norman boys who heard it retold by their elders. They may have listened with less interest—or, perhaps, have ceased to listen at all— when the talk turned to the long-drawn-out plots and struggles and clashes of arms that followed before Richard the Fearless sat securely on the ducal throne of stout old Rolf the Ganger ; but it would please them to know that luck turned against Louis d'Outremer, and to hear how Harald Blue-tooth, King of the Danes, came to the rescue of his young kinsman. Boyish justice would be satisfied too by the knowledge that Louis was fated to undergo a captivity every whit as wearisome as that from which Osmond de Centeville carried off Richard in a bundle of straw.

From his elders the Norman boy would hear of the great deeds of the Norman dukes and their barons ; from the quaint figures carved over the cathedral doors and the gaily hued scenes piled one above the other in the painted windows he would learn a certain amount of Old Testament history, would become familiar with Daniel's lions and Jonah's whale, and the angels and demons of heaven and hell. But he had other sources of information. From the jongleurs, the wandering minstrels who plodded from

THE CHÂTEAU DE COUCY

castle to castle, a straggling horde of Tom Tuckers, all singing for their supper, he heard the *Song of Roland,* and other old songs celebrating the valour and the victories of dead heroes. In their anxiety to please their audience the jongleurs were apt to cast historical fact to the four winds, and to mix up a round dozen of French monarchs, Clovis and Charles and Pepin, Hugues and Dagobert and Clotaire, ascribing all they did, and much that none

QUAINT FIGURES OVER THE CHURCH DOOR AT KENCOTT
The constellation Archer
From *An Illustrated History of England,* by W. S. Robinson (Rivington)

of them had ever done, to the Emperor Charlemagne. They were not easily daunted, the jongleurs. The fact that Charlemagne had been dead for two centuries at the date when they fixed his last battle against the Saracens did not trouble them in the least ; nor were they influenced by the plain truth that the enemies that fell upon Charlemagne's rearguard in the gorge of Roncevaux were Gascons, not Saracens at all. They got out of the difficulty by saying that the Emperor of the Franks lived for two hundred years, and they gave such a vivid description of the paynim host, of the dusky-skinned Huns, Moors, Persians, and Tartars, with their ruby-encrusted helmets and their prayers to Mahomet, that very soon everybody was firmly convinced of the solid truth of the story.

With Roland, Charlemagne's nephew, the hero of the favourite epic of the Normans, began the chivalric tradition which sprang

143

up and flourished wherever the Normans went. Without mounted warriors how could there be *chévalerie*? The Saxons hunted on richly-housed, lumbering horses; but they fought in battle on foot, while the men who served under the real Charlemagne learnt from the real Saracens the value of cavalry in war. This lesson was soon put into practice. And thus, through these stout fellows, the descendants of the sea-rovers, from these warriors who dwelt in castles, fought on horseback, and went far afield in quest of adventure, the knightly idea came to France and England. Orders of knighthood came later, but they came soon. One of the earliest—the order of the Star—was founded by King Robert the Pious in 1022, when the idea was already striking deep roots into the soil of Europe and spreading great branches far and wide. From those roots sprang all the valiant tales, all the chivalric visions, that have kindled the hearts of boys for more than six hundred years. A world that remained cold and unstirred at the legend of the young knight's oath and vigil, his golden spurs and emblazoned shield, his loyalty to his order, his tussles in the lists, and his lifelong quest of peril and adventure, would be a grey, frozen world, unfit for any boy to live in, and fit only to be swallowed up by the fifth and final Age of Ice.

In the time of the great-grandson of Richard the Fearless Normandy had come to be regarded as the centre of knightly ceremonial. Then it was that a tall Anglo-Saxon, with a drooping fair moustache and a slight cast in his blue eyes, arrived at the Norman Court to receive the honour of knighthood. His name was Harold, and later on he was not liked in Normandy. The oath of a knight was a very serious thing to the Normans, and Harold was tempted to break an oath which he ought never to have made. Not so, it was said in Normandy, would Charlemagne and his paladins have acted; never would Roland, the hero of one of the most stirring poems in the world, break his vow.

The boys of Normandy knew all about Roland—more, indeed, than Roland can have known himself, for legends clustered thickly round him after he fell in the gorge of Roncevaux. He stands out, a magnificent figure, with his golden-hilted sword, Durandel, his golden-tasselled lance with its fluttering white pennon, and his shield dight with flowers. Never very far away was his faithful friend Olivier. "Roland," says the ancient chronicle, "was valiant, but Olivier was wise." Neither valour nor wisdom saved the two paladins from disaster. The traitor Ganelon sold Roland to the Saracen King of Marseilles for " gold and silver, rich silken stuffs, horses and mules, lions and camels." To call anyone a ' Ganelon ' was, throughout the Middle Ages, the strongest possible way of calling him a traitor. It was Ganelon who persuaded Charlemagne to give his gallant nephew the command of the rear-guard as the Frankish army wound through the deep passes of the Pyrenees, homeward bound from the wars against the Saracens of Spain.

The vanguard, led by the Emperor himself, went safely through the dark gorge of Roncevaux and was some way ahead when Roland and the rearguard entered the doomful shadows of the mountains. Charlemagne felt vaguely disquieted. He strained his ears for the sound of Roland's horn ; but the horn was mute, and he gave the word to proceed.

From rising ground Olivier looked towards Spain—and he saw the army of the Saracens glittering and rippling in the sun. But the news did not daunt Roland. " God grant us to do battle here ! " he exclaimed. Roland was valiant, but Olivier was wise. Olivier urged that the horn should be blown to call back the vanguard to their aid. " God forbid," cried Roland, " that it should ever be said of me that I sounded my horn for fear of the paynims ! "

The battle which followed is told in the *Song of Roland* at great length, with great wealth of detail. We hear how the Saracens jeered at the French, crying that they had been abandoned by their crazy Emperor ; we hear how gallantly Roland fought, and Olivier, and the stout-hearted old Archbishop who first blessed the Christians and then joined in the fray. When some dark Saracen struck a mighty blow Roland would utter an impulsive word of praise ; at other times he mocked his foes, and told them that never would the day be won by a rascal like their Mahomet. Presently Olivier's spear was splintered to the grip, but he continued to wield it lustily. " Where is your sword, that you call Hauteclaire, with its golden hilt and its pommel of crystal ? " shouted Roland to his hard-pressed friend. " I have no time to unsheath it," returned Olivier, " I have got to keep on striking ! "

From the steep flanks of the mountains fresh forces poured down to swell the Saracen army, but still Roland and Olivier, the

K   145 dauntless Archbishop, and the Twelve Peers of France urged their men on, and fought like lions where the fight was hottest.

Meanwhile, in France, men asked themselves if the end of the world were at hand ; the sky was riven with terrible thunder, the sun grew dark at noon. Nature herself mourned for the death of Roland, though Roland was not dead yet. By his in-domitable courage he had almost turned defeat to victory. At one moment it seemed as if the Christians would be able to hew their way through the heathen hordes and gain the open country beyond the deadly gorge. But a certain King Margaris, one of the Saracens, seeing how the battle was turning in favour of Roland, galloped back to the King of Marseilles, and brought up the main body of the paynim army. Then there was no more hope for Roland. The brave old Archbishop lifted up his voice and urged the warriors not to recoil. " Truly," he said, " death is coming to us all. But to-morrow you shall be among the Saints in Paradise." Even then, when all hope had been aban-doned, the two heroic friends held their own against the waves of Saracen cavalry that rushed down from the mountains. The paynims called on Mahomet for aid ; the French replied with their battle-cry, " *Mont joie !* "

At last, when only three hundred weary and battle-stained warriors remained of the great and gallant company whom he had led to Roncevaux, Roland decided to sound his horn. " Too late," said Olivier ; " if you had sounded your horn when I ad-vised you to, we might have been saved. Your valour is a fatal gift, Roland. Our long friendship must end now. Before sun-set we shall be parted one from another, and that most cruelly."

Hearing the dispute between the two friends, the Archbishop intervened. Truly, it was too late for the Emperor to save them now. But if Roland sounded the horn, he might come in time to avenge them. Then Roland raised the horn to his lips, and blew so loud that the echoes were heard thirty miles away. Charlemagne heard ; but the traitor Ganelon swore that there was no such sound. Then Roland made a mighty effort and raised the horn again. And again the vanguard heard. " Nay," quoth Ganelon, " that is never Roland—the strong, the proud, the marvellous Roland ! If, indeed, it be his horn, then he is chasing hares, and laughing with his friends. Forward, Sire, Why should we halt ? Who would dare attack Roland ? "

A third time, and with even more desperate difficulty than before, Roland sounded his horn. The Emperor heard the note, like a cry of despair. And one of his loyal barons swore aloud that it *was* Roland, and that Roland was hard pressed ! Then, at last, the vanguard turned back toward Roncevaux. The trumpeters blew a blast, the knights relaced their helmets, and the horses broke into a gallop at the touch of the spur. Too late ! Too late !

Olivier was the first of the two friends to fall. When Roland saw him lying dead on the ground, his face toward the east, his hands folded in prayer, he swayed in the saddle and would have fallen also had not the high golden stirrups upheld him.

At last only Roland and the Archbishop were left to carry on the fight. And then, too late, when they were both wounded unto death, the Saracens caught the menacing notes of the French trumpets and knew that the vanguard was spurring to the rescue. Wisely the King of Marseilles decided to withdraw before the approach of Charlemagne. The glittering waves of the Saracen cavalry began to recede toward Spain, their wild cries grew fainter in the distance. Presently there remained upright in the dark gorge only Roland. At his feet lay the Archbishop, nigh unto death. Olivier he could not see, and, mortally wounded though he was, he dismounted and went to seek him among the grim brotherhood of the dead. Under a pine tree, near a wild-rosebush, he found Olivier, whom he lifted lifeless in his arms and bore back to the place where the Archbishop lay, that he might bless them both, the dead, and the living so soon to die.

Soon the brave old Archbishop rendered up his spirit. And then Roland, feeling death upon him, turned toward Spain, the land of his foes, and, holding in one hand his good sword Durandel and in the other his horn, he stumbled up a little slope on the crest of which were two beautiful trees flanking four marble steps. With his last flicker of force he tried to break Durandal upon the stone, so that no paynim hand should ever wield that famous blade. Thrice he strove, and thrice the stubborn, supple steel sprang back unbroken. Then, seeing that he had striven in vain, Roland laid himself down at the foot of a pine tree, with his feet toward France and his sword beside him. The French host was drawing nearer every moment ; the rearguard of the Saracens had vanished now. Roland raised the gauntlet of his right hand to the sky. It was the last act of his life. Murmuring a prayer for mercy on his soul and forgiveness of his sins, he joined his hands and died. So fell Roland, the first and the greatest of the heroes of chivalry, the story of whose life and death was the best-loved of all stories among the boys of Normandy. Those boys had other heroes, some living and real, some creatures of myth and legend ; but Roland remained the beacon of Norman boyhood, the warrior whose deeds they could never hear too often retold, whose valiant life and pitiful death thrilled the heart of all France ; the warrior whose fame the Normans spread

CRUSADERS EMBARKING
From a manuscript

wherever they went, in Sicily and Italy and in the island of Britain. No one could understand the mind of the Norman boy, who had never listened to the *Song of Roland*.

The idea that when he grew to man's estate he too might break a lance against the Saracen was never very far from the mind of a young Norman in the days of Duke Richard the Good, son of that Duke Richard whom men called ' the Fearless.' This second Richard encouraged his people to go on pilgrimages to Palestine, and by degrees the fame of his piety spread all over the Holy Land. The children of Rouen soon saw with wonder the dark-browed monks who had come all the way from Mount Sinai, the terrible mountain of the voice of God, to gather tribute from the faithful subjects of Duke Richard. When the Normans realized that not only the sacred earth of Palestine but also the island of Sicily and part of the southern sea-coast of Italy were in the hands of the Saracens, they began to murmur among themselves, and to say that Jerusalem must be cleansed of these miscreants, and that their Greek fellow Christians by the blue Italian foam must be delivered from heathen bondage.

Presently adventurous young Normans, who had nothing to do and nothing to gain if they remained at home, began to wend their way southward. That was the road followed by eleven of the twelve valiant sons of a certain Norman knight, Tancred de Hauteville by name. Tancred was more rich in children than in lands or gold. One by one the younger sons had to leave the castle in the Cotentin peninsula and set forth to seek their fortunes. Serlon, the eldest, was not the least brave, but it was his duty to remain at home. Guillaume, Drogo, and Humphrey departed betimes, and had hardly left boyhood behind them when they found themselves fighting the Saracens and the Byzantine Greeks in Apulia and Calabria, down in the jagged heel of the Italian ' boot.' It was to rescue the Greeks from the Saracens that the three young de Hautevilles drew their swords, but if any of the Christians proved stubborn or ungrateful, they, too, felt the weight of the de Hautevilles' anger.

Among the boys at home in Normandy who were thrilled by the tidings that came from Italy were the younger children in the de Hauteville castle, especially Robert, Humbert, and Roger. Robert early won the nickname of ' Guiscard,' or ' the Wise One.' Many Norman nicknames were less complimentary, and some notable Normans bore such quaint titles as ' Crooked-beard,' ' Iron-arm,' ' Tow-head,' and ' Long-neck.' But when Robert was still a boy among boys in the valley of the Cotentin, flying his falcon, training his hound, and learning between times those few but knotty lessons of Latin grammar and sacred philosophy that all well-born children had to learn, he was marked out by his quick wit and his eager intelligence.

The story of his far-wandering, hard-fighting elder brothers would reach Guiscard only in broken fragments, but as soon as he was old enough to piece those fragments together he determined to follow where Guillaume, Drogo, and Humphrey had led. Humbert declared he would go with him. Roger, the youngest of the twelve, was resolved not to tarry long behind. To the three elders, busy giving and taking hard knocks among the Tunisian Arabs and the Byzantine Greeks, the memory of the little boys at home must have grown hazy as the arduous years went by. But one day, after the eldest of the three had died and the next brother had taken his place in their stronghold at Amalfi, a company of fair-haired pilgrims, carrying their wallets and staves as warriors carry bucklers and spears, emerged from the ravine at the mouth of which the steep little town of Amalfi stands. They were led by two remarkably youthful leaders, in whom the bewildered Drogo recognised his two brothers Robert Guiscard and Humbert. Owing to Roman jealousy of Norman conquests they, and their thirty men-at-arms, had passed through Roman territory in the pious guise of pilgrims. When once they had joined Drogo they threw aside their staves and hastened to enrol themselves under him. Then began the warlike career of which Guiscard had dreamed as a child in the castle in the Cotentin—a career which brought him much heavy toil, many sharp perils, great struggles, and even greater rewards. The sixth son of the simple Norman knight became Duke of Calabria and Apulia, and Europe rang with the fame of his warlike deeds. The youngest son—it is always the youngest son who does best in the world—spent thirty years making himself master of Sicily—long enough for the boys of his native Normandy to hear of his doings all through their childhood and to rejoice at his final triumph over all his foes when they were grown men. Long before the First Crusade went forth, Norman knights had set out for Palestine in warlike mood. But, somehow, they halted on the way to exchange knocks with the heathen in those fair lands where the heathen had no right to be

A PILGRIM
Morris Meredith Williams

150

—as little right as the Normans themselves, who promptly proceeded to build castles for their own benefit on the soil which
they had redeemed from paynim thrall. Other Normans reached
Palestine in a peaceable humour, told their beads at the holy
places, and returned to Normandy. Others again—among them
a very famous Duke of Normandy—did not return. This
Duke, Robert, was the second son of Richard the Good, but he
bore no resemblance to his father. According to the legends,
which gathered thickly round him, he was a fierce and unruly
fellow from his childhood. When his monkish tutor rebuked
him for his idleness he is said to have drawn his dagger and
thrust it between the poor man's ribs. Then with a band of
youths as reckless as himself he took to the greenwood, and led
much the same sort of life that Robin Hood did in England
some two hundred years later. Only Robert's career in the forest
had none of that merry good fellowship about it that made
Robin's sojourn in Sherwood seem like a perpetual picnic enlivened by an occasional charade. Robert had no friends so
respectable as Friar Tuck. One of his oddest acquaintances was
a certain Ermenoldus, a Breton, who had once sailed with a
pirate fleet toward the rising sun and had learned strange
magical lore from the Wise Men of the East. When Richard
the Good died, his elder son, yet another Richard, succeeded
to the dukedom. Then Ermenoldus began to stir up strife
between the new Duke and his brother Robert. In the records
of that time so many legends are mixed with sober truth, it
is difficult to disentangle them from each other. It seems,
however, that Richard's sudden death, as he sat at a banquet
with his brother in the great hall of Rolf the Ganger's castle at
Rouen, was believed by the people of Normandy to have been
caused by Robert, probably with the aid of the magic arts of
Ermenoldus.

Robert, now Duke, soon forsook Rouen for Falaise. He
shunned the grim old castle where he had heard, above the
shouts of the revellers and the clash of the tankards, the solemn
throb of the bell that marked the passing of his brother's soul
from the world.

Like Richard III of England, whom in some ways he resembles,
Robert was a good ruler, even though the shadow of dark sus-
picions deepened over him as the years passed. The people gave

him two nicknames—' Robert the Magnificent ' they called him, when they saw with what splendour he held his Court ; or sometimes, if they happened to remember the grim stories that clung round his youth, they called him ' Robert the Devil.' It was like him, mysterious, mocking, picturesque, and sinister fellow that he was, to set out on a pilgrimage to the Holy Land when

WILLIAM'S CASTLE AT FALAISE
Photo Neurdein

he felt that he was sick unto death, and to leave his kinsfolk and his barons ireful and perplexed.

The assembled barons told him roundly that he did very ill to leave the dukedom leaderless. His kinsfolk all believed themselves to have equally good claims to the ducal throne, and it was clear that they would rend Normandy asunder with their disputes should it stand empty. Then Robert reminded them that though his Duchess, Estrith, the sister of King Cnut, had been childless, he had, none the less, a son. The barons received this reminder without enthusiasm. Never would they regard as their sovereign lord the grandson of a tanner of Falaise ! If their magnificent Duke should leave his bones in paynim earth, they must find some other member of Rolf the Ganger's line to rule over them. But Robert, by sheer force of will, overcame their angry reluctance. Before he sailed for Constantinople, the ' Mikkelgaard ' of his Viking forbears, he called the barons together and made them do homage to his seven year-old son William, whose mother, Arlette, had been a tanner's daughter.

" He is but little, my lords," said Robert, lifting the boy in his arms, " but he will grow."

Of all the boys ever born in the dukedom of Normandy this William was the most interesting, and grew to be the most re-nowned. He gave the first proofs of his strong will almost as soon as he was born, when he took a tight hold of the rushes which strewed the floor where he lay. From his childhood his father trained him to be a leader. At the age of five he was placed at the head of a band of boys as small as he, whom he drilled and governed and dominated with wonderful decision and skill. At the age of eight he could read Cæsar's *Commentaries* ; and a taste for learning never left him. Indeed, he was wont to declare that an ignorant king was nothing better

HAROLD'S VISIT TO NORMANDY
From the Bayeux Tapestry

than a crowned donkey. Alone among envious kinsmen and scornful barons, the position of young William was almost as perilous as had been that of his great-grandsire, Richard the Fearless. Some impatient and unscrupulous enemy would most probably have got rid of him without remorse, had it not been that for a long time nobody knew what had happened to Robert the Devil. Many people believed that he was dead ; but no one could be quite sure. A pilgrim from the Cotentin, Pirou by name, had a glimpse of the mysterious Duke, and heard him crack a grim joke under the very walls of Jerusalem. There, said Pirou, he had encountered four swarthy paynims bearing a litter on their shoulders ; and the man in the litter, wasted and broken by disease, was none other than Robert of Normandy. Pirou then told how the Duke had called out to him to go home and tell the valiant peers of Normandy that he had met their liege-lord being carried to Paradise by four demons. Yet not for a long time, not till William was old enough to be safe from their malice, could the barons feel assured that Robert had really died, as

153

rumour said he had, at Nicæa, in Bithynia, and that he would never return.

The prophecy of Robert the Devil soon reached fulfilment.

HALLEY'S COMET
From the Bayeux Tapestry

The little boy grew, in body and in spirit, until he reached the stature of a great warrior and a great king. When Harold, the moustached Anglo-Saxon, came to visit his future conqueror in Normandy he was received by a powerful fellow more than six feet in height, broad-shouldered and keen-eyed, clean-shaven and with his hair cropped close on the nape of the neck after the Norman fashion. So much had the tanner's grandson grown!

The boys whose fathers he had drilled, in his childhood and theirs, heard and saw something of the excitement which thrilled all Normandy in the memorable year 1066. There was a great deal to see, not only on land and on water, but in the sky, where

NORMAN SHIPS
From the Bayeux Tapestry
The end ship on the right is William's. At its mast-head is the banner blessed by the Pope.

Halley's comet (only it was not Halley's then) was trailing its fiery tail. A year of wonders! But when in the autumn of that wonderful year William set sail for England the boys who had the good fortune to go with him were not the sons of nobles, nor even of merchants. In the crew of every ship was at least one boy, probably the son of some fisherman or boatman, used from his cradle to the sights and sounds of the sea. Such a boy, though he would not be strong enough to pull an oar, could slip up the rigging like a squirrel and perch on the cross-beam like a bird. From that perch he would see the Norman fleet, " seven hundred ships save four," in the bustle and stir of departure, when stacks of arrows and sheaves of nine-foot spears were hauled aboard, and coats of mail slung on poles, long, kite-shaped shields, and mighty barrels of crimson wine.

All the ship-boys of the fleet would be proud and joyful when at last it set sail, even though they had had to brave the buffeting of the autumn tempest that broke when the ships lay at anchor off St Valery. Nobody knew then that the tempest was doing yeoman service to William by holding him back till his enemy, Harold of the crooked blue eyes, had marched north, and till Southern England lay open and unguarded before him.

When once Harold was well on his way to Stamford Bridge, the wind dropped to a friendly breeze and the waves moved quietly round the painted keels of the Norman fleet. Then with what a beating heart must the ship's-boy of the *Mora*, Duke William's own ship, have perched himself above the cross-beam and high above the gently swaying deck. Looking down, he could see Odo, Bishop of Bayeux, that doughty churchman who loved hard knocks as well as any fighting-man, and Taillefer the minstrel, that same Taillefer who rode along the ranks before the battle fifteen days later, singing the *Song of Roland* with a loud voice and tossing his sword in the air. The boy's eyes would not follow the Bishop or the minstrel, however : they would be fixed rather on the tall form of Duke William himself, clothed in glittering grey mail. After a time there would be something else to do besides watching William as he donned his close-fitting steel helmet with its peaked nose-guard. A look-out must be kept for the first faint peep of English land. Like a streak of cloud on the horizon appeared the cliffs of Sussex : then, farther to the east, the green marshes of Pevensey, and the low, jagged fragments of Roman wall where once the fortress of Anderida had stood.

Soon the sharp, golden prows of the Norman fleet ran into the sandy shallows. Then, looking eagerly shoreward the ship's boy of the *Mora* saw the great Duke give a headlong leap, and stumble, and clutch at the sloping shingle with both hands. He could see the sudden fear in the faces of the bystanders turn to smiles

and happy nods as the Duke told them, with his deep laugh :
" By the splendour of God, I have taken seizin of England."
Then, from all the ships, men rushed and poured to the land,

THE BATTLE OF SENLAC
From the Bayeux Tapestry

with a great clashing of steel and clanking of wood and rumbling
of barrels.

Soon after all Europe knew how true were the words spoken
of his little son William by Robert the Devil, sometime Duke of
Normandy.

THE FIRST FALCON
A.D. 1122

How many days till Martinmas ?
I wonder !—Will they ever pass ?
Not yet have we reached Michael's day,
And Martin's seems so far away.

Of us five brothers I alone
Have not a falcon of my own
That I can bear abroad and fly,
Because the youngest son am I.

Roger and Humphrey, Hugh and Piers
Upon their wrists bear falcons fierce ;
If I had one on mine, maybe
They would talk falconer's lore with *me*.

My father said, " At Martin's tide
With them a-hawking you shall ride " ;
And never would he break his vow.
How many days till Martin's now ?

A glove of Roger's I have got ;
(It is too big, but I care not !)
And Hugh's old jesses I can chime
Upon my wrist at any time.

I'll smooth my hawk, and talk to her
As doth our wise old falconer ;
I've learnt the call to lure her home.
Will Martin's morrow *never* come ?

CHAPTER VIII

The Mediæval Boy

IN the Middle Ages—that is to say, in the thirteenth, fourteenth, and fifteenth centuries—a boy of noble birth had usually to look forward either to the golden spurs of knighthood or the solemn vestments of a priest.   A boy born in the class immediately below had a much wider choice, since from that class came the merchants, the lawyers, the traders, and citizens who formed the broad foundation of the many-coloured fabric of mediæval life.

Sometimes it befell that a poor knight might be glad to place one of his younger sons in the household of some wealthy merchant, as in the case of Richard Whittington's father ; but boys of good family more often passed their early years in the house of some great man, if not the King himself, then his chancellor, or some other prelate or peer.   Even the sons of merchants, if they had remarkable talents and powerful patrons, might be trained in courtly and knightly lore, as was young Thomas à Becket by the Anglo-Norman baron de Aquila at Pevensey Castle.   When Becket was at the summit of his splendour he was constantly attended by a throng of boys, sons of English and French nobles, whom he " trained in honourable learning and accomplishments." A lover of music and sweetmeats and silken attire like Chancellor Becket is not likely to have been a harsh master ; but of Cœur-de-Lion's Chancellor, Longchamps, Bishop of Ely, the son of a Beauvais ploughman, it is recorded that so stern was he that the boys of *his* household never dared meet his eye unless when he spoke to them by name.   Far more fortunate were the young Londoners who went to one of the three great church-schools of London.   On Shrove Tuesday these boys played football, school against school, at Smithfield ; in winter, if it froze hard they went and slid with skates made of sheeps' bones on the ice-filmed marshes north of the city.   On summer evenings they went for pleasant walks in the outlying meadows, where there were springs of crystal-clear water bubbling over bright pebbles.   One of these springs was so much haunted by scholars that it came to be dubbed ' Clerkenwell,' and, though the waters of that well, and the well itself, have vanished as utterly from sight as have the schoolboys of mediæval London, the place bears that name still.

THE SEA-FIGHT OFF SLUYS
Morris Meredith Williams

For a boy of noble descent the best possible fortune was to be numbered among the pages of some magnificent prince. There were many such princes in the Middle Ages, and, just as the colours of the western sky grow more vivid and more varied toward sunset, so does the life of Europe in Court and camp wax more and more gorgeous as the long day of chivalry begins to wane.

If a boy were not set apart for a priestly career, manners and accomplishments were often regarded as more useful and important than bookish learning. Thus, in the very ancient ballad of " King Horn " we are told that as a child the hero was handed over to the Steward of " Aylmar the kyng " to be taught the lore of woods and rivers, how to act as cupbearer and carver at the royal board, and how to play the harp " with his nayles scharpe."

Many princes, among them the valiant sons of Edward III of England, were trained almost from the cradle in the arts of war. The eldest was only fifteen when he won his spurs at the battle of Crecy ; the fourth, John of Gaunt, was only ten when he took part in a stirring sea-fight off Sluys, and followed his doughty father into action to the tune of the latest dance-music favoured at Court, played by the royal trumpeters aboard the King's own ship.

In the old story of " Petit Jehan de Saintré " we get a glimpse of the education of a typical French page at the end of the fourteenth century. Like many another stout-hearted fellow, Jehan was short of stature and slightly built. When, at the age of thirteen, he became page to King John of France he threw himself with ardour into all manly sports, riding on horses almost too large and too lively for him to manage, playing paume (a sort of tennis), jumping, running, and practising feats of arms. A beautiful lady of the royal household took a kindly interest in the little page, whose spirit was so much more powerful than his body, and she gave him good advice upon subjects as far asunder as the necessity of keeping his nails clean and the importance of avoiding the deadly sins of anger and pride. She counselled him to fill his mind with the true and marvellous doings of the Romans, and planned a course of reading for him which was nothing if not solid, for it included the works of Livy, Suetonius, Sallust, and Josephus.

We are not told where or how Petit Jehan learnt to read : perhaps from his father's chaplain, perhaps at some modest school kept by the village priest under the shadow of his father's castle in Touraine. From the life-story of another fifteenth century boy, Olivier de la Marche, it is clear that the sons of knights *were* sent to such schools to learn the first elements of their education. In his old age Olivier wrote down, at great length, the memories of his long life, and from his book, which has never been translated into English or published in modern French, we can catch several picturesque peeps of Burgundian boy-life in the days of Good Duke Philip.

When Olivier was nine years old his father was Governor of the Castle of Joux, in Franche-Comté, and the boy was sent, with the sons and nephews of neighbouring families, to the school at Pontarlier. There they would learn their catechism and creed in Latin, reading, writing, and the chants to which the psalms were sung in church. Ancient history, quaintly coloured and twisted by the simple-minded translators, also formed part of their education, so that Julius Cæsar, that worthy peer, and Pompey, that proud baron, became familiar figures, and they were able to imagine Messire Hector, in a plumed helmet, sallying forth from a moated and many-turreted Troy.

When Olivier de la Marche had been for about three years at the school at Pontarlier, and had seen the bonfires blazing to

L

celebrate the conclusion of peace between Duke Philip and Charles VII of France (Jeanne d'Arc's King), his father died, and, after a time, the Duke, mindful of the loyal services of the dead de la Marche, took the boy to be one of his pages. Philip was far more powerful than many of the kings of his age. His broad domains included the lands now called Holland and Belgium, and much of what was really French territory. Though he had to do homage to the French King as a vassal of the French Crown, he was actually so wealthy and so strong that timid and greedy monarchs strove against each other to win his friendship. The life which young Olivier led at his Court was one that would have appealed to any boy. Those long-drawn-out banquets at which it was his duty to serve his master were often enlivened by pageants, acrobatic interludes, and short, exciting plays. Sometimes the pages themselves were ordered to 'dress up' and take part in these performances, to wear the beard of Hercules and slay a stuffed lion, or the helmet of Jason and march in bearing the golden fleece. The banquets, however lengthy, were never tedious. Sometimes a huge pie would suddenly open, and—not four-and-twenty blackbirds, but a band of fiddlers and bagpipers would be revealed, scraping and blowing with all their might. The long tables, covered with black velvet embroidered in flame-colour and gold, were decorated with many marvellous objects,

A MEDIÆVAL BANQUET

Morris Meredith Williams

A squire of the Earl of Pembroke bringing a message to Sir John Chandos as he is about to dine —*Froissart*

162

THE MEDIÆVAL BOY

mostly models, made of wood, wax, or painted glass : windmills
with sails that went round, churches with bells that rang, tigers
that wagged their heads, and falcons that beat their wings.

From time to time Duke Philip would amuse himself by riding
forth on a warlike expedition against any neighbours who had
happened to annoy him, or any subjects who had dared murmur
against his decrees. Then all the high-hearted members of his
Court rejoiced, and none more than the pages, who thought it

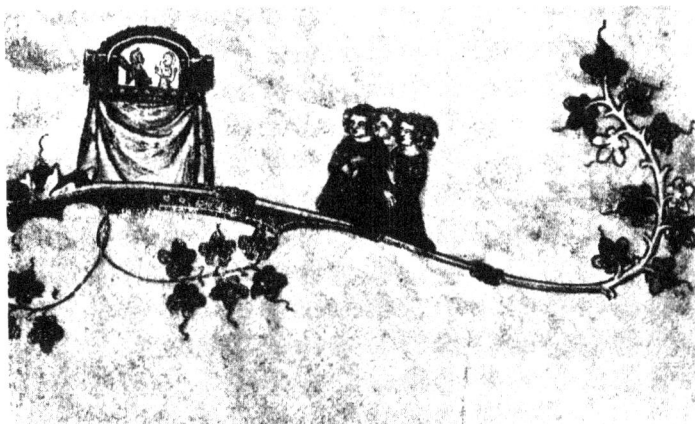

A MEDIÆVAL PLAY
From a manuscript in the Bodleian Library
This shows a stage with curtained lower room

rare sport to set off on horseback, wearing helmets inlaid with
pearls, in the train of those Burgundian knights whose prowess
they had seen so often proved in tournament and who were all
heroes in their boyish eyes. Occasionally the pages were so fool-
hardy that steps had to be taken to prevent their falling into the
hands of the enemy. They would lead the Duke's horses to the
watering-pond under the very noses of the archers of the rival
army, and whenever a castle was captured, by ruse or by assault,
the pages were always among the first to scale the walls and
explore the inner ward.

The wages of these boys were only about three halfpence a
day, but they can never have been hard up, for they were lodged
at one of the most gorgeous Courts in Europe, and their master
constantly rewarded good service with princely gifts. A boy like
Olivier, with a taste for martial pageantry, must have been in

his element there, for the knights of the ducal household were always jousting and tilting and arranging tournaments. When Olivier, in his old age, wrote his memoirs for the benefit of the great grandchildren of Duke Philip, the pages of his book glowed and clanged with the colours and sounds of those knightly frays. With lingering delight he tells of the challengers and the heralds,

A TOURNAMENT
From *Scenes and Characters of the Middle Ages,* by the Rev. E. L. Cutts

the pavilions and the lists, the gaily hued housings of the horses, the courtesy and courage of the combatants. Only—what seems rather strange—after all the whacking with swords and galloping with lances nobody seems to have been one penny the worse! The only casualties of which we hear are those of a warrior the peak of whose helmet stuck in the sand when he fell, so that the heralds had to help him to rise, and of another, even more un-lucky, who wounded himself in the wrist with his own lance when he was putting it in rest.

Philip the Good had a brave and reckless only son, Charles, Count of Charolais, some years younger than Olivier. Perhaps it was because the young page had shown a taste for Roman history as well as for jousting that he was placed in the household of the Duke's heir. When we first meet Charles in Olivier's memoirs he is a fiery-tempered, ruddy-locked youth of fifteen or sixteen. It was at Brussels in the year 1451 that a Tournament was proclaimed in which the Count was to run the tilt for the first time. The bravest of all the Duke's knights, Messire Jacques de Lalain, was chosen to tilt against him. They rode two preliminary courses before the Duke and Duchess, and in the first encounter Charles splintered his lance full on de Lalain's shield, while the knight passed him with his weapon in the air. When the Duke saw this, and saw that de Lalain was deliberately sparing his son, he sent word to him that if *that* was how he

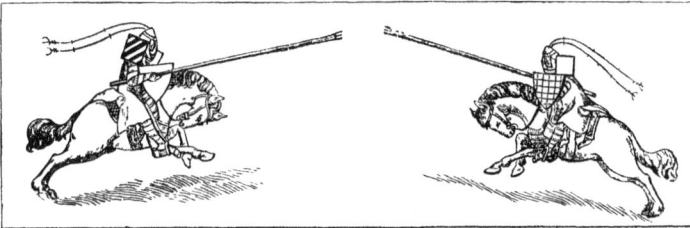

THE JOUST
From a manuscript in the British Museum

meant to fight he need not trouble to fight any more. "Fresh lances were then brought," writes Olivier de la Marche, "and Messire Jacques rode against the Count, who spurred eagerly toward him. They met with such a shock that both their lances were shivered to fragments. At this the Duchess was a little wroth with Messire Jacques ; but the Good Duke only laughed."

To Philip and Margaret, the grandchildren of Count Charles, Olivier, when an old man full of honours—knight, councillor, and chamberlain—spoke of the boyhood of their grandsire who, when he became Duke of Burgundy, won for himself the nickname of ' the Bold.'

" The Count of Charolais," says he, " was hot-tempered and restless. As a child he always wanted to have his own way in all things, and was very impatient of control ; yet he had an excellent understanding, and overcame his temper so well that no more courteous and gentle prince than he was ever known." Moreover, he was quick at his lessons and had a good memory. From his youth he loved to read, or to have read aloud to him, the lives of the famous Romans or " the gay and pleasant histories of Lancelot and Gawain." Above all things he loved the sea and ships. He delighted in hawking and hunting, was the best chess-player of his time, could beat all his courtiers at tennis,

THE GAME OF CHESS
From a manuscript in the British Museum

and shot with the long-bow better than any archer. Unfortunately for him, his voice was not naturally very sweet, but he was well skilled in music, and composed many songs to be sung by voices more tuneful than his own. Truly a delight-ful sort of grandfather to have! When Philip and Margaret listened to the memories of Messire Olivier, they must often have wished that Charles had lived to play games with them and to tell them about the Romans, or about Lancelot and Gawain, instead of dy-ing on the battlefield at Nancy in a last, desperate stand against that much more clever and much less attractive prince, Louis XI of France.

At the Court of King Edward IV of England, who was far more lucky in his dealings with the wily Louis, six small boys, known as the Gentlemen-henchmen, were educated. Their tutor, called the Master of the Henchmen, had many duties and re-sponsibilities. He had to keep them " in the rules of goings and sittings," to teach them courtesy in " words, deeds, and degrees," to show them how to wear armour and how to joust. They also had to learn " sundry languages and other learnings virtuous," harping, piping, dancing, and correct behaviour at table.

To help their tutor—and them—some old fellow who had a knack of rhyme translated from a Latin original a treatise on courtesy which he called *The Babees' Book.* He tells his " sweet children " that if they should find any words in it which they cannot quite understand they must keep on asking till they have discovered the meaning, and when they *have* discovered it let them remember it well ! Very rightly he thinks that the laws of good manners are among the first lessons which the King's little hench-men ought to master. " When you enter the great hall," he says, " bow to every one whom you find there, and say ' Godspeed ! ' Come in quietly, hold up your head, kneel on one knee when you salute your lord. If any one speaks to you, look at him steadily, listen attentively ; don't chatter, or let your eyes wander all over the place. Don't sit down till you are told,

A MEROVINGIAN
CHESSMAN

Such as those used at the French and Burgundian Courts in the Middle Ages

don't fidget, don't loll against a pillar ! " All this is sound advice but, except for a few small details, it might be given to any boy in any century. A little farther on we get a touch of more

A STATE BANQUET
From a manuscript of the fifteenth century in the Bibliothèque Nationale, Paris

definitely mediæval colour. The henchman is reminded that he must always be on the alert to hand the cup, hold the candle, or otherwise make himself useful. If during the banquet the King should give him a drink from his own cup, the boy must receive

it standing up, take it in both hands, and on no account offer it
to anyone else.   Then, when the time comes for the King to wash
his royal fingers, one boy will hold the bowl while another pours
out the fresh water, and a third stands hard by with a napkin over
his arm.   Some of the warnings sound quaint in modern ears.
The " babee " must not lap up his soup, but use a spoon ; he must
not dip his meat in the saltcellar or put his knife in his mouth.
The advice to keep his hands clean may have been the hardest to
follow when the fingers of the left hand had to do duty as forks.

Encouraged by the success of *The Babees' Book* an enterprising
rhymester produced a rival treatise called *Urbanitatis*, in which

A FOOLS' DANCE
From *The Sports and Pastimes of the People of England*, by Joseph Strutt

the counsels proffered are even more startling.   The reader is
urged not to sniff, not to smear the cloth with his fingers, and
not to use it to wipe his nose !   Soon followed yet another manual
put together by some conscientious person who was anxious to
say anything that by any chance the earlier authorities had left
unsaid.   The student of this last *Lytyl Boke* would soon realize
that courtesy forbids a boy to open his mouth too wide, to fling
himself upon the cheese, or to cast the bones from his platter on
to the floor.   " If," says the author " you remember all these
good counsels, people will exclaim, after you have quitted their
company, ' A gentylman was heere ! ' but he that despiseth this
teaching is unworthy to sit at a good man's table."

All these writers agree in impressing upon their young pupils
the importance of avoiding brawls and quarrels.   That their
warnings were by no means unnecessary is proved by a true story
told of himself by Gotz von der Berlichingen, that picturesque
ruffian, one of the last of the great robber-barons of the Middle

THE MEDIÆVAL BOY

Ages. Some twenty years after *The Babees' Book* was written Gotz, being then a page in the castle of the Margrave of Anspach, had a sudden dispute with a fellow-page which nearly had serious results for both of them. This fellow-page came from Poland, and was on that account a favourite with the Margrave's Polish

LADY TEACHING HER SON
From a manuscript in the British Museum

wife. He happened to have anointed his hair with eggs one day when Gotz was wearing a new broad-skirted coat that had been specially made for him at Namur. As Gòtz rose from his place at table his gorgeous coat ruffled up the sticky locks of the young Pole who, losing his temper, made a swift stab at the offender with his bread-knife. The blow glanced aside, but it was now Gotz's turn to wax warm. He drew his dagger " and therewith smote the Pole about the pate." This was a most reckless thing to do, the sticky-locked youth being, as we have said, a fellow-countryman of the Margravine. Next day, when the household were on their way back from church, the Provost-marshal attempted to arrest Gotz, but the boy defied him, and dashed upstairs to appeal to the young Princes. At their suggestion he hid himself while they went and pleaded his cause with their father and mother. The Margrave was inclined to mercy, but his wife insisted that Gotz should be cast into a dungeon forthwith. This did not seem fair to Gòtz, as the Pole had begun the quarrel, but the young Princes promised him that his imprisonment should last only a quarter of an hour, and one of them offered to lend him a velvet cloak lined with sable in case the dungeon should be damp or cold. " The princes kept their word," wrote Gòtz, many years later, " for I lay but a bare quarter of an hour in that tower. Then my brave captain, Paul von Augsberg, came and delivered me, and bade me tell him again how the trouble began. Then this loyal knight led me before the Margrave's Council and sought to find excuses for me, and all the squires and pages of the Court, as many as fifty or sixty, ranged themselves on my side. Von Augsberg swore roundly that it was the Pole who ought to be locked into the tower ; but he did not have his way."

PREPARING A SQUIRE FOR
KNIGHTHOOD
From *In Feudal Times,* by
E M Tappan (Harrap)

It does not seem as if *The Babees' Book* had been translated into German, and it is clear that its warnings against quarrelsomeness were needed at other Courts than that of the English King.

However the childhood of a page was spent, whether he learnt his letters at home, or at school, or not at all, the end and aim of his whole training was to fit him to wear the golden spurs. His life as a page usually began when he was eleven or twelve years old and continued till, at the age of sixteen or seventeen, he became a squire. He was then only one step from the climax of his career, and every day brought him nearer to that solemn day when he should take the vows of knighthood and don the garb of a knight, the white tunic, symbol of honour, the red robe, symbol of the blood he must be ready to shed in a good cause, and the black hose, symbol of that end which awaits all men, both the humble and the proud. The squire's duties were more arduous than those of the page. He had not only to bear

the shield and lead the spare chargers of the knight whom he served, but also to buckle on his spurs, close the rivets in his armour, and, if necessary, comb and curl his hair! A squire whose knight was more than usually warlike, or more than usually dandified, may sometimes have looked back regretfully to the time when he was a silk-clad page playing a hundred pranks with pages as merry-hearted as he. He may have forgotten for the moment that a page's duty was sometimes wearisome enough, when the banquets were long, and if there were stubborn birds to carve, peacock,

A KNIGHT
From a French bronze of the fourteenth century in the National Museum, Florence
Photo Brogi

partridge, heron, and crane, and when the heavy two-handled tankards brimmed over with the sharp-scented hippocras.

But the squire, poor fellow, was not released from the work of a carver when he ceased to be a page. He still had to carve, before his King or his liege-lord, or, as in the case of Chaucer's musical, gaily garbed young squire, " before his father at the table." O happy day, when he should be a knight, and have a page to bring him his tankard, and a squire to cut up his dinner and carry his shield!

171

What of the boy who was not destined for knighthood, but whose fate it was to be a priest, a schoolmaster, or a doctor, a merchant or a man of law ? From the far-off times when the half-legendary Irishman Maidulf kept his simple school on the edge of the greenwood, there had always been schools, and often very good schools, scattered here and there in the towns and villages of England wherever there was a church or a monastery or some other pious foundation. Chaucer gives us a fleeting glance at one of these mediæval schools in the *Prioress's Tale*, when he tells us about a " heepe " of children who

> learnèd in the scolé yeer by yeer
> Such manner doctrine as men usèd there,
> That is to say, to singen and to read
> As smallé children do in their childheed.

From what follows it is clear that the children did not always understand what they were singing, for when one of the smaller boys asked the meaning of the words of a hymn which he heard the elders learning, his school-fellow was able to give him only a vague idea, and had to add apologetically :

> I can no more expound in this matter :
> I learn song ; I know but small grammar.

A little later in date, but very similar in type, was the school attended by John Lydgate. This worthy fellow afterward became a monk and wrote, long before *The Babees' Book* was thought of, a book of rules for good behaviour. From his own account of his schooldays he seems to have been anything but a model scholar. He tells us that he went unwillingly to school and wasted his time, running wild " like a young colt without a bridle " ; also, he arrived late, and " jangled and japed " instead of fixing his mind on his lessons. Worse still, he stole apples and grapes from gardens, mocked the passers-by, hated getting up and going to bed with equal intensity, and preferred playing with cherrystones to going to church !

In mediæval England a poor boy's chances of picking up some crumbs of learning were rather unequal. Until the Statute of the Apprentices, which became the law of the land in 1406, a villein could be fined for sending his child to school instead of keeping him labouring in the fields, and this cruel decree may have robbed many intelligent boys of their one hope in life. On the other hand, it does not seem that the fines were imposed very freely or very frequently ; otherwise why should William Langland, the grim contemporary of cheerful Chaucer, have complained so bitterly that " every cobbler's son and beggar's brat goes to school nowadays " ?

Still, in their humble way, the village schools of the Middle Ages kept the torch of learning alight in dark and desolate places, and though the precious flame sometimes sank to a flicker it never died. Toward the end of the fourteenth century there arose a great man who upheld that torch in England and made it shine with a clearer light than ever before. That man was William of Wykeham, the founder of Winchester College.

At Winchester itself, that wondrously ancient town, the legendary Camelot of King Arthur, there had been schools of divers sorts from very early days. In addition to the novices' school of St Swithin's,

A FIFTEENTH-CENTURY GRAMMAR-SCHOOL
From a manuscript in the British Museum

there was a grammar-school whence thirteen poor scholars went daily to dine in the Hundredmen's Hall of St Cross Hospital. This free dinner, which they shared with a hundred poor wayfarers, consisted of a loaf of coarse bread, three quarts of weak beer, a herring or two pilchards, or two eggs, and a deep ladleful of porridge or soup. Among the boys at this old grammar-school, though probably not among those who enjoyed the weak beer at St Cross, was a certain Geoffrey whose school expenses were paid by no less a person than King John. The air of Winchester was friendly to learning. More than a hundred years before the Statute of the Apprentices, John de Pontissara, Bishop of Winchester, desired that every boy in his diocese should have an opportunity to learn to read and to sing. Nineteen years after that kindly Bishop's death a boy was born in that diocese who was destined to fill his throne most worthily, and yet whose parents were so obscure that he took his name from his birthplace, the village of Wykeham. Some powerful friend seems to have made it possible for young William of Wykeham to be "imbued with the first learning" (*primitivis scientiis*), but beyond that point he never advanced. Whether it was at the old Winchester grammar-school that he received that scanty dole of education is not quite clear, but it is certain that part of his boyhood must have been spent in

TOMB OF WYKEHAM
Winchester Cathedral
Photo Valentine

that beautiful little town in the hollow of the green Hampshire hills, for it is recorded that he used to rise early in order to attend what was called the "Morrow Mass," sung in the small hours for the benefit of pious townsfolk who had to set off to work betimes. When William of Wykeham was still a young man he entered the service of King Edward III, probably through the intercession of the Constable of Winchester Castle, for whose soul he caused masses to be sung in after-years. By the time he was thirty-one he was surveyor of the works at Windsor Castle, a position of honour and responsibility under the eye of the King himself. Though Wykeham wore the tonsure, that is to say, the shaven crown, of a clerk of the first degree, he did not actually become a priest till 1362. Four years later he was chosen to fill the bishop's throne of Winchester. Few fairy-tales relate a more romantic change of fortune than this—that the Hampshire village-boy should come to rule over the stately church where he used to kneel in the grey dawn among the workmen with their tools and the pedlars with their wares. At the very spot where the Morrow Mass was chanted Wykeham's tomb now stands, and there you may see his carven effigy, with mitre and crozier, and two little monks kneeling at his upturned feet.

174

When Wykeham became Bishop of Winchester great wealth passed into his hands. Mediæval prelates had many sources of revenue, and, to their credit be it remembered, many of them made noble use of their riches. Surely no man ever turned a stream of gold into a better channel than did William of Wykeham ! His first foundation for the benefit of young students hampered by poverty was not at Winchester but at Oxford,

ENTRANCE GATEWAY TO NEW COLLEGE
Photo Frith

where, within seven years of his elevation to the bishopric, we find him buying land for his college, now called New College, but dedicated by him to St Mary the Virgin. A little later he was paying for the maintenance and education of four poor scholars at Winchester. His plans were interrupted by changes of fortune and by unforeseen difficulties, but, at last, in 1378–79, he was able to begin the great work of his life, the erection and endowment of " a college for seventy poor scholars who should live college-wise and study grammar near the city of Winchester." The " seventy poor scholars " were not drawn from the highways and hedges, or called from following the plough ; they seem to have been, for the most part, sons of merchants, squires, farmers, burgesses, and even of younger branches of noble families, boys whose parents could not afford to give them the full training

175

of a scholar though they had already " imbued them with the *primitivis scientiis.*" What made Wykeham's foundation memorable and important was the fact that up to that time no one in England had conceived the idea of an independent collegiate school on such a large scale, or, indeed, the idea of anything like a big school for boys on the lines which he traced out.

Another motive besides his interest in clever children prompted Wykeham to found Winchester College. In 1348, and again in 1361, England had been so ravaged by the Black Death that the result was a serious lack of lettered men, and a very real danger that the next generation might grow up ignorant and uncouth for want of teachers. Wykeham sought to do something to fill that perilous gap by training successive bands of scholars, first at his college and then at Oxford University, so that they might bear forth the lamp of learning unto places left dark and desolate.

Wykeham planned every detail of his foundation with loving care. On fair parchment he caused to be written the rules and statutes governing the Warden, the Fellows, and the seventy scholars. The boys were to be between eight and twelve years old at the time of their admission, of good behaviour, apt to study, and well versed in reading, plain-song, and "Old Donatus." Clearly the good Bishop hoped and expected that most of his scholars would enter the priesthood. Within a year of his entrance each boy was to receive the clerkly tonsure, though, as in the case of young Wykeham himself, this did not mean that he *must* be fully ordained in course of time ; many shaven clerks never were, and some even fought for the King with helmets on their monkish-looking heads. The Winchester scholars must be staid and sober in their dress and bearing, however ; their dress— each received enough cloth to make a gown and a hood—was to be plain, without pied or striped colours ; they were forbidden to have fashionable turned-up peaks to their shoes, to wear red or green garters, or to decorate their hoods with elaborate knots or tassels. They must not play ball-games in chapel, cloister, or hall, lest the rich carvings and the fair painted windows should be harmed. Neither must they keep hawks, dogs, or ferrets as pets. " Manners makyth man " was Wykeham's motto, and he was anxious that his boys should practise what he preached. At Winchester may be seen to-day a Latin inscription which, even if it be not as old as the older buildings, sums up the spirit

WINCHESTER COLLEGE

From a drawing by Warden Chandler in the manuscript Life of Wykeham at New College, Oxford

From *Schools of Mediæval England*, by A F Leach (Methuen)

By permission of the Warden of New College

(See poem at the end of this chapter)

of the founder's will: " *Aut disce, aut dicede ; manet sors tertia, cædi.*" Modern Wykehamists translate it: " Work, walk, or be whopped." The " third fate " was assuredly the fate of all in-attentive pupils in the fourteenth century, not only among the seventy original scholars, but also among the " sons of noble and powerful persons, special friends of the said college " who, " to the number of ten," were also to be " instructed and informed in grammar within the said college." These ten were the real forerunners of the many thousands of their type and class who have since been educated at Winchester and the other great and famous English schools built on Wykeham's model.

Not for nothing had the worthy Bishop directed the labours of the King's architects and masons at Windsor ! The college which he planned was as magnificent as any palace, shining with jewelled windows, fretted with delicate tracery, roofed with cunning work in wood and stone. Until their new home was ready for them the first masters and boys dwelt in the parish of St John-on-the-Hill, whence they could watch the masons at their task in the meads below, and whence they marched down, in 1394, with swaying banners and clinking censers, to take possession of their goodly heritage. St John's Church stands on the lower slope of St Giles' Hill, on the summit whereof used to be held, all through the Middle Ages, a busy and famous fair to which pedlars, merchants, jugglers, and rogues used to flock from all over the country. The boy-monks in the fourteenth and fifteenth centuries were given a yearly gift of money with which to buy themselves knives at this fair, and it was there that in 1394 were bought the first tablecloths, 40 ells at 7d. an ell, and the first iron candlesticks, for the use of Wykeham's boys.

There were no regular holidays then, but Saints' days were kept with much festivity. When such days fell in winter-time the founder decreed that the Fellows and scholars should remain after supper in the great hall, singing songs and reciting " poems, histories, and wonders of the world." Then every December there was the Feast of the Boy-bishop. This feast was kept throughout Europe in the Middle Ages and did not fall into dis-use till the Reformation ; it is thought to have originated in the Roman revels called the " Saturnalia " which were held at the same season in pre-Christian days. At most of the mediæval monasteries, abbeys, and cathedral-schools the ceremonies were very similar. At vespers on the Eve of St Nicolas, when the choir chanted the words " He shall put down the mighty from their seat," the Abbot or Warden descended from his carven stall, and it was at once occupied by a boy, previously chosen from among the younger boys, robed like a miniature bishop, with a mitre of cloth-of-gold and a copper-gilt pastoral staff. For twenty-four hours, from vespers to vespers, children filled the places and played the parts of their elders, while the grave Canons acted as incense-bearers and candle-holders. The Boy-bishop clambered up into the pulpit and preached a sermon, probably written for him by his schoolmaster. He solemnly blessed the assembled people. Then he went on horseback in procession through the crowded streets, and at night he supped with the clergy of the Abbey or Cathedral. Even then his brief span of glory was not ended. It was his privilege to go on a sort of tour among the castles and monasteries round about, collecting gifts and faring sumptuously on plovers, woodcocks, and pears.

Twice in the course of the year 1441 the Warden of Winchester College received an illustrious visitor, none other than that pious, well-meaning shadow of a king, Henry VI, then nineteen years of age. Henry had resolved to found at Eton, in the pleasant meadows at the foot of Windsor's castle hill, a college on the plan of Wykeham's great foundation, and he was anxious to see for himself how that plan worked in practice.

If, in the manner of the Norse Norns, a fairy came to the cradle of Henry VI at Windsor she must have been a very different sort of fairy from her sister who hovered over the fluted oaken cradle of Henry V at Monmouth. The fairy in the Welsh castle foretold a life short, indeed, but brimful of glory, blithe in its dawning, brilliant in its noon, though its sunset came all too early. To Henry VI it was granted to achieve little, to do few things triumphantly well, to be remembered for nothing much—save for two things most memorable and worthy of praise. Those two things were the founding of Eton College and of King's College, Cambridge. The royal foundation at Eton was not on such a magnificent scale as Wykeham's at Winchester. It provided for only twenty-five poor scholars at first ; but on the other hand Henry wanted the school chapel to be larger than any other church in England except York Minster. The first headmaster, Waynflete, was a Winchester man, and on the death of Cardinal

Beaufort in 1449 Henry wrote to the monks at Winchester urging them to elect Waynflete as their bishop, which they dutifully proceeded to do. The boys there must have enjoyed the ceremonies of the installation at which the King himself was present, and when the Archbishop gave forty shillings—equal to forty pounds of modern money—for refreshments for the scholars of the new Bishop's old school.

Wykeham had admitted only ten boys of gentle birth in addition to the poor scholars " on the foundation " : Henry,

ETON COLLEGE
The quadrangle, with chapel on the extreme right
Photo Valentine

however, raised this number to twenty, and desired that instruction should also be given to " any other scholar who might resort thither from any part of England." Thus Eton from the beginning held a freer, more open, and more varied community. The boys who went there in the palmy days of Henry VI felt his grave eye almost constantly upon them. When they climbed, as so many generations of Eton boys have climbed since, up the castle hill they often encountered a spindle-shanked gentleman with broad, unfashionable shoes on his feet and a prayer-book in his thin white hand, one whom they would never have guessed to be the King had they not known him well by sight, and unless the golden collar of the Garter on his homely tunic of dark woollen stuff had been there to show that it was truly he. From this lean gentleman they would receive much good advice, not all of it unwelcome, for one of the things that Henry liked his boys to do was to practice archery in the pleasant meadows that were afterward the playing fields of Eton, famous in song and story.

It seemed for a time as if the defeat and death of this unhappy King and the triumph of his light-hearted rival, Edward IV, would bring to nothing all the plans that were being carried out at Eton. Edward had no reason to look with favour upon any foundation which was likely to remind England of the good deeds—and even better intentions—of his predecessor. The worst that happened, however, was that the staff of chaplains was reduced, the idea of the huge church was abandoned, and Henry's desire that an almshouse for aged poor men should be attached to his college was set aside. Edward stayed his hand, and Eton survived; but he never showed the same favour to the younger school that he did to Winchester. In 1471, when a fine lion was landed at Southampton on its way to the royal menagerie in the Tower of London, the King gave orders that one of his servants should take the beast to Winchester so that the boys might have a look at it. The Fellows rewarded the lion's keeper with a ' tip ' of one shilling and eightpence.

A YOUTH OF THE PERIOD
From a manuscript in the British Museum

One of the boys who was at Winchester when that lion visited the college, a certain William Horman, filled the headmaster's chair at Eton from 1485 to 1494, and then returned to rule over his old school from 1494 to 1502. After he retired Horman published a collection of the Latin and English sentences which he had used when teaching at the two great schools, and from the dusty, discoloured pages of his book we can learn much about school life at the end of the fifteenth century. They are critical about Latin, Horman's boys ; they know the difference between a sound scholar and a "smaterar " ; they laugh at him who " hath gyven up gramar because he cannot away with it." "I have left my boke in the tenys-playe," says a forgetful boy; "he hit me in the yie with a tenys-ball," laments another. "He is a royall coyter," and " We will playe with a ball full of wynde," are sentences that tell us that quoits and football were both

played at English schools five hundred years ago.   We hear also
of a boy who cast away his gown lest it should hamper his running,
and of another who " ruffelled all the game with his boistrusness."
   What were the feelings of mediæval youngsters toward their
teachers ?   Many of them, no doubt, would have joined heartily
in the song invented by one of them :

> I would my Master were a hare,
> And all my bookés houndés were !
> And I myself a jolly hunter—
> To blow my horn I would not spare !

Doggerel, in Latin or in English, or in both, was dear to them all.
They prodded their memory with such jingles as " *Pulso, pulsas*,
for to ring, *Canto, cantas*, for to sing, *Hic Rex* for a King ; *Hec
tibea* for a leg, *hoc ovum* for an egg, *hec Margarita* for Meg."
Where an impatient scribe had written on the margin of his book,

> *Est mala scriptura*
> *Quia penna non fuit dura*

(It is badly written because the pen was not hard), a later
student added the following comment :

> *Penna non valet*
> *Dixit ille qui scribere nescit !*

(The pen is no good, quoth he who cannot write).
   While the sister-colleges of Winchester and Eton were springing
up, like lilies wrought of grey stone, from the green meadows of
England, another great experiment in education was in progress
in another part of Europe.   To the court of Gianfrancesco Gonzaga, Marquis of Mantua, toward the year 1425, came a short-
legged, quick-witted schoolmaster, wearing a dangling dark robe
and a quaint peaked hood.   His name was Vittorino da Feltre.
In his youth he had been a poor student at Padua—so poor that
in the hope of picking up a few crumbs of learning he entered the
service of the mathematical professor as a footman.   Later he
betook himself to Venice and learned Greek, which was then no
common accomplishment, and was not taught at Oxford till
1491.   All this time Vittorino was thinking about education,
and dreaming of a system which should break the chains of stiff
and rusty old traditions, a system that would help to mould and
strengthen both the minds and the bodies of youth.   Thanks to

the Marquis of Mantua, he was able to see his ideas put into practice. In a charming pleasure house called La Giocosa, standing in a large meadow bordered on one side by the river Mincio, Vittorino started his school. Only promising children were accepted. Rich men offered him much gold in vain if the looks and manners of their sons did not satisfy him ; on the other hand, he would receive free of charge poor boys whom he believed to possess rare gifts of mind and character.

Vittorino did not approve of the rigid and formal system

A SCRIBE AT WORK
From *The Arts in the Middle Ages*, by Paul Lacroix

followed in the older schools. He encouraged his pupils to talk about all sorts of wonderful and beautiful things ; he took them for country rambles, he showed them the treasures of his library, and he made them practise exercises that taught them endurance and self-control. When they were handed over to his care many of his boys were spoilt and lazy little fellows. Carlo, the younger of the Gonzaga princes, was so fat that he could hardly move. Vittorino thought of a sly way to win the greedy boy from his gobbling. When Carlo was deep in his dinner his master would begin some subject of conversation so fascinating that the young glutton, eager to listen and to join in, but too polite to speak with his mouth full, was forced to halt from time to time ; or such delightful music was played that Carlo would lay down his knife

183

and spoon to listen. And so young Gonzaga developed from a podgy, slow-witted child into a scholarly and athletic young man. A triumph for Vittorino !

All these boys of the later Middle Ages, Wykeham's at Winchester, King Henry's at Windsor, Vittorino's at Mantua, were living on the eve of great and wonderful events. A new age was at hand, when heaven and earth were to be unfolded before the

YOUNG SFORZA READING LIVY
Wallace Collection
Photo Mansell

eyes of poets and seafarers and men of science. In the fifteenth century the wisdom of the Greeks had been rescued from its long sleep in the dust and, under the name of the New Learning, had begun to transform Europe. Art and poetry and philosophy took new forms and colours in that golden light. Vasco da Gama rounded the Cape, Columbus reached America. Horizons were widening and receding. It seemed as if the world were reborn.

Then came the century of still greater discoveries, when men pierced the mysteries of the seas and the skies : then Copernicus showed the true place of the sun among the stars, and Kepler traced out the rules which all the planets obey ; then Drake circled the terrestrial orb and Shakespeare sailed the uncharted oceans of the soul.

THUS WYKEHAM WILLED

IN darkling winter-time there fall
  Both feast and holy day ;
Then late within the firelit hall
  The Warden lets us stay ;
And there we sit, while dusk grows deep,
  And list to tale and song—
(Sometimes the younger boys will sleep
  If the tale be over-long).

Wot you, 'twas Bishop Wykeham's will
  That these things should be so
When first from good St Giles his hill
  Unto the meads below
His scholars marched to this same place
  Where we are met in school,
He willed that we should have this grace
  Toward the time of Yule.

Thus Wykeham willed—that we should speak
  Of wonders wild yet true,
The Warden and the Fellows eke,
  And we elder boys thereto ;
Yea, all the marvels that men find,
  Whose hap it is to roam
Far off, in Araby and Ind,
  Beyond the perilous foam.

The shining wonders of the sky
  The Warden will expound,
And how in unheard harmony
  The planets wheel around.
" The notes upon the scale," saith he,
  " Are writ in starry fire ;
So soundly birched that boy should be
  Who sings amiss in quire ! "

And then the Senior Fellow tells
  Of beasts most fierce and strange,
Of dolphins long as seven ells
  Whose scaly colours change,

185

Or of the basilisk, whose blink
    Can slay a stalwart man,
Or him who frights the ocean-brink,
    The fell leviathan.

We never glance behind or quake
    To hear that Fellow's tale,
Though basilisks and dragons make
    The younger boys turn pale ;
We know such creatures are not seen,
    And haply never were,
In the grey walks and meadows green
    Of our own Winchester.

After a while the talk will pass
    To ancient towns of fame :
One had an hundred gates of brass
    And Babylon was its name ;
In Thrace, built all of burnished steel
    Did Mars his temple rise ;
In Ægypt to the Nile men kneel,
    For it flows from Paradise.

O great flat world, so richly wrought
    Beneath the planets small,
'Tis thanks to Bishop Wykeham's thought
    We know your wonders all ;
Or if some two or three remain
    Which we have yet to learn,
The Warden, sure, will make them plain
    When winter shall return.

CHAPTER IX

The Renaissance Boy

A VERY wise historian once declared that the Renaissance, the intellectual rebirth of Europe, " signifies the renewed study of Greek and the consequences ensuing from it " during the years that divided the Florentine poet Petrarch from the Dutch scholar Erasmus of Rotterdam ; that is to say, from the seventh decade of the fourteenth century to the **third** decade of the sixteenth.   This great movement began in Italy, and its full force was not felt in Northern Europe until it had almost spent itself in the South.   We have already seen the boys of the Italian Renaissance studying Greek at Mantua with Vittorino da Feltre. Now we will betake ourselves to England, Scotland, and France a century later.   In northern Europe, strangely enough, this gain of culture and knowledge meant the loss of much of that easy good-humour which went far to atone for the roughness of the Middle Ages. Splendour now became rather tawdry. Learning led more often to angry arguments than to pleasant talks.   Colours were deeper and gaudier, shadows longer and more profound.   This spiritual change was reflected

SLASHED COSTUME OF THE SIXTEENTH CENTURY

From Boxgrove Church Sussex

in the costume of the period, which became more and more stiff, heavy, and magnificent.   Instead of the graceful, long-sleeved, girdled gowns of Plantagenet days men now wore slashed and padded doublets and breeches, trimmed with bars of velvet or fur. Ruffs began to rise and choke them.   Peaked shoes broadened into clumsy, square-toed slippers.   Learned men took to wearing severe robes sewn with rows of bristling buttons.   Brilliant hues gave way to lurid crimson and sombre black.   Solidity and splendour succeeded to gaiety and grace.

At the end of the reign of Henry VII and during the early

187

years of Henry VIII a Londoner was carrying on the fine tradition begun by William of Wykeham and Henry of Windsor. His name was John Colet, and he was the eldest of the twenty children born to Sir Henry Colet, Lord Mayor of London, and the only one to survive childhood. In the fifteenth and sixteenth centuries boys were admitted to the Universities at an age when they would now be still at school. Colet was probably not more than seventeen when he began his studies at Oxford, and among the teachers there was a certain clever Ipswich man who had taken his degree of Bachelor of Arts before his sixteenth birthday. This man's name was Thomas Wolsey, and when in 1515 he received the Cardinal's Hat with great pomp in the Abbey of Westminster Colet preached the Latin sermon in honour of the occasion. After an interval of travel in Italy John Colet returned to Oxford, and began to lecture on the epistles of his favourite apostle, St Paul. His fearless originality and his deep learning made a great impression on those who heard him, notably upon a certain sharp-featured, keen-eyed Dutchman, Erasmus of Rotterdam, afterward his close friend, and famous among Renaissance thinkers in northern Europe. In 1505 Colet became Dean of the Cathedral dedicated to his beloved apostle, and threw himself with ardour into his new duties, though without losing a jot of his love for learning. One of his first steps was to reduce the magnificence of the banquets at the Deanery, where his predecessors had kept a bounteous table. No doubt his guests were disappointed; but Colet did not turn aside from his purpose, which was to use the money thus saved for the benefit of poor scholars. There was already, and had been for more than three hundred years, a school attached to the cathedral, and this school, the pupils of which were known as the Children of Paul's, continued to exist after the Dean had accomplished the great work of his career—the foundation of the school still bearing the name of the apostle he loved best. In 1509, when he inherited considerable estates at the death of the old Lord Mayor, his father, Dean Colet began his school " for a hundred and fifty-three boys to be taught free in the same." Like Wykeham before him, he made his plans with elaborate care. For the first headmaster he chose William Lilly, formerly his fellow-student at Oxford, author of the first Latin grammar written by an Englishman, and a far-travelled man, who had

climbed the hills that stand about Jerusalem, and had tarried in
the rose-sweet island of Rhodes. The day's work began at seven
in the morning (at Winchester it was half-past five !), and
continued till eleven ; then it began again at one, and ended at
five in the evening. The boys were forbidden to bring meat,
drink, or bottles into school, and their parents had to supply
them with wax candles for use during lesson-hours in winter.
Cock-fighting, which had long been a popular sport with young
Londoners, and remained in vogue at Eton till the eighteenth
century, was not allowed by the gentle Dean ; on the other hand,
he wished his boys to attend the festivities of the Boy bishop at
St Paul's Cathedral, and that each one should make an offering
of one penny to the youthful ' prelate.' Finally, he not only
persuaded his learned friend Erasmus to write Latin discourses
for those boys to recite, but himself drew up a short elementary
grammar for their use, saying that he had tried to make the
Parts of Speech " a lytel more easy to yonge wyttes than, me-
thinketh, they were before . . . in whiche lytel boke I have left
many thynges out of purpose, considering the tenderness and
small capacyte of lytel myndes " ; and he ends by addressing his
scholars in tones of half-playful kindliness that are strangely like
the tones of a living voice : " Wherefore I praye you, all lytel
babys, all lytel chyldren, lerne gladly this lytel treatyse . . .
trustynge of this begynnynge that ye shall procede and grow to
parfyt lyterature,[1] and come at the last to be gret clarkes. And
lyfte up your lytel whyte handes for me, which prayeth for you
to God."

From the *Precepts of Living* which Colet set forth it is clear
that he remained unaffected by the recent revival of the classical
idea of physical culture. He says nothing about exercises or
sports ; he warns his boys to beware of " ryot," to love peace,
to persevere, to be always well-occupied ; but, his aim being to
train them as " gret clarkes " he did not, as learned laymen of
his age soon began to do, hold up for their imitation that type
of scholar who was an athlete and a sportsman as well. Before
he became too fierce and too fat Henry VIII was a good example
of this type. In his young days he was equally vain of the
elegance of his Latin and the shapeliness of his leg. He thought
himself a prince of wrestlers till, at the Field of the Cloth of Gold,

[1] Culture, education.

189

he was overthrown in a friendly bout by François I. He could wield the two-hand sword, a mighty weapon with a blade six feet in length. He played tennis to the admiration of the foreign ambassadors who gathered round the court to watch him. Then, following the Renaissance ideal, he showed that he could use his wits as well as his muscles; he wrote books on subjects that far wiser men than he were afraid to handle, taking now one view and now another; he dabbled in the physician's art; he composed songs both merry and grave.

When his only son was about five years old Henry caused *An Introduction to the Eight Parts of Speech* to be printed for the children of his loving subjects who, in the foreword, are invited to imitate the little Prince. " Let noble Prince Edward encourage your hearts; a prince . . . framed of such perfectness of nature . . . that he is now almost ready to run in the same race of learning with you." Of course such a pearl of wisdom and learning as Henry must have children worthy of him. And, indeed, he was disappointed neither by his daughters nor his son. So great and goodly a tree, declared his admirers, could bring forth none but noble fruits ! The men who served this Tudor prodigy never wearied of telling him, nor he of hearing, that he combined in his bulky person all the gifts and accomplishments that went to make a model for mankind to wonder at and—as far as possible—to imitate. Behind all this flattery the new idea was moving and stirring, the idea that only by a due balance of bodily against

EDWARD VI AS AN INFANT
Holbein
Photo Bruckmann

190

spiritual achievement can a boy be trained into the finest type of man.

Schoolmasters continued to knock Latin—and Greek, now, as well—into the heads of their pupils with good hard knocks, but thoughtful people here and there were beginning to ask themselves whether, after all, beating were the best way to make a child remember and enjoy his lessons. Among the first of the great Tudor Englishmen to devote his attention to this subject was Sir Thomas Elyot, man of law, Member of Parliament, and ambassador, whom the King sent as far afield as Brussels and Ratisbon, Tunis and Naples. How in the course of his eventful life Elyot found time to write and to study as much as he did remains something of a mystery. He himself tells us that he was never robust, and that once he had a cold in his head which lasted for four years. At Windsor Castle there is a drawing of Elyot done in chalk and watercolour by Holbein. It is an interesting face, with its dreamy, far-gazing eyes and its strongly

AN EARLY SIXTEENTH-CENTURY SCHOOLMASTER

From a woodcut title-page of a grammar printed in 1516

hewn nose and chin. Looking at it we can understand why this man was loved by such men as Erasmus and Thomas More ; we can understand his gentle idealism, his tenderness for young children, his hatred of all cruelty, violence, and wrath. Elyot wrote an astonishing number of books and pamphlets in addition to the first Latin-English dictionary and a treatise—*The Castell of Health*—in which he relates how he cured himself of his four-years'-long cold ; but his greatest work was *The Boke Named the Governour*, a discourse on the best method of training a boy to serve the state. Strangely enough he, who had so much to say about the bringing up of children, had never a child of his own. It must have been his nephews, the sons of his sister Margery,

whom he saw " playing at churches," and holding up their little hands as if they were praying, or " going and singing as it were in procession." Their kindly uncle would not have small boys " forced by violence to learn, but sweetly allured thereto with praises and such pretty gifts as children delight in " ; and he would have the alphabet painted for them in gay colours. So anxious is he that the boy should learn early to speak pure Latin he gravely suggests that his nurse should learn to speak it too ; or, at least, that she should be taught not to mangle the English language with playful ' baby-talk ' in the nursery. Music the good knight thinks a most necessary accomplishment, though he wisely adds that amateur musicians ought not to " show off " in public. When a child is " of nature inclined, as many be, to paint with a pen or form images in stone or wood," he must not be rebuked. The art of drawing is pleasant and profitable ; it is helpful to students of geography, astronomy, and algebra. But Elyot hastens to make it clear that he would not approve of a noble youth appearing " stained with sundry colours . . . or powdered with the dust of the stone that he cutteth " ; which is exactly what a boy would like to do.

SIR THOMAS ELYOT
From the portrait by Holbein in Windsor Castle

Though Elyot would have the first lessons made easy, and urges teachers not to keep their pupils too long at grammar (" a gentle wit is therewith soon wearied," he says), he disapproves of extended holidays. " If," he remarks, probably with a twinkle in his far-gazing eyes, " the children be absent from school for the space of one month the best learned of them can scarce tell whether the *Fato* whereby Æneas was brought in to Italy was a man, a horse, a ship, or a wild goose ! " None the less, he would not have his imaginary boy kept too strictly to his task. He must learn to wrestle, to run, to dance, and to shoot with the longbow. Swimming is a useful art to possess ; remember Horatius Cocles who " by his feate of swymmynge saved the city of Rome from perpetuall servitude " ! But Elyot will not have football at any price, for he can see in it nothing but " beastly furie and exstreme violence."

The broad-built, puffed and bepearled English king had a nephew, the son of his sister Margaret, who early showed as much delight in music as little Prince Edward did in Latin grammar. This nephew was James V of Scotland, a monarch more lively than lucky, of whose childhood we catch a most attractive glimpse in the verses addressed to him in after years by his gentleman-usher, Sir David Lyndsay :

> I take the Queené's grace thy Mother,
> My lord Chancellór and many other,
> Thy Nurse and thy old Mistress,
> I take them all to bear witness
> How, as a chapman bears his pack,
> I bore thy grace upon my back,
> And sometimes straddling on my neck,
> Dancing with many a bend and beck.

Lyndsay reminds the King that the first words His Majesty ever spoke were " Pa, Da Lyn,"—Play, David Lyndsay—and how he would obey, and play more than twenty jigs upon the lute to please him :

> From play thou never let me rest ;
> And aye when thou camest from the school
> Then I behoved to play the fool.

The schooling and the fooling were both over betimes, for the boy who romped with " Da Lyn " was crowned King of Scotland when he was only twelve years old. When James had been some four years on the throne Lyndsay wrote to him :

> When thou wast young I bore thee in mine arm
> Full tenderly, till thou began to gang,
> And in thy bed oft happéd thee full warm,
> With lute in hand syne sweetly to thee sang ;
> Sometimes in dancing fairily I flang
> And sometimes playing farces on the floor ;

N

But now, he adds:

> But now thou art by influence natural
> High of ingyne [1] and right inquisitive
> Of antique stories and deedés martial.

Very different was the childhood of James's Tudor cousin four years younger than himself. We cannot imagine little Edward riding pick-a-back, or clamouring for jigs and yet more jigs. When he was less than a year old Chancellor Audley wrote of him as having " so earnest an eye, as it were a sage judgment towards every person that repaireth to his grace." He was, indeed, a grave and sedate child, cooler and wiser when he became King at the age of ten than his Stuart cousin was at the end of a lifetime almost thrice as long. There is little that is attractive though there is much that is impressive in the vision of this Tudor prince, with his top-heavy, sandy-haired head, his frigid, watchful eyes, writing his diary with calm precision and recording the execution of his uncle, the Protector Somerset, thus stonily: " The Duke of Somerset had his head cut off on Tower Hill between eight and nine in the morning." This Duke was his mother's brother, and must have been as familiar a figure to Edward in his childhood as " Da Lyn " was to James, though perhaps a less jovial companion.

HENRY STUART, LORD DARNLEY (17)
AND HIS BROTHER CHARLES (6)
Lucas de Heere
Photo T. & R. Annan and Sons

Two years after Sir Thomas Elyot's *Boke Named the Governour* appeared, a worthy gentleman of Périgord was applying, though

---

[1] Spirit, invention, wit.

probably without knowing it, many of Elyot's ideas to the education of his son Michel. The Seigneur de Montaigne had begun to wonder whether a mental diet of Donatus, seasoned with liberal thrashings, were really the be-all and the end-all of a child's training. So he made several startling and perfectly new experiments. He placed the little boy first of all in the care of a humble family in the village of Papessus, hard by the peaked and turreted roof of the Château de Montaigne, so that he might learn to enjoy simple things—plain food, homely surroundings, the quiet life of a French village. Then, in order to make sure that Michel should hear no other language than Latin when his mind became active, he gave him a German tutor who knew not one word of French, and taught the members of his household enough Latin phrases to carry on short conversations with the child. Instead of being aroused in the morning by knocks on the door, commands to get up, or any other prosaic sound, Michel opened his eyes to the strains of sweet music.

CHÂTEAU DE MONTAIGNE, PÉRIGORD

When, at the age of six, he entered the Collège de Guienne at Bordeaux, where quite small children were received in the lower forms to learn their alphabet, he was miles ahead of any boy of his years, and had to be placed in a higher class to study Cicero, Quintilian, and Ovid with pupils far older than he.

Among the professors at Bordeaux was a tremendously learned and tremendously grim and grumpy Scot, George Buchanan by name. This professor wrote, in Latin so perfect that he was suspected of cribbing from a long-lost classical original, stodgy, stately plays to be acted by the boys of the Collège de Guienne. In these plays young Michel de Montaigne often took a leading part, from which it would seem that he had a good memory and a clear voice, and spoke with the correct accent and emphasis.

When his schooldays were long past Michel de Montaigne retired into one of the turrets of his château in Périgord, surrounded himself with books, and devoted himself to those meditations which afterward, under the name of *Montaigne's Essays*, made him famous. It was an age in which men went forth on perilous voyages over unknown seas. Montaigne thought " the proper study of mankind is man," and devoted his attention to the man of whom he knew most — himself. Among the thoughts and ideas which it amused him to jot down were his views upon the training of little boys. Like Elyot, he had none of his own upon whom to try experiments. But the young Montaignes, had they ever existed, would have had a much more easy and amusing childhood than most boys of their century—always supposing that the good-humoured old philosopher had been faithful to his own plan !

In the meantime, Montaigne's old teacher, George Buchanan, had found another task, not in France, but in his own grey native land. The Renaissance was closely followed by another great spiritual and intellectual movement —the Reformation. Few scholars of Buchanan's quality had accepted the Reformed doctrines unreservedly, and the Scots lords left in charge of Queen Mary Stuart's small son after her flight to England were anxious to find worthy tutors for him whose Protestantism was beyond doubt. Therefore, in the year 1570, George Buchanan was appointed one of the principal preceptors of James VI.

In the National Portrait Gallery, London, there is a quaint picture of the little King of Scots, painted when he had been four years Buchanan's pupil. He stands with his legs curiously slanting, as though on a slope, one hand on his side and the other holding his tame falcon. The high-perched hat a-nod with plumes, the strangling ruff, the tight-waisted doublet of quilted white satin, and the vast padded breeches of green velvet, seem quite suitable trappings for so unboyish a boy, though his grand-

JAMES VI AS A BOY
National Portrait Gallery
Photo Mansell

father, James V, would have found them irksome in his romps with
" Da Lyn." James VI, we are sure, never romped ; perhaps
because he had no one to romp with, for he was very far from
being a priggish prodigy like his kinsman Edward VI. He was a
nervous and intelligent child, very much in awe of the well-
meaning but rather fearsome elderly people who watched over
his youth. But despite his dread of his grim tutor he delighted
in his studies, and took very kindly to even the driest and tough-
est of them. A worthy Scot recorded his impressions of the little
monarch when he saw him at Stirling in 1574. " We remained
two days," he wrote, " and saw the King, the sweetest sight in
Europe that day for strange and extraordinary gifts of judgment,
memory, and language. I heard him discourse walking up and
down in [*i.e.*, holding] the old Lady Marr's hand, of knowledge and
ignorance, to my great marvel and astonishment." In the same
year James edified the English Ambassador by translating so well
a chapter of the Bible out of Latin into French and then out of
French into English " that few men could have added anything
to his translation." It was three years before this and one year
after he became Buchanan's pupil that little King James astonished his subjects by his gravity and his mysterious words
when he went in state to open Parliament at Stirling. Upon
taking his place at the high table he spied a hole in the table-
cloth and began to poke at it with his finger, at the same time
asking one of the lords-in-waiting what house it was in which
they found themselves. " The Parliament House," he was told.
" Then," remarked the five-year-old King, " this Parliament has
a hole in it ! " Less than a week later his grandfather, the
Earl of Lennox, who had been the leader of that Parliament,
was murdered, and then the superstitious Scots remembered the
words so gravely uttered by their little sovereign, and saw a
dark significance in them.

In 1564, two years before the only son of Mary Queen of Scots
first saw the pale sunlight of a northern June, a boy was born on
an April day in the west of England whose education was to be
very different, who was destined to learn small Latin and less
Greek, and yet who came to rule over a vaster kingdom than
James or any other king had ever recked of. At Stratford-on-
Avon, where this boy was born, there had been a little school
attached to a church guild ever since the thirteenth century. At

the Reformation this school, like many others, was broken up and then refounded as one of King Edward's grammar-schools.

It was not intended for boys of any particular class or of any especial promise; it received " all sorts of children to be taught, be their parents never so poor and the boys never so unapt." John Dalam, the last master of the old guild-school, does not seem

STRATFORD-ON-AVON GRAMMAR SCHOOL
Photo Frith

to have done his work very well, for Alderman John Shakespeare, the poet's father, and a number of his fellow-burgesses could neither read nor write. Perhaps Dalam was of one mind with that other sixteenth-century schoolmaster, who would never teach any scholar more than his father had learnt before him, lest he should prove a " saucy rogue." After King Edward's commissioners had overhauled the ancient foundation better schoolmasters were employed, with the result that a larger proportion of the townsfolk were thenceforward able to sign their names instead of merely making their marks.

Even in this simple and humble country school Latin was the chief study. Before a boy began his regular lessons there he would have to learn to read elsewhere. In Shakespeare's *Henry VI*, Part II, we come across a Town Clerk of Chatham who set copies for boys, and it was probably from some such worthy that the sons of the Stratford people learnt their letters. Printed books were still scarce and costly. The A B C was conned in a horn-book, a little flat box with a handle, holding a printed leaf cased in transparent horn.

Towards the year 1571 the seven-year-old son of Master John Shakespeare might have been seen,

> . . . with his satchel
> And shining morning face, creeping like snail
> Unwillingly to school.

Most of the allusions to schools and schoolboys in Shakespeare's plays suggest that not only young William himself but most of his fellows must have been reluctant scholars. In *The Taming of the Shrew* he makes Gremio speak of coming from church " as willingly as e'er I came from school." In *Henry IV*, Part II, Lord Hastings thus describes the dispersal of a defeated army :

> . . . like a school broke up
> Each hurries toward his home and sporting-place

In *Romeo and Juliet* we have both images, the regretful approach and the eager departure :

> Love goes toward love as schoolboys from their books ;
> But love from love, towards school with heavy looks.

What were the lesson-books of these reluctant scholars in Elizabethan Warwickshire ? We know from the evidence of the greatest of them that they must have plodded through the Latin Grammar of Dean Colet's friend Lilly, and then through a phrase-book called *Sententiæ Pueriles*. From both these books Shakespeare quotes in one of his earliest comedies. And old Priscian had not been entirely shouldered out by Lilly. Of him also young Will Shakespeare had certain rather hazy notions, while Horace and Ovid were something more—though perhaps not much more —than names in his remembrance.

What manner of man was Master Walter Roche, under whose stern eye and even sterner rod Alderman Shakespeare's auburn-haired son had to learn that *mons* meant " the hill," *cœlum*, " the sky, the welkin, the heaven," and *terra*, " the soil, the land, the earth " ? If—as seems most likely—Master Roche was the

original from which his famous pupil drew the two schoolmasters
Holofernes and Parson Evans, we feel as if we had met him and
paused to talk with him many a time on Hugh Clopton's fair
stone bridge across the Avon.   Both these portraits of country
schoolmasters are so vivid that it is impossible to doubt that the
model was the Stratford dominie.   In *Love's Labour's Lost*, the

HUGH CLOPTON'S FAIR STONE BRIDGE
Photo Frith

third of the light-hearted comedies which Shakespeare wrote after
he had gone to seek his fortune in London, we make the acquaintance of two village worthies, Holofernes the schoolmaster, and
Nathaniel the priest.   Each is mighty proud of his learning, but
neither has any real reason to be proud.   All that *they* knew
young Shakespeare knew when his schooling was cut short by
his father's fall in fortune.   And that ' all ' was so little that the
more fortunate poets of Tudor London used to sneer at the youthful Westcountryman's lack of culture in words not unlike those
which he makes Nathaniel use of Dull, the village constable:
" He hath not fed of the dainties that are bred in a book ; he hath
not eat paper, as it were ; he hath not drunk ink ; his wit is not
replenished."   Holofernes' own wit was replenished with odd
scraps of Lilly's Grammar, with a few morsels of the poems of

Mantuanus, a mediæval poet once admired but now long forgotten, and some confused ideas concerning Alexander, Judas Maccabæus, Pompey, and Hercules. But the simple fellow made a great show with his modest store of learning. He sprinkled his conversation with Latin words ; and greatly did he rejoice when a visit from the King of Navarre gave him an opportunity to display his gifts in the Pageant of the Nine Worthies which he set forth for the entertainment of his Majesty.

When little Will Shakespeare was eleven years old Queen Elizabeth visited Kenilworth Castle, and he was probably taken by his father to see some of the gorgeous pageants with which the Earl of Leicester then greeted his splendour-loving sovereign. These pageants included a Lady of the Lake, a Savage Man, fireworks, morris-dances, and a mock fight between Saxons and Danes. Poor Master Holofernes could not be expected to produce such impressive performances as these ; but he grapples with his task so engagingly, with such childish confidence, that we are quite annoyed when the courtiers make fun of him, and try to put him out of countenance. Even in the verses which he composes for the Nine Worthies the schoolmaster cannot resist the temptation to show off his learning. The part of Hercules was taken by a small, pert page, and as he made his entry Holofernes recited these lines :

> Great Hercules is presented by this imp,
> Whose club killed Cerberus, that three-headed *canis ;*
> And when he was a babe, a child, a shrimp,
> Thus did he strangle serpents in his *manus.*

Though the scene of Master Holofernes' activities is stated in the play to have lain in the kingdom of Navarre, it has been suggested that the school in which he taught was really the older school at Harrow. He is asked by an absurd Spanish knight, Don Armado, " Do you not educate youth at the charge-house on the top of the mountain ? " and replies learnedly, " Or *mons*, the hill." If the " mountain " alluded to by the highfalutin Don were in truth the hill on which Harrow now stands it seems certain that there must have been a fairly well-known school there before John Lyon's foundation. That worthy yeoman had applied to Queen Elizabeth as early as 1571 for a charter for his grammar-school, but the oldest of the existing brick and timber buildings was not begun until 1608, in the

201

reign of James I and VI, and some twelve years after the appearance of *Love's Labour's Lost*. The principal study of the first
Harrovians was, of course, Latin, and the work of the day began
with the peep of dawn in winter and at six o'clock in summer.
" Tossing a hand-ball," whipping tops, and archery were their
chief pastimes, but some of the delight of their play-hours must
have been spoiled by the rule which bade them talk Latin even
when at play.

Chance has preserved the name of the first scholar of Lyon's

HARROW SCHOOL
Photo Valentine

completed foundation—a picturesque name, Macharie Wildblood,
round which it would not be difficult to weave a stirring tale.
Young Macharie began his life as a Harrovian in 1615, just one
year before the death of Shakespeare.

Though there may be some doubt as to the actual hill which
the poet had in mind when he was writing of Holofernes, there
can be none as to the whereabouts of the school where reigned
his other famous country dominie, Parson Evans in *The Merry
Wives of Windsor*. This second portrait is in many ways like
the first. But Hugh Evans of Windsor was a Welshman ; he
combined the duties of schoolmaster and parson, and seems to
have been on excellent terms with his flock. He too loves to
slip in a word of Latin here and there ; he too is very scornful
about the ignorance of others, and ready to cry " Fie ! " at any
lapse. In an age when Eton boys used to run away from school

to escape flogging, when Elizabeth's tutor, Roger Ascham, needed all his courage to lift up his voice in praise of gentler methods, it is pleasant to find that not far from Eton, and under the shadow of the royal castle, there was a dominie who dealt good-humouredly with his pupils, even though he *did* perplex one of them with questions on a holiday. Young William Page, walking abroad with his mother on a day when his sister's wooer, Master Slender, had won leave for the boys to go and play, encounters Parson Hugh. Mistress Page then begins, " Sir Hugh,[1] my husband says my son profits nothing in the world at his book. I pray you ask him some questions in his accidence." " Come hither, William," cries the parson with alacrity; " hold up your head, come." " Come on, sirrah," interrupts Mistress Page; " hold up your head, answer your master, be not afraid." Then poor William has to struggle with a string of questions made all the more puzzling by Parson Hugh's Welsh accent. He is made to decline " *Singulariter, nominativo, hic, hæc, hoc.*" " Well, what is your accusative case ? " " *Accusativo, hinc.*" " I pray you have your remembrance, child; accusativo, *hung, hang, hog* ! " Then, " what is *lapis*, William ?" asks Parson Hugh. " A stone," answers William promptly. " And what is a stone ? " " A pebble." " No, it is *lapis*. I pray you, remember in your prain." " *Lapis*," murmurs William and he is rewarded by a cheery " That is a good William ! " from his teacher. But when he is bidden to " show me now some declensions of your pronouns," he falters, " Forsooth, I have forgot." Still, he cannot have acquitted himself very badly, for when his mother remarks, " He is a better scholar than I thought he was," Parson Hugh answers, " He has a good sprag memory." With the possible exception of Arthur in *King John* the boys in Shakespeare's plays are natural and likeable boys. Macduff's small son is inclined to be pert, but when Macbeth's hireling calls Macduff a traitor he bursts forth, " Thou liest, thou shag-haired villain ! " and when he himself falls stabbed to death his last words are :

He has killed me, Mother :
Run away, I pray you !

Before we meet Mamillius, in *The Winter's Tale*, we hear that he

---

[1] All priests were called " Sir " in mediæval and Tudor England.

is a gallant child, and though we do not see much of him we see
enough to be sure that he was indeed. We catch fleeting
glimpses of several little boys in this play, of the two kings,
Leontes and Polixenes, when they were

> Two lads that thought there was no more behind
> But such a day to-morrow as to-day,
> And to be boy eternal ;

of Leontes, not yet promoted to breeches :

> In my green velvet coat, my dagger muzzled
> Lest it should bite its master ;

of Polixenes' small son Florizel, of whom his father says :

> He's all my exercise, my mirth, my matter,
> Now my sworn friend and then mine enemy . . .
> He makes a July's day short as December.

Even in those stern and stately times fathers sometimes laid
aside their state and played delightfully wth their children.
Leontes calls Mamillius his " squire," his " rover," his " captain,"
his " honest friend." When asked if he would " take eggs for
money "—evidently a way of ' playing at shop '—the boy replies
sturdily : " No, my lord ; I'll fight." But he had imagination,
too, and that love of the grim and mysterious characteristic of
imaginative children. When we last see him he is beginning to
tell a story to his mother, who says :

> Come on, sit down ; come on, and do your best
> To fright me with your sprites ; you're powerful at it !

and then Mamillius begins, with bated breath :

> There was a man
> Dwelt by a churchyard ; I will tell it softly.
> Yon crickets shall not hear !

But there the tale breaks off for ever and we hear no more of
it than the crickets did.

French as well as Latin was studied by the small sons of
London merchants in Shakespeare's day. A certain Huguenot
refugee, Claude Desainlieus, who kept a school in St Paul's
Churchyard, wrote for the benefit of his small scholars some
lively colloquies. We see (or, rather, hear) the reluctant young

Londoner getting ready to set out betimes. " Where have you layde my girdle and my inckehorne ? " he asks, " Where be my sockes of linnen ? Where is my cap, my mittayns, my slippers, my handkarchif, my sachell, my penknife, and my bookes ? " School-fees were not high—" A shilling a weeke, a crown a moneth, fourtie shillings a yeare." The boys who dined at school instead of at home had " herbes or every one a mess of porridge—sometimes turneppes, coleworts, wheat and barley in porridge. Fresh fishe—or salt fishe well wattered." A scholar rebuked for arriving late excuses himself on the grounds that he met another boy " by the way which did slide upon the ice, which did cast snow, which fowght with his fist and balles of snow, which did scourge his top, which played for pennies, cherie stones, counters, dice, cards." Quite unmollified, the master answers grimly, " Enter in, gallant, I will teach you a game which you know not ! " But it is probable that the tardy pupil knew the ' game ' of being birched all too well.

Shakespeare understood boys ; and to understand them is to like them. But there came a time when his feelings toward certain young Londoners were somewhat mixed ; for the Children of Paul's and the Children of the Chapel Royal were such clever actors, and acted so well in ' grown-up ' plays that their popularity began to make their elders angry and alarmed. " Gentle Shakespeare," as growling old Ben Jonson called him, seems to have steered clear of the quarrels in which most of his fellow-poets were constantly involved, but even *he* threw a little gibe at this " aery of children, little eyases [*i.e.*, young hawks just taken from the nest] that cry out on the top of question and are most tyrannically clapped for it." One of these boy-actors, Salathiel Pavy, was the subject of an elegy by Ben Jonson when he died, after three years of triumph, at the age of thirteen. Ben whimsically says that Salathiel

> . . . did act (what now we moan)
> Old men so duly
> As sooth the Parcæ [1] thought him one,
> He played so truly.

In the days of Queen Elizabeth we are told by old John Stow,

[1] The three Fates of Greek and Latin mythology, the Norns of the Norsemen.

the tailor-chronicler, that " the scholars of Paul's, meeting them of St Anthony's, would call them Anthony Pigs, and they again would call the others pigeons of Paul's, because many pigeons were bred in Paul's church and St Anthony was always figured with a pig following him : and, mindful of the former usage,

did for a long season disorderly in the open street provoke one another with *Salve, tu quoque ! Placet tibi mecum disputare ? Placet.* [" Greeting ! Doth it please thee to dispute with me ? It doth."] And so proceeding from this to questions in grammar they usually fell from words to blows with their satchels full of books." The " former usage " dated from Norman times, and from the fact that Dean Colet expressly forbade his boys to take part in these public " disputations," which he called " foolish babbling," it is clear that the " pigeons of Paul's " to whom Stow refers were the choristers from the older school and not scholars of Colet's foundation.

A DANDY OF SHAKE-
SPEARE'S TIME

From *British Costume*, by
Mrs Ashdown (Jack)

It was not only on account of their skill as actors that these singing boys of old St Paul's became powerful and important toward the end of the sixteenth century. The nave of the great cathedral was then, even during service-time, the haunt of all sorts of worldly-minded people. Men-servants in quest of masters rubbed shoulders there with poets in quest of patrons, horse-dealers in quest of customers, and gorgeous young dandies anxious to see the newest fashions or to hear the latest gossip of the hour. From beyond the choir-screen the chanting of the choristers rose high above the buzz and clamour of the crowd, yet even there the vision of the busy world outside would sometimes penetrate. Dekker, a fellow-poet of Shakespeare's, has recorded that the young dandy who wished to be known for his elegance often thought it worth while to win the goodwill of Paul's choristers, who could so easily spread his fame throughout the City. So he would go up into the chancel, holding his perfumed and embroidered purse ready to " quoit silver into the boys' hands," and they would swarm about him " like so many white butterflies " when they heard the clash and jingle of his spurs.

206

A CHILD OF THE CHAPEL ROYAL

A.D. 1586

Upon her Grace's birthday
  To Windsor we shall fare
And play a Masque before her
  And all her gentles there,
With painted cheeks and posies,
Lath swords and silken roses,
  And cork-heeled shoes to wear.

Last year I was too little
  Before the Queen to play ;
I had to stand all silent,
  Holding a laurel-spray ;
But now that I am older,
And bigger far and bolder,
  I have long lines to say.

Yet must I play *Scintilla*
  With ruff and fan and veil ;
I'd liefer play *King Priam*,
  And clank in silver mail,
Or crawl as half a dragon,
Or bear a torch or flagon,
  Than wear a farthingale.

I fain would play *Cambyses*
  And clatter to and fro ;
'Tis sport to be a tyrant,
  As all we players know,
To be a fearful fellow,
And roll your eyes and bellow
  As doth *Geronimo*.

Next year it hath been promised,
  If I am tall enough,
That I shall act some monarch
  Most terrible and gruff ;
Farewell, then, to *Scintilla*,
Timoclea and *Flavilla*,
  Farewell to hoop and ruff !

Oh, rare to be *Cambyses*
And wear a yellow crown,
And wave my glistering sceptre,
And see my foes fall down,
And make the good folk wonder
And quake to hear me thunder,
The folk of London Town.

We Children of the Chapel
Learn leagues of verse by heart ;
I would not grudge the labour
Were mine a tyrant's part ;
Better I love such playing
Than whipping tops or maying,
Cob-nuts or damson-tart.

CHAPTER X

The Seventeenth-Century Boy

NEITHER Sir Thomas Elyot nor Michel de Montaigne, as we have seen, had a small son of his own upon whom to try his educational ideas; the Englishman had no children, the Frenchman, daughters only. But more fortunate was King James the First of England and Sixth of Scotland, who not only had much to say about the training of boys, but had two of his own upon whom he never wearied of showering good advice with tongue and pen. He was a quaint fellow, this one-time pupil of the grim George Buchanan, and when Sully, the French statesman, dubbed him the " Wisest Fool in Christendom " he summed up the royal character in four words. Yet James had a good store of common sense and homely humour, and, in his youth, was not incapable of dashing deeds. He braved the autumn fury of the North Sea in a cockle-shell of a boat to bring home his Danish bride, storm-bound at Oslo on the craggy Norwegian coast, though he had other troubles than angry waves to struggle against—croaking councillors, rebellious subjects, and such a woeful lack of coin that he had to borrow a pair of silk stockings for his wedding from a loyal lord.

The eldest son of the British Solomon, born at the Castle of Stirling in 1594, was an important boy for more reasons than one. With every year that passed it became more and more likely that when Elizabeth Tudor should die the son and grandson of Mary Stuart must follow her on the throne of England. Though the stubborn, suspicious old Queen would never speak her mind on the subject, her intentions were made fairly clear when she sent as a christening gift to the first grandson of the lovely and luckless Mary certain massy cups of gold so heavy that a strong man could hardly lift them with both hands. The baby received the name of Henry, after his ill-fated grandfather Darnley, and was placed in the care of the faithful old Countess of Marr who had watched over the childhood of his father. His younger brother and sister, Charles and Elizabeth, were also confided to

o   209 ancient Scottish families, until the death of the last Tudor monarch of England left the way clear for the first Stuart, and the three children were reunited in their new southern home. Henry was ten years old when this great change in the fortunes of his family occurred. In such haste did the excited James set off for England he had no time to visit his son at Stirling first, but he wrote him a long, wise letter, and sent it by Sir Robert Carey, that same Carey who had waited, booted and spurred, under the window of the room where Elizabeth lay dying so that he might be the very first to gallop north with the news of her death.

" Let not this news make you proud and insolent," wrote the King, " for a king's son and heir were ye before, and no more are ye yet. Be therefore merry, but not insolent . . . be resolute, but not wilful. Look upon all Englishmen that shall come to visit you as your loving subjects, not with ceremony, as towards strangers, but with such heartiness as at this time they deserve . . . I send you herewith my book, lately printed. Study and profit in it, as you would deserve my blessing. Be diligent and earnest in your studies that at your meeting with me I may praise you for your progress in learning. Be obedient to your master for your own weal, and to procure my thanks, for in reverencing him ye obey me and honour yourself."

In the green midsummer days of 1603 Queen Anne and her eldest son and daughter made their way slowly southward, welcomed everywhere with masques and pageants and songs of joy. The three-year-old ' Babie Charles ' was left in Dunfermline Castle, whence his guardian, Lord Fife, wrote : " He continues, praised be God, in good health, good courage and lofty mind, though yet weak in body, and is beginning to speak some words."

That same growling old poet, Ben Jonson, who had written a lament for Salathiel Pavy, now bestirred himself to write a *Masque of the Fairies*, to be acted in the wooded park of Althorp before the dark-eyed, fair-haired Danish Queen and her eldest son. Mab, Pan, and a dancing throng of green-clad foresters and glittering elves played this light-hearted English pageant on the dewy grass. It must all have been marvellous and enchanting to the serious little Prince, brought up among learned Scotsmen in the grey old Castle of Stirling. In July the royal family reached the much more magnificent Castle of Windsor, and there Henry was invested with the Order of the Garter, beneath the fretted tracery of St George's Chapel and the solemn splendour of the banners of the knights. The English courtiers, looking with critical eyes at the little Prince, were impressed by his " quick, witty answers and princely carriage."

The " book, lately printed," which King James commanded his son to study was the *Basilikon Doron*, or Kingly Gift, and was

STIRLING CASTLE
Photo Valentine

rather heavy reading for a boy of ten. Like his father before him, Henry was intelligent beyond his years, but we do not know when he applied himself to this ponderous volume, nor what he thought of it when he did. He early developed vigorous opinions of his own, and it is not impossible that he smiled sometimes at the anxious cackling of his sire. James began the *Basilikon Doron* with a cheerful sonnet, ending :

> Your father bids you study here and read
> How to become a perfect King indeed !

Clearly, the royal author believed himself to have mastered the whole art and craft of kingship, a most comforting belief, even when people and events refused to be guided by his will, and when his dearest purposes came to naught. James believed most sin-

ST GEORGE'S CHAPEL AND BANNERS OF THE KNIGHT

Photo Valentine

cerely, and his unfortunate younger son inherited his belief, that kings are the representatives of God on earth,

> For on this throne His sceptre do they sway,

and are responsible to Him only for their actions as His viceroys.

This idea runs through all that the Wisest Fool in Christendom wrote, or said, or did, as King; it was this idea that raised the scaffold on which died Charles I. But, apart from his fatuous faith in the Divine Right of Kings, James has much to say that is wise and true, and he says it in a quaint way that is quite his own. He loses no opportunity to show off the classical learning so hardly acquired under George Buchanan's ever-ready rod, and his pages are peppered with quotations from Greek and Latin. Now and then he pauses to shake his head over the barbarous Highlanders or the recalcitrant Puritans. Then he seems

PRINCE HENRY STUART AS KNIGHT
OF THE BATH
In the collection of Viscount Dillon
By permission of the Owner

to lower his voice as he speaks of a terrible, an unpardonable crime: " It is the unreverent writing and speaking of your parents and predecessors." No doubt it is a serious sin to break your word, to murder, or to steal ; but to criticize your father ! James shudders at the very thought. Unfortunately, this is one of the precepts which we know that Henry did *not* lay to heart. It is recorded that the Prince of Wales, when he was older, used to inquire into his father's actions, and often to disapprove of them too, though good manners prevented him from showing his disapproval too openly.

Learned though King James was, and eager to display his learning, he was no dull, dusty old scholar, and he tried, to the no small wrath of the Puritans, to encourage the people to enjoy " plays and lawful games in May and good cheer at Yule." In this he must have had the full sympathy of all schoolboys, for nobody can have resented more than they the Puritanical attempts to frown down all jinks and jollity. The King urged his eldest son to practise running, jumping, wrestling, fencing, and dancing. " The honourablest and most commendable games that ye can use," he wrote, " are games on horseback, for it becometh a Prince best of any man to be a fair and good horseman ; " and he counsels Henry to ride and master "great and courageous horses," a thing that he himself, strapped to

BOYS' SPORTS IN THE SEVENTEENTH CENTURY

From a woodcut in the first picture-book ever made for children

From *Mediæval and Early Modern Times,* by Professor Hutton Webster (Heath)

TILTING AT THE RING

From *The Sports and Pastimes of the People of England,* by Joseph Strutt

the padded saddle of his quiet nag, did not aspire to do. Tilting at the ring, and sports apt to teach skill with arms on horseback the King chiefly praised, and his words were quite as welcome to the seventeenth-century Prince of Wales as they would be to the present bearer of the Three Feathers. De la Boderie, the French Ambassador, wrote of young Henry in 1606 : " None of his amusements has any smack of childishness. He is a fervent

lover of horses, though he does not care much for hunting.   When
he hunts it is chiefly for the joy of the gallop.   He enjoys tennis,
and a Scots game very like mall [probably golf].   After two hours
devoted to study he spends the rest of his time tossing the pike,
shooting with the bow, vaulting, or some other exercise.   He is
never idle.''

James had no need to urge the boy to be earnest and diligent
in his studies ; he was earnest and diligent in everything.   Nor

A TENNIS-COURT

does it seem that the King's remarks about dress and deportment
were much to the point.   It is a little curious to find a monarch
whose own gait and gestures were so strikingly ungraceful, who
waddled and gabbled, as Sir Walter Scott said, " like an old
gander," holding forth with eloquence on the importance of a
kingly demeanour.   Here Henry was better able to obey than he
to command, though neither he nor his-brother Charles was quite
so " homely and hearty " as their father held that even kings
should be sometimes.   Like nearly all the Stuarts, Henry took a
keen practical interest in science, more especially in the sciences
connected with navigation.   His astrolabe, with which he mea-
sured the courses of the sun and stars, may still be seen in the
British Museum.   He encouraged the great naval architect,
Phineas Pett, standing by him through thick and thin, and

roundly declaring that those who plotted against him " deserved hanging."

Meanwhile the younger brother, Charles, was growing in grace and in inches. When he was brought from Scotland the little prince stumbled if he tried to walk and stuttered if he tried to speak. The alarmed James wanted to encase the child's legs in iron boots and to have his tongue cut by a surgeon, but Lady Carey, the Prince's governess, stoutly opposed the King, and had the happiness of seeing her gentler methods succeed. The legs of "Babie Charles" must, however, have remained somewhat unimpressive, for Henry chaffed him about them, and told him that when he, Henry, should be King he would make him Archbishop of Canterbury so that any imperfections might be hidden with stately, trailing robes. By the time that Charles reached the age of ten,

PRINCE HENRY STUART'S ASTROLABE
British Museum

however, this handicap seems to have been completely overcome, for when Henry was created Prince of Wales his brother took a leading part in the beautiful *Masque of the Rivers* which one of the Court poets wrote to grace the occasion. The Queen herself took part in this masque, garbed as Tethys, with a murex-shell for a helmet and silver seaweed trailing from her blue robe. At her feet sat Henry's beloved sister Elizabeth as the Nymph of the Thames, while young nobles garbed as Tritons gambolled round them among silver dolphins and many-coloured shells. Wearing a tunic of flower-embroidered green and a pair of gauzy silver wings, "Babie Charles" led twelve little blue-clad girls in a dance which enchanted all the beholders. At the end he stepped forward and handed a gilt trident to his father, the Ruler of the Waves, while to the newly created Prince of Wales he offered a jewelled sword and a scarf richly wrought by the hands of their mother, the Queen, who thereupon descended from her throne of silver rocks and mingled in the Naiads' dance.

In spite of Henry's chaffing of him, Charles seems to have been devoted to his elder brother, as many of his childish letters bear witness. " Sweet, sweet brother," one of them runs, " I will give anything that I have to you, both my horse, and my books, and my pieces [*i.e.* fowling-pieces, small guns], and my crossbows, or

ST JAMES'S PALACE
Photo Valentine

anything that you would have." At nine years old he was writing in Latin to tell his *Frater carrissime* that he had begun to study the colloquies of Erasmus.

In the meantime Henry was preparing himself, in his serious way, for the destiny which seemed to lie before him. Though he did not meddle in affairs of State, neither did he hold himself aloof. The Lord Chancellor Bacon described him as " slow of speech, pertinent of his questions, patient in listening, and of a strong understanding." Sometimes this earnest young Prince could not refrain from making his real feelings known. Of Raleigh's long imprisonment he said, " No man but my father would keep such a bird in such a cage ; " and once, when the French Ambassador asked him what message he wished to send to the King of France, he answered more energetically than prudently—" Tell him," he said, " how you found me employed." The Ambassador had found him tossing the pike.

Every year that passed increased Henry's popularity with the English nation. When he was given a household of his own, and held his separate Court at Richmond or St James's, so many of his future subjects flocked to honour him that the poor old King felt more than one sharp twinge of jealousy. " Will he bury me alive ? " asked James in dismay. But the King was fated to outlive his brilliant first-born son for thirteen long years.

On the night of October the 29th, 1612, a lunar rainbow was seen, bending its pallid, eerie colours over the dark red turrets of St James's Palace. Londoners looked up at it with troubled eyes, for it was known that the Prince lay ill there. The nature of his illness baffled the Court doctors, but on the chance that it might be infectious they forbade his sister, Elizabeth, to visit him. Then the undaunted Princess disguised herself, and tried in vain to slip through the watchful line of attendants mounting guard by her brother's door. On November the 5th, the King's loyal subjects were celebrating the seventh anniversary of Guy Fawkes's famous failure. The streets of London were full of excited people, carrying torches, and marching, or jigging to the " squeaking of the wry-necked fife." At midnight, when the joyous bonfires were blazing from one end of England to the other, the noble spirit of Henry, Prince of Wales, flickered out, and all the high hopes centred in him lay shattered in the dust.

On the other side of the Channel another young heir-apparent was then passing through childhood to boyhood—Louis the Dauphin, afterwards King Louis XIII. With him Henry had

CELEBRATING GUY FAWKES' DAY
May Gibbs

exchanged stately letters and gifts of horses, guns, and hounds. The letters were probably composed by the boys' respective tutors, but the gifts must have made each Prince seem very real to the other. The Dauphin was as unlike the Prince of Wales as the gay, breezy, fearless Henri of France was unlike the quaint,

LOUIS THE DAUPHIN AS A BOY
Painter unknown
Photo Alinari

fussy, pedantic James I of England. While Henry was tall, hand-some, and graceful, Louis was an unchildish-looking little fellow, heavily built, with a tongue too large for his mouth, reddish hair, and cold dark eyes. Henri IV's ideas were very far removed from those of his " good cousin of England." He cared little for mere bookish learning, but it pleased him to see his son drink wine and eat oysters like a man, and stand the sound of gunfire without flinching, like a soldier. He would romp with his children in a way that shocked and amazed the stately Ambassador of Spain ; but he did not sit down and write a book for their guidance !

The Dauphin's chief fault, for which he had to be whipped almost every day, was a tendency to be *opiniâtre*, or self-willed. On New Year's day and other solemn occasions he would make tremendous resolutions to behave better ; and once when his nose began to bleed he remarked to his governess that he was sure it must be because he had been *opiniâtre* again. Whipping, though perhaps not very severe, formed an important part of his training. He also had to learn to jump over ditches, to hand his father's cup to him at table, to receive bishops gravely and ambassadors with smiling politeness, and to hold out his small hand with a good grace for the bristling salutes of moustached courtiers.

This Dauphin early showed a marked gift for drawing, and he loved to watch the movements or play with the colours of the artists who came to paint his portrait. When he was five years old a painter called Martin was painting him in a gorgeous military dress, with a golden cuirass, a crimson cloak, a sword on his side, and a spear in his hand. The boy insisted that his favourite hound should appear with him in the picture. When it was pointed out to him that warriors do not usually take their hounds with them into battle he retorted : " But this will be to seize the legs of the enemy ! "

Lessons were not made very difficult for the little Prince (his father was not like the Wisest Fool in Christendom), and dancing seems to have been one of the most important. For toys he had drums, guns, trumpets, and little clay monkeys with which he played military games. He also had a tiny silver saucepan in which he used to cook morsels of beef or bacon, and sometimes he and his pages used to amuse themselves stringing coloured glass beads to make collars for his pet hounds. With his younger brothers and sisters he played a game called *La compagnie vous plait-elle ?* and another, called *Ils sont à St Jean des choux*, which may have been French versions of universal old games like " Nuts in May " and the " Mulberry bush."

One of the Dauphin's favourite pranks seems to have been to ' play at ' various grown-up doings. Sometimes he would gather his brothers and pages round him and pretend to hold a council, " like Papa." His little sister was not allowed to join in. " Go away," he said to her, " girls can't be councillors." At other times he would say that the carpet was the sea, and swim or sail across it, or pretend to be an astrologer, a robber, or a runaway horse. When he was only three years old a strolling troupe of English actors paid a visit to the palace of Fontainebleau and gave a performance at which he was present. The little Dauphin listened patiently to the unfamiliar language, and gravely watched the strutting and flourishing of the players. Three days later he was striding about with his pinafore wound round his head, growl-ing out, " Tiph, toph, my lord ! " and saying that he was an English actor. The words re-tained in the quick memory of the child seem to suggest that the play acted at Fon-tainebleau in 1604 was the Second Part of Shakespeare's *Henry IV* where (Act II, Scene 1) Falstaff says to the Lord Chief Jus-tice : " This is the right fencing grace, my lord ; tap for tap, and so part fair."

BOY WITH A HAWK
Joannes van Noordt
Wallace Collection

Although there was in the Dauphin, as there was in him after-ward as Louis XIII, a certain strange reserve which often made it difficult to guess his real thoughts and feelings, he showed some engaging touches of pity and kindliness when he was a boy. Once, seeing a gang of wretched convicts being driven on their way to become galley-slaves, he began to cry, and said to his governess, Madame de Montglat, " Mamanga, I want them to be set free ! " He often interceded for soldiers who had been locked up for some fault of discipline. " Be good now," he said to two who had been placed under arrest for brawling, " Don't quarrel any more. Off with you ! " At other times he would ask " Mamanga " for money to give to the poor people whom they passed on the road. Though he was a little afraid of his father's teasing, he had a great admiration for him and tried to imitate him in all things, to the occasional alarm of his attendants. If he were told that he ought to say, " Please," or that he ought not to call for wine with his breakfast, he was always ready to retort, " But Papa doesn't ! " or " Papa does ! " He had, indeed, an answer for almost everything. When he was informed that bread was meant to give to the poor and not to dogs, he asked : " Then, are dogs rich ? "

For birds, whether in picture, story, or real life, he had a singular affection. During the severe winter of 1608, when the ink froze in the palace inkpots at St Germains, several wild birds were caught, stupefied with cold, in the wooded park. These the Dauphin gathered together in a large enclosure on the terrace outside his window, " I have," he told his doctor, " a battalion of little birds in my aviary. I put them there during the frost. The captain is a chaffinch, and so is the lieutenant, and so is the ensign. The drum-major is a lark, and the piper is a gold-finch. Every day I had a brazier put in the cage, and the birds used to come round, two by two, and warm themselves, and chirp." Another bird in whom the Dauphin felt a keen interest was the tame eagle in the legend, who when the Roman lady, its mistress, died sacrificed itself on her funeral pyre. " Tell me again about the eagle ! " he commanded, on the same day that he had first heard the story ; and when it had been told again he said : " *I* should like to have a tame eagle. But is it a *true* tale ? "

As a child this King, afterward so cold and dull, was observant and inventive. One day M. de Vic, Governor of Calais, dined with the Dauphin, who noticed the absence of a spur from one of his boots and demanded the reason. De Vic explained that a spur would be useless as on that side his leg was of wood, and could not be bent." You must put a little peg under the knee," said the Dauphin, crooking his finger on the table to show what he meant, " and then it will go *crac* ! " Next day he asked the Governor if he had yet followed his advice. De Vic confessed that he had not, and the seven-year-old Prince proceeded to explain his idea. " You must have a little wheel to make your leg bend," said he, " And then a peg to stop the wheel. Will you race me along the gallery ? I will give you a start of fifty feet."

While the boy-princes of Europe were being trained for their future tasks according to the ideas of their various fathers, the small boys, their future subjects, struggled with the Latin grammar, climbed apple-trees, whipped tops, flew kites, were birched, and soon forgot their birchings, like their fathers before and their sons after them. School life, except for the changes in chapel at the Reformation, altered very little between the sixteenth century and the eighteenth. Only, here and there, among the light-hearted little rascals of Stuart England, there would be some finer spirit making itself ready for a higher destiny. Foremost among these we must set John Milton, most famous of all the famous men educated at Dean Colet's school. So intense was this young Puritan's passion for study he would sit up, poring over his books, while the bells of St Mary le Bow clanged the night hours above his head, and the unfortunate maidservant waiting to light him to bed nodded and dozed in her chair. Milton was so early

A FAMILY DINING

and so keenly conscious of his great poetic mission that he can never have been a very boyish boy. " To walk the studious cloisters pale " must always have appeared to him a far more pleasant way of spending his time than flying kites or tossing balls. The rod, ever ready to descend upon the inattentive and the idle, can seldom have touched so ardent and so apt a scholar, though when he himself in after years undertook to teach his young nephews he followed the example of Orbilius with a thoroughness that would have delighted that stout-armed trumpeter of Beneventum. Another great Englishman of the seventeenth century, Isaac Newton, was a much less serious student than the son of Mr Milton, scrivener, of Cheapside. At Grantham grammarschool Isaac was regarded as a very ordinary and quite unambitious sort of boy until, one fine day, he emerged victorious from a tussle with a schoolmate bigger than himself. This victory stirred him up to such good purpose that he began to pay more heed to his neglected books, and soon made up for lost time. When,

owing to a fall in the family fortunes, he was sent to work for
a little while on a farm, young Isaac turned out to be an oddly
absent-minded and awkward farmer, owing to the fact that his
mind was busy with mathematical problems instead of with the
duties of the barn, the stable, and the field.

Though the boy for whom the *Basilikon Doron* was written
did not live to "become a perfect King indeed," his younger
brother bore the imprint of its narrow philosophy all his life.
Prince Charles fully shared his father's views upon kingship ;
and he shared his scholarly tastes as well. There is in the
British Museum a wonderful volume prepared by this Prince as
a gift for his learned parent, full of quotations from classical
authors copied in an exquisite flowing hand. When the sad-
eyed, stiff-willed Prince of Wales succeeded to the throne and
had, in his turn, a small son to train for the succession, he went
about the task in the spirit neither of James I nor of Henri IV.
For his little boy's governor he chose William Cavendish, Earl
(afterward Duke) of Newcastle, a great noble of the old school
who knew more about the art of riding than of any other. This
art he imparted to his royal charge, who became one of the most
accomplished horsemen of his time ; but some other branches of
the royal education seem to have been neglected, for it was recorded of Charles II that he had some difficulty in reading " a
plain Latin book," a difficulty which would have been felt by
few gentlemen of his reign. Though Newcastle affected to despise
bookishness, he himself dabbled in authorship, and wrote some
pompous, stilted plays in addition to two massy tomes on horse-
manship. He drew up, for the enlightenment of the future
Merry Monarch, a very curious letter, containing much advice
that must have appealed strongly to the young prince.

" I would not have you too studious," wrote Newcastle, " for
too much contemplation spoils action—and virtue consists in
that. . . . The greatest clerks are not the wisest men . . . the
greatest captains were not the greatest scholars," and he adds
slyly that, the Prince not being very " apte " to his book, no
long discourse was needful to deter him from excessive study !
On the other hand, he is anxious that Charles should read
history, so as to be able to " compare the dead with the living,"
and that he should be always ready to doff his hat, smile, bow,
say a tactful word. A knowledge of men and manners, a fair

acquaintance with history, and perfect good-breeding—these, thought my lord of Newcastle, were the qualities most necessary to a king. He may not have been far wrong ; for it was mainly by dint of following his advice that Charles II contrived to hold on to the throne from which the far more earnest, cultured, and thoughtful Charles I was so rudely cast down.

The little Prince of Wales was strikingly unlike his handsome father, and so dark that his mother, Henrietta Maria (sister of Louis XIII), wrote that she was ashamed of him. In his infancy his best-loved plaything was a block of wood, to which he clung affectionately both day and night. As he grew older he was inclined to be, like his French uncle, *opiniâtre*, and in the first letter she ever wrote to him his mother had to chide him for re-fusing to take his medicine and to threaten to come herself and make him take it. Some connection must exist between this letter and the comical little note which the Prince wrote to his governor :

CHARLES II AS A BOY
After Van Dyck
Photo Mansell

My Lord,
    I would not have you take too much physic, for it does always make me worse and I think it will do the like with you. I ride every day and am ready to follow any other directions from you. Make haste to return to him that loves you.
                      CHARLES P.

For my lord of Newcastle.

P

225

In Holland little Charles had a company of cousins rather older than himself whose childhood was spent less merrily than his and whose education was far more serious a matter. These were the sons and daughters of his Aunt Elizabeth, Queen (for a short time) of Bohemia. This Queen, without a crown, without a kingdom, without revenues, and her unlucky young husband, King Frederick, were poor in everything but children. When

the family fortunes began to topple down the Stadtholder of Holland had lent Elizabeth a house at Leyden, and there, while she held her gay, shabby Court at The Hague, her hand-some, quick-witted boys and girls spent their childhood. Of the six boys by far the most picturesque and interesting was the third, Prince Rupert, famous while he was still young as the dashing cavalry-leader of the Civil War. Though their mother seems to have found more amusement in her pet dogs and monkeys than in her children, she was too true a daughter of her father, the author of the *Basilikon Doron*; to let the family grow up un-taught in their home beside the glassy canals and grey-green

PRINCE RUPERT AS A BOY
Van Dyck
Photo Bruckmann

osiers of Leyden. Their life was very strictly regulated, and they never lacked tutors though they often had to be content with plain fare. A certain degree of courtly ceremony was observed among them. When the girls entered the dining-room with their governess they always found the boys, with their tutors, drawn up in a stiff row, and there was a solemn exchange of bows and curtseys between the brothers and sisters before they sat down to their simple, and sometimes meagre, repast. The day began with prayers and a Bible-reading in English. Then the boys had to study four or five modern European languages in addition

226

to the inevitable Latin. Then came history, geometry, juris-
prudence, fortification, fencing, and dancing. At eight years
old Prince Rupert, already tall and active, could handle pike,
musket, and sword with the skill of a veteran. The lore of the
chase formed a necessary part of a gentleman's education in the
seventeenth as in the sixteenth century, and Elizabeth of
Bohemia's sons were early skilled in it. Sometimes she would

BEAR-BAITING

take the elder boys hunting with her, and once Rupert came near
returning no more. This was when the fox went to ground and
his favourite hound followed. Rupert saw the hound vanish
down the fox's hole, and, after waiting in vain for it to reappear,
decided to creep into the earth and pull it out. He managed to
grip its hind-leg, and then he found that he himself could not
get out again. Most luckily his tutor happened to see a pair
of princely feet sticking out of the hole and hastened to seize
them, when the Prince was dragged forth still gripping the
hound, and the hound still gripping the fox.

It was well for young Rupert that he was given many lessons,
and hard ones, in his childhood, for his lesson days were soon
over. He was only thirteen when he had his first taste of real
war. The luckless Frederick of Bohemia had died in the interim,

227

and the Stadtholder, Henry of Orange, took two of the fatherless
Princes, Charles Louis and Rupert, with him on the campaign
which ended in the capture of Rhynberg. Two years later the
younger brother was again on active service, and fitting himself
for the career of a soldier of fortune—that career which he was
destined to pursue with a chivalrous unselfishness of purpose
very rare in warriors of that breed. The happiest time in the
boyhood of this most gallant of seventeenth-century boys came
in the year 1636, when he paid his first visit to England. Charles
Louis, a sedate and rather sly youth, was already at the English
Court, but Elizabeth hesitated to send her fiery, impetuous
third son, nicknamed ' *le Diable*,' to join him. Her hesitation
was groundless. Finding himself in a new, more sympathetic
atmosphere, Rupert lost all the awkwardness and brusqueness
which had annoyed his mother and quickly won the first place in
the affection of his grave uncle, Charles I, and his charming aunt,
Henrietta Maria. Before the creeping shadow of the Civil War
had touched it, the Court of Charles I was one of the most
delightful in Europe. Under a King who loved and understood
art and music, who gathered round him sculptors, artists,
musicians, and poets, Windsor and Whitehall were the centres
of all that was gracious, lovely, and of good report during those
brief days of quiet light before the destroying tempest broke.
Rupert revelled in that golden air. On the last day of his
sojourn, when he was out hunting in Windsor forest, he exclaimed passionately that he wished he might break his neck and
so leave his bones in England. It was in England that his dust
was laid forty-six years later, after a career as rich in adventures
as any boy ever dreamed of. Does it not stir the boyish imagination even now, after almost three centuries, to hear how, when
Charles I had fallen and his children were penniless exiles,
Rupert took command of a handful of battered royalist ships
and steered for the Indies, to wage war on the merchant fleets
of Cromwell and all Cromwell's allies ? The young prince and
his even younger brother Maurice, who went with him but never
returned, were dubbed pirates by the indignant English Parliament. But history tells us of no other pirate so chivalrous as
Rupert, of no other who, after capturing many rich cargoes,
came home as poor an adventurer as he had set forth ; so came
Rupert, handing over all his spoils to the widowed Queen of

England and her children, and keeping as his share only a monkey or two and an adoring little African page !

As we have already said, boy-life in school and playground was much the same in the seventeenth as in the sixteenth century, and in order to get a clear and vivid impression of the Stuart boy it is often necessary to seek him in courts and camps, where life was more full of colour and action.   Houses were changing, the solid, brick-built, comfortable type taking the place of the timbered and gabled dwellings ; costume was changing, and the cavaliers crowded more and more feathers on to their hats, while the Puritans buckled themselves grimly into buff and steel.   But boy-life changed little.   At the great English schools, Eton, Harrow, Winchester, Westminster, St Paul's, lessons and games differed hardly at all from the lessons and games of the Tudor period.   The discoveries of Galileo, Kepler, and Copernicus had revealed to astonished Christendom that this world was not, after all, the centre of the whole universe ; the voyages of dauntless seamen, English, Spanish, Portuguese, and Dutch, had taught Europe that there were other marvels in other far-off continents and islands than

OLD TIMBER HOUSE

Type of building in London before the Fire

those that the mediæval travellers had described ; the triumph of the Reformation in England had altered the form of worship in college-chapels.   These were the chief changes which affected the outlook of the seventeenth-century dominie and his boys.

Under Charles I the Etonians were very fortunate in their Provost, Sir Henry Wotton, poet, traveller, ambassador, and dreamer of dreams.   It was he who had fixed to the wooden pillars in Lower School " choicely drawn pictures of divers of the most famous Greek and Latin poets, orators, and historians."

During the twenty years which Wotton spent as English Ambassador at Venice he must have entertained a large number of English boys making the Grand Tour of Europe with their tutors. The Grand Tour long remained a favourite way of finishing a

young Englishman's education, though stern stay-at-homes sometimes declared that foreign travel did more harm than good, and
that the youthful travellers got into a great many scrapes, and
played a great many pranks, which would have been impossible had they remained quietly in England.   Still, Shakespeare's
opinion that " home-keeping youths have ever homely wits " pre-
vailed during his lifetime, and for nearly two centuries after his
death.

Some of these travelling students seem to have given no little

COSTUME OF THE NOBILITY AND GENTRY IN THE
TIME OF CHARLES II

trouble to English ambassadors on the Continent, and to have
taken up their quarters quite calmly in the various embassies,
often uninvited.   In a play called *Monsieur d'Olive* one of these
harassed diplomatists utters this complaint : " Gentlemen send
me their younger sons . . . to learn fashions, forsooth ; as
if the riding of five hundred miles and spending a thousand
crowns would make 'em wiser than God meant to make 'em !
Three hundred of these goldfinches have I entertained. . . . I can
go in no corner but I meet some of my young Wifflers in their
accoutrements. . . . Six or seven of them make a perfect
morris-dance ; they need no bells, their spurs serve their turn.
I am ashamed to trail them abroad ; they'll say I carry a whole
forest of feathers with me, and I should plod before 'em in plain
stuff, like a writing-school master before his boys when they go
a-feasting ! "

THE SEVENTEENTH-CENTURY BOY

Life at Eton was pleasant under Charles I, anxious under Cromwell, and both pleasant and anxious, in other ways, under the Merry Monarch. When, in the year 1662, the plague was raging the boys were ordered to puff at pipes of tobacco in class in order to disinfect the air, and woe unto the boy who disobeyed this startling order ! Three years later Mr Samuel Pepys, Secretary to the Admiralty, recorded in his *Diary* that he had visited Eton College and found " all mighty fine." He read the Latin verses made by the scholars as a Shrove-tide exercise, and thought them better than any he himself had written when he was at St Paul's School ; he then went to see the boys disporting themselves in the playing-fields, and " did drink of the college beer, which was very good."

A friend and fellow-diarist of Mr Pepys, by name Mr John Evelyn, had a small son who, though a seventeenth-century boy, was not typical of that age or of any other. With wonder and with a touch of pity we read how little Richard Evelyn, at two and a half years old, " could perfectly reade any of the English, Latine, French, or Gothic letters, pronouncing the three first languages exactly." When, just two and a half years later, his brief life ended, his disconsolate father recorded that the boy had " a strong passion for Greeke," and knew by heart " divers propositions of Euclid that were read to him in play." Yet this unchildish load of learning seems to have been lightly borne, for we are assured that he was " all life, all prettinesse, far from morose or sullen in anything he said or did." Mr Evelyn, who was delighted with Richard's precocity, might have been wiser had he locked up Greek grammars and mathematical text-books, and *shoo'd* the child out to fly a kite or spin a top with children less brilliant but more sturdy than he. It was that sturdiness, with its accompanying buoyancy of spirit and elasticity of mind, characteristic of the average boy which kept the essential qualities of boyhood unquenched during the long centuries when King Solomon's maxim about the rod and the child was the guiding principle of parents and teachers alike. Here and there a frail or nervous little fellow might be warped or broken ; but that indomitable average boy was too much for Solomon and all Solomon's disciples. Undefeated, he survived ; undaunted, he always forgot the bitter swishing of yesterday in the joyous pranks of to-day, and asked nothing better than " to be boy eternal."

PIPES IN SCHOOL
ETON, 1662

THE plague's abroad in London
  From Lambeth to the Pool,
And lest it come to Eton
  They've made a rare new rule ;
    Nay, wot you what ?
    Now have we got
  To smoke long pipes in school !

And since our worthy Provost
  Has issued this decree
Blue curling clouds of vapour
  In Lower School you see,
    And there we puff
    The fragrant stuff
  As if grown men were we.

Fair fortune to our Provost
  For taking such a whim !
Now can we eat green apples
  In class unseen of him ;
    He, too, must play
    On a pipe o' clay
  That makes the eyes wax dim.

Like any learned greybeard,
  My plug of leaf I roll,
With wax I tip the pipe-stem,
  With chalk I clean the bowl ;
    And, once well lit,
    I breathe till it
  Glows like a burning coal.

But only in the classroom
  We play these brave new games ;
We may not burn tobacco
  I' th' houses of our Dames,
    For many folk
    Do hate such smoke
  As much as did King James.

233

THE BOY THROUGH THE AGES

We may not walk through Eton
With fuming bowls alight,
We may not flaunt in Windsor
    Their stems all long and white
        Nor puff our weeds
        On Datchet Meads,
    But—how I wish we might !

CHAPTER XI

The Eighteenth-Century Boy

WHEN the eighteenth century began, a lean, hawk-eyed little Dutchman sat on the English throne. Louis XIV, the Sun-king, still shed his gilded rays over the continent of Europe. America, not yet called the United States, belonged to England, and Canada to France. In dress, in literature, and in art taste had grown prim and pompous and severe. Just as Wren's solemn domes and pillars took the place of the clustering pinnacles and spires of Old St Paul's, the flowering, rambling richness of English poetry narrowed and stiffened into lines of formal grace. It was an age of gay colours and grim shadows. Magnificence and misery rubbed elbows, even as in Hogarth's prints you see elegant ruffled and brocaded gentlemen jostling with beggars and footpads of the most ruffianly aspect. The elegant people were very elegant indeed ; one almost hears the click

VAUXHALL GARDENS
May Gibbs
Showing costume of the period

of their high scarlet heels, the snap of their enamelled snuffboxes, between the leaves of the books they loved best. Such people tripped on tiptoe over the ugly, muddy realities of the world ; but before the century closed men and women had been born who were not afraid to face these things and who tried courageously to make them different. Such men were Wilberforce, the champion of the slaves, and Buxton, who carried on the noble work he began, and Raikes, founder of the first Sunday Schools in England ; such women were Elizabeth Fry, the friend of " all prisoners and captives," and Hannah More, whose rather self-conscious goodness *did* express itself sometimes in practical good deeds. Sports were brutal, laws were harsh, but the new spirit of compassion gradually made itself felt; hospitals, orphanages, and missions to the heathen multiplied, and a trail was blazed for the feet of the great humanitarians of the nineteenth century.

When the last stroke of midnight died away on the 31st of December 1799, a century closed which had brought many and marvellous changes to Europe and to the whole world. No continents now remained unknown. The voyages of Captain Cook in the Pacific had made all old maps look as out of date as that Anglo-Saxon map in which the Danube, due south of Constantinople, flowed into a nameless sea opposite the Plain of Troy. A red-haired, snub-nosed boy born in 1727 in a Kentish parsonage had won Canada for England ; a grave-eyed, strong-jawed boy born in 1734 by the Potomac had won America for herself. Wolfe and Washington had thus changed the face and the fortunes of the Western Hemisphere not less drastically, and more enduringly, than those of Europe were changed by the little Corsican born on the craggy shore of Ajaccio in 1769. The dawn of the century had been gilded by the rays of the French Sun-king : its sunset was red with the fire and blood that blotted out kingship in France. And the first day of the nineteenth century found that

PRINCE JAMES FRANCIS
EDWARD STUART
Painter unknown
Photo T. and R. Annan and Sons

Corsican as First Consul at the helm in Paris, an Anglo-Virginian
President ruling the new United States, and a good old blundering
fellow, mostly German by race, but wholly British at heart,
planted more or less firmly on the English throne. Outwardly
the age then closing had been one of paved paths and clipped trees,
powdered wigs, silken knee-breeches, tulip-tinted brocades ; but
as it closed new influences were at work ; the daisies began to peep
between the flagstones, the clipped trees were returning to their
natural form, unpowdered heads were seen here and there among
the stiff, floury curls, and those most unclassical garments,
trousers, were beheld with little pain and less surprise. The age
of stove-pipe hats and steam-engines was at hand. How did all
these changes affect the daily life of the eighteenth-century boy ?
At first, not much, and in one way not at all. King Solomon's
remark about the rod still rang in the ears of parents and peda-
gogues, drowning the gentler voices of Elyot and Ascham. Except
in a few cases where a boy was delicate, or parents were tender-
hearted, nobody thought of sparing the rod, and everybody was
heroically resolved not to spoil the child.

King Solomon's philosophy was put into practice with great
vigour in the home of one of the most remarkable Englishmen
of this epoch—one of those Englishmen to whom the cruelty and
evil of the world seemed neither natural nor incurable. This man
was John Wesley. Born in 1703, in the Rectory of Epworth, a
thatched and timbered house garlanded with climbing fruit-trees,
John and his numerous brothers and sisters were brought up with
a strict hand by their mother. It was to her training and influence that he owed both the high idealism and the physical toughness which afterwards led him from one end of the kingdom to the
other in his famous preaching tours ; from her, too, he may
have inherited the dauntless spirit which enabled him to stand
alone and unafraid on the hills of Cornwall and the moors of
Northumbria among people as rough and untaught as any of
the South Sea Islanders encountered by Captain Cook.

As each of the Rectory babies reached the age of one year it was
taught to join and raise its hands during family prayers, and to
bear the rod without loud weeping. For breakfast and supper
they had " some broth without any bread " (can Mrs Wesley
have been the original of the Old Woman who lived in a Shoe ?),
but at dinner they fared better, and were allowed to drink as

237

much weak beer as they pleased. These children, in their quaint home on the lonely Lincolnshire fens, were trained to be almost as ceremoniously polite to each other as were the young Princes and Princesses at Leyden some seventy years before. Three hours in the morning and three in the afternoon were devoted to lessons, over which the " Rectoress " presided. On its fifth birthday each child was expected to master the alphabet. Some of the little girls, to their mother's pained surprise, took a day and a half,

CHARTERHOUSE SCHOOL
From an old print

but John needed only half a day, and at once flung himself eagerly upon the first chapter in Genesis.

Solomon, King of Israel, would have found a fellow-philosopher in the mother of the Wesleys. She held that early indulgence was really a form of cruelty, since it breeds faults of character which must be severely corrected later on, but, on the other hand, she never punished a child twice for the same misdeed, never recalled a past lapse, never refused pardon when it was sought truly.

When John was six years old the Rectory was burned to the ground and he himself had a narrow escape from death. " A brand plucked from the burning ! " his father did not fail to declare. Various kindly neighbours took charge of the children till the house could be rebuilt, but when the family were reunited

Mrs Wesley was alarmed to find that the good results of her strict training had been almost undone, and that her small boys had learnt rough games and rough ways, spoke with a broad Lincolnshire accent, and whistled frivolous airs. Their mother girt herself for the fray with Satan who, as she believed, was trying to snatch the souls of her children from her. Life at the Rectory became an almost continual round of prayers, meditations, pious discourses, and readings from serious books. The worthy Rector found it necessary to be absent rather often and to pay long visits to London about this time; he knew that his wife was quite capable of managing both the children and the parish unaided. On one of these visits to London he obtained, through a noble patron, a scholarship at Charterhouse for his son John. The rough-and-tumble of school-life must have seemed strange at first to the eleven-year-old boy fresh from the severe, and yet gracious and tranquil atmosphere of home, but John did well at school, and never forgot his father's earnest advice to take a brisk run round the playground the first thing in the morning. Discipline was as

GRAY AS AN ETON BOY

From an engraving by J Hopwood, after an oil-painting by J Richardson

From *A History of Eton College*, by Lionel Cust (Duckworth)

harsh in the eighteenth as in the fifteenth century, but a spirit of rebellion gradually developed among the English schoolboys, and found vent from time to time in upheavals and revolts which, for the moment, the masters were powerless to repress. As conditions improved, these incidents became less frequent and finally ceased.

Eton in the eighteenth century was chiefly interesting for the great number of boys among the pupils who were destined to become famous in one field or another when they reached manhood. Such boys were William Pitt, afterward Earl of Chatham, of whom his tutor wrote that he " never was concern'd with a

WELLINGTON ENTERING THE MILITARY ACADEMY AT ANGERS
AFTER LEAVING ETON
George W. Joy

young Gentleman of so good Abilities "; Henry Fielding the
novelist, who, apostrophising learning in *Tom Jones*, wrote,
" Thee . . . where the limpid, gently rolling Thames washes
thy Etonian banks have I worshipped " ; Arne, the composer of

" Rule Britannia," who tormented the other boys by practising night and day on a " miserable, cracked, common flute " ; Earl Howe, hero of the great sea-fight off Ushant on the " glorious first of June," 1794 ; Fox, Canning, and Wellington.

The Iron Duke's remark that Waterloo was won on the playing-fields of Eton is well known, but he himself had given no hint of future greatness in his Etonian days. He was an awkward youth, with a tongue too big for his mouth, and an unsociable disposition ; his only memorable exploit at school was a stand-up fight with a boy called " Bobus " Smith, whom he defeated in three or four rounds. But in later years, when he was at the summit of his glory, the Duke revisited Eton, and, forgetting his age and his dignity, astonished the bystanders by climbing the wall and running along the top, as the boys had been wont to do in his Eton days.

Many Etonians have left on record their abiding love for their old school, but Gray's " Ode on a Distant Prospect of Eton College " is something more than a mere expression of personal feeling. His ode has the true flavour of the time—its eloquence, its richness of thought and phrase, its occasional lack of humour. It seems strange that the same poet who wrote so whimsically of a " Cat drowned in a Bowl of Goldfish " should have written such pompous lines as these when contemplating the scenes of his youth :

> Say, Father Thames, for thou hast seen
> Full many a sprightly race
> Disporting on thy margent green
> The paths of pleasure trace,
> Who foremost now delight to cleave
> With pliant arm thy glassy wave ?
> The captive linnet which enthrall ?
> What idle progeny succeed
> To chase the rolling circle's speed
> Or urge the flying ball ?

From this we learn that the Etonians of Gray's time did not think it beneath their dignity to bowl hoops, and were permitted to keep pet birds. This permission must have been especially welcome to Gray's schoolfellow, Horace Walpole, who for the whole of his long life was a fervent lover of animals, and whose collection of pets, dogs, cats, squirrels, birds, and goldfish made his charming villa at Strawberry Hill resemble a toy menagerie.

THE BOY THROUGH THE AGES

Horace had been a fragile sprig of a child—he remained a queerly slim and unreal-looking person, and was said to walk like a peewit !—so he escaped the rigours of the rod, and was petted and indulged by Lady Walpole his mother, the wife of George I's ruddy-cheeked, broad-built, fox-hunting Prime Minister, Sir Robert. His early love both for his friends and his pet animals, his " cruatuars " as he quaintly calls (and spells) them, is shown in this letter written to his mother when he was eight years old :

DEAR MAMA,
        I hop you are wall and I am very wall and I hop Papa is wal. . . . My cosens like there pla things vary wall
And I hop Doly phillips is wall and pray give my duty to Papa.
HORACE WALPOLE.

and I am very glad to hear by Tom that all my cruatuars are all wall. and Mrs Selwyn has sprand her Fot and gives her Sarves to you and I dind ther yester Day.

Despite his delicacy, which prevented him from excelling at even such mild sports as " chasing the rolling circle's speed," Horace Walpole seems to have liked his life at Eton " vary wall." From Cambridge he wrote to an old schoolfellow in 1734 : " Gray is at Burnham, and, what is surprising, has not been at Eton. Could you live so near it without seeing it ? " And a few years later he was writing from the Christopher Inn at Eton itself : " Lord, how great I used to think anybody just landed at the Christopher ! Here I am like Noah, just returned into his old world again, with all sorts of queer feels about me. By the way, the clock still strikes the old cracked sound. . . . I recollect so much, and remember so little, and want to play about, and am so afraid of my playfellows, and am ready to shirk Ashton [another schoolfellow, who had become a Fellow of Eton and a noted preacher]. . . . In short, I should be all out of bounds if I were to tell you half I feel, how young again I am one minute and how old the next. If I don't compose myself a little more before Sunday morning, when Ashton is to preach, I shall certainly be ' in a bill ' for laughing at church : and how to help it, to see him in the pulpit, when the last time I saw him here he was standing up funking over against the conduct [1] to be catechised ! "

At Winchester the early years of the eighteenth century were

---

[1] " Conduct "—Etonian slang for a chaplain.

242

A BOY IN RED

Madame Vigee Le Brun
Wallace Collection

marked by some very necessary reforms in the boys' diet. Partly owing to the Civil War and the 1688 Revolution, partly to the pilfering of minor officials, this branch of the school government had fallen into a most unsatisfactory state. Beer seemed to be the only refreshment of which the boys got anything like enough ! For breakfast they had weak broth, " made of the dinner beef " ; on the first four days of the week, beef, cold or " sodden," was their portion. Though they had roast meat on Sundays, they had hardly any breakfast and only a meagre dinner on Fridays and Saturdays, no supper on Friday, and only " a baked pudding made up with water " on Saturday. One of the most popular reforms was the addition to the school menu of a " baked pudding made of flour, bread, fruit, spice, and milk," on at least two days out of seven. Wykehamites continued to breakfast on beef and beer till well into the nineteenth century ; and they liked their wooden platters so well that when china plates were introduced every boy, with one common impulse, cast the new-fangled object upon the ground ! The " ten young noblemen's sons " who lodged in the house of Dr Burton (headmaster 1724–66) may have fared more elegantly. It is certain that on half-holidays the worthy Doctor used to take these fortunate youths out hunting with him much as John of Beverly had taken *his* boys for a gallop more than a thousand years before.

Though books had been written to improve the minds of the young in Plantagenet times, and children had figured in many Elizabethan plays and poems, it was not until the Georgian period that anyone wrote books for the *amusement* as well as for the instruction of the small boys of England. In 1719 appeared the first volume of the greatest of these Georgian stories —*Robinson Crusoe* ; seven years later Dean Swift brought out a book which was not meant to amuse children, but rather to startle and rebuke their elders ; but *Gulliver's Travels*, with its giants and dwarfs, was so like a fairy-tale that it soon had to do duty as one, and, shortened and simplified, has held its own in English nurseries for nearly two hundred years. There was more edification than amusement for the buckled and ruffled little boys in Dr Isaac Watts' *Divine and Moral Songs for Children* ; but a generation which knows not Isaac knows the parodies made by Lewis Carroll of two of his songs : " 'Tis the voice of the sluggard " and " How doth the little busy bee." The first line of another of his stanzas, " Let dogs delight to bark and bite," has become a proverb ; but forgotten are his lurid pictures of the " blood and groans and tears " awaiting naughty children in the world to come.

Among the pompous and portly forms of their elders we catch brief glimpses of little boys, some merry and some sad. Saddest of all is the picture of the son of the Rector of Berkhamsted, William Cowper. We see him happy in his childhood, tucked up in his go-cart, or sitting on his mother's knee and pricking the embroidered flowers of her dress on to paper with a pin, or enjoying a " confectionery plum " ; but after her death the picture is very different. At Cowper's first school there was a big bully of a boy whose face he could not afterward remember, so seldom had he dared to raise his tear-dimmed eyes from the buckle of the bully's shoe. Yet this quivering and tortured junior lived to write " John Gilpin," one of the blithest ballads that ever charmed the mind of a child. Happier than Cowper, and only a little less happy than Horace Walpole, was another frail little fellow, seven years younger than the poet. Edward Gibbon, though nobody expected him to survive the perils of his early days at Putney, grew up a perky, podgy person, and wrote an enormous and eloquent book in many volumes—*The Decline and Fall of the Roman Empire*. His mother was too fond of amusement to spend much time with her odd little elf of a son, but he had a devoted aunt, " at whose name," he wrote years later, " I feel a tear of gratitude trickling down my cheek." This excellent lady watched over his childhood with anxious care ; she encouraged him to talk to her with a happy confidence unusual between children and ' grown-ups ' in that rigid, chilly age ; and when, finally, he went to Westminster School she took a house in Dean's Yard so that (as he puts it) " instead of audaciously mingling in the sports, the quarrels, and the connections of our little world," he might be " still cherished at home " under the wing of his aunt. Perhaps it was owing to the bountiful fare with which this indulgent aunt plied her nephew that he afterwards possessed " cheeks of such prodigious chubbiness that they enveloped his nose so completely as to render it in profile absolutely invisible."

In the spring of 1748, when Edward Gibbon was in his first term at Westminster, young George Washington was on a surveying expedition in the wild, beautiful forests of Lord Fairfax's Blue Ridge estates in Virginia. Two years earlier, when he was fourteen, George had been gazetted midshipman in the Royal Navy, but at the last moment, with the ship in which he was to have made his first cruise actually at anchor in the Potomac, his mother was seized with misgivings, and England lost a great sailor while America gained a great soldier and a great man.

The boys of Virginia had few educational opportunities in those early days. Washington learnt the first elements from his mother and from one Hoby, who combined the *rôles* of sexton and schoolmaster ; all the additional schooling he ever had was at what was called an " old-field " school at Fredericktown, under a certain Parson Marye who had been a pupil of the French Jesuit missionaries.

TWO BOYS AT THE END OF THE EIGHTEENTH CENTURY
Sir Henry Raeburn
Photo T and R Annan and Sons

From him the " Father of his Country " probably learnt to write the graceful, flowing hand in which he wrote his letters and dispatches. The boy filled thirty folio pages with " Forms of Writing " in his fourteenth year, and carefully copied out one hundred and ten " Rules of Civility and Decent Behaviour in Company and Conversation," of which the last is not the least important : " Labour to keep alive in your Breast that little Spark of Celestial Fire called Conscience." To a boy of this practical and precise temperament no studies appealed so strongly as arithmetic and mathematics. Washington was gravely occupied in land-surveying when an Etonian would still

245

have been " chasing the rolling circle's speed and urging the flying ball." Earnest and self-possessed though the future first President seems to have been, even in his boyhood, he must have felt a thrill of boyish excitement when he set off one March morning with Mr George Fairfax, a kinsman of the owner of the estate, to survey these wildly beautiful and almost pathless tracts of Virginian forest. Robert Beverley had written in 1705 of the wonders of these woods, their murmuring brooks, their marvellous fruits and flowers, their throngs of humming-birds

THE BIRTHPLACE OF WASHINGTON
From *Elementary History of the United States,* by A. C. Thomas (Heath)

" not half so large as an English wren . . . but a glorious shining mixture of scarlet, green, and gold." Added to these delights there was the knowledge that in the deepest shadows of the trees dwelt tribes of plumed and painted redskins who might emerge at any moment, with friendly intentions—or the reverse !

Prudent beyond his years, George Washington kept a journal in which he noted the crops and trees which he saw, the " most beautiful Groves of Sugar Trees," the " abundance of grain, hemp, and tobacco." He records, with evident satisfaction, that at Frederick-town, their first halt, they had " Wine and Rum Punch in plenty " and a " good Feather Bed with clean sheets, which was a very agreeable Regale." On March the 23rd there is a more boyish and picturesque entry : " Raind till about 2 o'clock and cleard, when we were agreeably surprised at ye sight of thirty odd Indians coming from war with only one scalp." The palefaces gave these braves some refreshment which, " elevat-

246

ing their spirits, put them in ye Humor of Dauncing." A war-dance followed which Washington was boy enough to watch keenly and to describe at some length. " The manner of Dauncing is as follows : viz. :—They clear a large Circle and make a great Fire in ye Middle. Men seat themselves around it. Ye speaker makes a grand speech, telling them in what manner they are to daunce. After he has finished, ye best Dauncer jumps up as one awaked out of a sleep, and Runs and Jumps about ye Ring in a most comicle manner. He is followed by ye Rest. Then begins their musicians to play. Ye music is a Pot half full of water, with a Deerskin stretched over it as tight as it can, and a gourd with some shott in it to rattle, and a Piece of an horse's tail tied to it to make it look fine. Ye one keeps rattling and ye others drumming all ye while ye others is Dauncing." This seems to have been the most exciting incident of the trip, though the young surveyors underwent various ordeals, such as having their bedding set alight and their tents blown away, and crossing swollen torrents with their horses swimming after their canoe ; they also shot (and ate) many wild turkeys, and saw (and probably heard) a " Rattled Snake."

A YOUTH OF " TOM JONES " PERIOD

In the same year that young Washington was surveying the backwoods of Virginia, Henry Fielding, the old Etonian, was finishing a novel which, though it is quite a ' grown-up ' one, contains an interesting account of the boyhood of two boys of very different characters. The elder, Tom Jones, was a merry youth, always in mischief, often in disgrace. He paid scant heed to the discourses of Mr Thwackum, his tutor, but delighted in going out shooting with Black George, the gamekeeper. On one of these secret expeditions Tom followed a partridge into a wood belonging to a neighbour and shot it there, though his guardian, Squire Allworthy, had sternly forbidden any one on his estate to poach or trespass. Nothing would induce the boy to betray the gamekeeper who had gone with him. The truth, however, was let out by the other boy, young Blifil, a sly and pious youth, prime favourite with Mr Thwackum, but called by the villagers and tenants a "sneaking rascal." Sad to relate, Tom laughed at this playmate of his, and once even punched his head and caused his nose to bleed. Down came Thwackum's rod ; and down it came again when it was discovered that Tom had ridden off alone on market-day and sold the pony which the Squire had given him. Surely an ungrateful thing to do ! But when the Squire learnt that Tom's object had been to get some money to give to the starving children of Black George, the dismissed game-keeper, he intervened, and Thwackum's rod was turned aside for the time being. Master Blifil was a model pupil ; he could talk like a copybook for hours on end ; he never amused himself by jumping five-barred gates, or climbing trees, or otherwise endangering his neck or his raiment. He is altogether unconvincing, altogether unlikeable. He turns out, indeed, to be the villain of the piece. Yet, strange to say, there is a marked family resemblance between him and the *hero* of a book which appeared toward the end of the same century—*Sandford and Merton*. This queer, stodgy story was written by a crotchety philosopher called Thomas Day, for the "Amusement and Instruction of Juvenile Minds." It is only in his priggish way of talking that the hero, Harry Sandford, is like Master Blifil; never would Tom Jones's playmate have rescued *him* from a snake as Harry rescued Tommy Merton, whose "female attendant" had fled from the reptile with loud cries. Mr Merton, a rich planter from Jamaica, was so much impressed by the noble sentiments of Harry that he at once sent his son to the same clergyman to be educated. Parson Barlow's system was simplicity itself ; it consisted in making the boys hoe the garden, rewarding them with cherries (to Tommy's "inexpressible joy" !), and then telling them, or hearing them read aloud, fables and allegories and edifying tales. One such was the tale of Androcles and the Lion. The grateful animal, the boys were told, " put itself into many attitudes of joy " when the thorn was extracted from its paw. Other stories described more or less alarming adventures in Gambia and Mexico, Russia and Switzerland. Small wonder that Tommy Merton one day exclaimed, " O dear Sir, what a variety of accidents people are exposed to in this world ! " We like Tommy better, and he seems far more real, when we hear how, inspired by some of good Mr Barlow's narratives, he tried to tame a reluctant young pig, and to teach an astonished dog to pull him along in an improvised sleigh, and came to grief in both experiments.   Finally, after Harry has rescued him once more (this time from an infuriated bull), and after Tommy has combed the powder out of his hair as a token of his resolve to lead the Simple Life, the two boys part, each shedding " a tear of sincere friendship " as they do so.

Schoolmasters of the Orbilius or Thwackum type were still all too numerous, and found champions even among the most humane. Dr Samuel Johnson, that growling sage who was so playful with his cat Hodge, so gentle with small children, declared that in school " Severity must be continued until obstinacy be subdued, and negligence be cured." The tradition was a strong one.   For the greater part of the seventeenth century Westminster School had been governed by Dr Busby, a famous wielder of the birch, whose successor, Dr Markham, was following his example with vigour some fifty years later. The Westminster boys seem to have been a peculiarly lively company under Markham.   One of them, William Hickey, known as " Pickle," has left a record of his schooldays which would have shocked and grieved the author of *Sand-ford and Merton*. " Instead of preparing my Theme, verses, or construing Virgil,"

A GUARDSMAN OF THE PERIOD

(See poem at the end of this chapter)

wrote " Pickle " Hickey, " I loitered away my time in Tothill Fields and St James's Park, or if I could muster cash, hired a boat to cruise about Chelsea Reach, in most of which excursions my friend Henley accompanied me and consequently came in for his share of stripes.   One of our chief amusements was going to the parade at the Horse Guards to look at the soldiers exercising, and at nine o'clock accompanying the daily relief in their march to Kensington, where his Majesty [George II] then resided."   Many years later a group of old Westminster boys, of whom Hickey was one, met round a dinner-table in India and fell to talking of their old School.   Their happiest memories were of the apple-tarts sold by an aged dame outside the gates.   When it occurred to them that this benefactress of boyhood might be alive and in poverty,

249

they collected a sum of money for her among themselves and sent it to the then Headmaster of Westminster, to be doled out in quarterly instalments lest the poor old lady should squander her unexpected wealth. We get a glimpse of another type of schoolmaster, the country dominie, in Goldsmith's " Deserted Village." " A man severe he was and stern to view," and, like Shakespeare's Holofernes, a little vain of his superior knowledge :

> Yet he was kind, and if severe in aught
> The love he bore to learning was at fault.

Anxiously the boys would watch his morning face to see if he were in a good humour ; eagerly they laughed at his jokes, and " many a joke had he." On the whole, he sounds a more genial type than his contemporary at Norwich High School, Mr Jones, who had among his pupils two boys from a Rectory in the neighbourhood, William and Horatio, the sons of Mr Nelson of Burnham Thorpe. " I well remember," wrote a former schoolfellow to the great Admiral, " where you sat in the schoolroom . . . between the parlour-door and the chimney. Nor do I forget that we were under the lash of Classic Jones . . . as keen a flogger as merciless Busby, of birch-loving memory."

Horatio's schooldays were soon cut short. He had an uncle in the Navy, Captain Maurice Suckling, called by the sailors " Fine Bones " on account of his liking for perfumes and elegant attire. In 1771 this uncle was surprised to receive a letter asking if he would take with him on his next cruise the least sturdy of his many young nephews at the Rectory. " What," wrote " Fine Bones," " what has poor Horatio done, who is so weak, that above all the rest he should be sent to rough it at sea ? But," he added cheerfully, " let him come : and the first time we go into action a cannon-ball may knock off his head and so provide for him."

It was a sunless, chilling April day when Horatio Nelson's fragile little person and his very modest amount of luggage were dumped at Chatham by the stage-coach. No one had come to meet him. Captain Suckling was not aboard the *Raisonnable* ; indeed, he was absent on leave and did not return till two days later. Helpless and forlorn, the boy sat on the quay, among the unfamiliar bustle and stir, watching the warships lying at anchor with their black-and-white painted timbers and their clustering masts, watching the pig-tailed sailors rolling along the

NELSON'S FIRST FAREWELL
George W. Joy

harbour edge, and waiting for someone to have pity on him. All his life Nelson remembered that miserable day at Chatham. Not until he had sat there many hours, with a sinking heart, did a kindly officer pause and question him. Most fortunately this blue-and-gold Samaritan knew " Fine Bones " Suckling. He took the hungry, homesick Horatio to his house, which was near at

WATT AND THE TEA-KETTLE
Marcus Stone, R.A.
By permission of Virtue and Co , Ltd

hand, gave him a much-needed meal, and finally saw him safe aboard the *Raisonnable*, little thinking that the timid boy with the tumbled fair hair, woefully bewildered by the strange scenes and faces round him, and speaking with the queer twang of his native Norfolk, would become in course of time the greatest sailor in the history of the world.

As the century draws near its close, visions of famous boyhoods crowd so fast that they blot each other out. Now we see James Watt chalking geometrical problems on the floor, or called an "idle boy " by his aunt because he spent so much time holding a spoon or a cup over the steam of the tea-kettle to count the drops of condensed moisture as they fell ; now we see Walter Scott dragging his lame foot along the carpet, in pursuit of a gold watch dangled before him by a white-haired old soldier in an embroidered scarlet waistcoat, or listening wonderstruck to the old Scots ballads sung to him by his aunt (yet *another* aunt !) at Sandyknowe.

In the darkest days of the French Revolution a schoolmaster called Fréville was putting together for the benefit of his little son, Émilien, a collection of stories drawn from the lives of famous children. It is a wonderfully varied crowd which he has called up ; we recognise there our old friends Publius Valerius Pudens, and Edward VI of England, but we also meet many boys of whom we have not heard before—the twin Neapolitans who made a large fortune by playing duets on the flute and were killed by a thunderbolt, the eleven-year-old Ambroise de Bouflers who fought and fell at the battle of Dettingen, the Irish cabin-boy who throve upon biscuit so hard that it had to be broken up with a hatchet, and who was devoured by the shark from which he rescued his father, and another Irish boy who set up as a wool-merchant at the ripe age of twelve and prospered mightily.

BOY WITH LESSON-BOOK
Greuze
Photo T and R Annan and Sons

Émilien, the little son of the author, did not live to read all the wonderful stories thus diligently gathered up for his amusement. He died in 1793, at the age of seven, and his heartbroken father added to the *Enfants Célèbres* a sketch of the short life of this most engaging child.   We see Émilien first as a baby, trying to share his supper with the little Chinese figures on his nursery screen ; then,

253

later on, we hear him bubbling with laughter over the terrestrial globe, following his finger round the world, and crying gleefully, "Here I am in Paris! I've just come from Lyons. . . . Ah, now I have tumbled into the Mediterranean!" Later still there is a charming picture of Émilien and his father's three American pupils, nick-named Dédé, Coco, and Doudou, going out botaniz-ing in the woods. "Often," writes Fréville, "our young naturalists would still be hunting for specimens when the sun had dipped below the horizon. Dusk warned them to turn homeward, but they were reluctant to leave their innocent sport. Then they filled their hats, their handkerchiefs, and their pockets with their rich spoils and returned, each one eager to plant his precious roots in his own garden-plot."

NAPOLEON AT BRIENNE
Réalier Dumas
Photo Neurdein

Shortly after Émilien's death, at the height of the Reign of Terror, poor Fréville was arrested, and haled before the Revolutionary Tribunal, charged with being an " Enemy of the People." Fouquier-Tinville, the President of the Tribunal, was sending hundreds of innocent com-patriots to the guillotine every day; he was famous for his utter lack of pity. Yet even *he* could not listen unmoved when Fréville asked him how a bereaved father, then occupied in writing the story of his child's brief life for the benefit of the children of France, could pos-sibly be an "Enemy of the People?" Above the roar of the mob, above the roll of the tumbrils, that appeal was heard, and thus, as Fréville himself says, " le petit Émilien " saved his father's life.

There was at Brienne, in the province of Champagne, at the end of the eighteenth century a great military college,

under the direct patronage of Louis XVI. After six years'
training the pupils were drafted into the French army or
navy as gentlemen-cadets, but during those six years they

GEORGE III AND THE DUKE OF YORK AS BOYS
R. Wilson
National Portrait Gallery

were not allowed, unless for very special reasons or as a very
signal grace, either to see their parents or to go home. This
rule weighed heavily on boys who came from a great distance
or who, for one reason or another, were not liked by the masters

nor by their schoolmates. Such a boy, the ten-year-old son of a Corsican gentleman called Bonaparte, donned the blue-and-crimson uniform of Brienne in May 1779. He was a slight, wiry boy with a bronze-tinted complexion, tightly-folded lips, and curiously piercing grey-blue eyes. To his schoolfellows he was not only a stranger, but a foreigner; he could hardly speak their language, his Christian name, Napoleon, was an outlandish name, and could not be translated into French. His Corsican accent, his abrupt manners, his aloofness, all combined to annoy the French boys, and for the first year or two they did everything they could to make him realize that he was hopelessly unpopular. But the despised intruder had qualities in him that could not remain hidden long. There was a heavy fall of snow one winter, and the whole college was allowed to build model fortifications and fight mimic battles; and then the Corsican cadet asserted himself and took the lead. It was he who planned the trenches, the battlements and sally-ports with the instinct of a born engineer; it was he who directed now the attack, and now the defence, with the resourcefulness of an inspired commander. And then it began to dawn upon the other boys that Bonaparte was not a barbarian and a blockhead after all!

DANCING DOLLS

There was a time during his schooldays when it seemed as though the Navy instead of the Artillery would be the destination of this sallow, silent youth. For either career he was well equipped by the knowledge of mathematics and geography which he had gained at Brienne. In history also, more especially military history, he had done well there; but he never mastered the art of penmanship. Indeed, when he revisited his old college as Emperor he chaffed his old writing-master for having turned out such a " duffer of a penman " as himself.

Some of Napoleon's school notebooks still exist, and in one of these he has written, in his characteristic sprawling, spluttering hand, a note concerning a certain craggy speck of an island in the South Atlantic. " *Ste Hélène, petite île appartenante aux Anglais.*"

KING GEORGE'S GUARD
A.D. 1758

NINE o'clock—soon time for school—
   (*Tirr-ra-ra*, can you hear the drum?)
Let us go by St James's Park
   And watch the soldiers come,
Let us follow as they swing round,
Let us go by the drilling-ground,
   Through the trees, where we've often been,
     As far as to Knightsbridge Green.

After nine, and time for school
   (*Wheetle-whee*, do you hear the fife?)
I wish *I* were one of those red-coats tall
   That guard King George's life—
That's what they march to Kensington for,
That's why they stand at the palace-door;
   Let's march with them, but not beyond
     The bench by the half-way pond.

Quarter-past—how far to school
   Down by the Cockpit, through Dean's Yard?
Nay, it is worth a swishing or two
   To follow King George's Guard.
Try to keep in step as we go—
Look how their legs all swing in a row,
   Spatterdashes all pipe-clayed white,
     And buttons all blinking bright.

Half-past nine—too late for school;
   (*Whew!* What *will* our master say?)
We've marched all the way to Kensington
   In step for *most* o' the way;
If we had caps all flat and high
With a great ' G.R ' in stitchery,
   And long white gaiters and bandoliers,
     They'd think *we* were Grenadiers.

Ten o'clock—to-day in school
   None will speak when they call our names;
I'm glad King George lives in Kensington
   Instead of at St James',

R

For two good miles the Guards must swing
When they go marching to guard the King
At his house with the clock and the creaking vane
And—we'll go with them soon again !

CHAPTER XII

The Early Nineteenth-Century Boy

THE first sixty years of the nineteenth century were the last of King Solomon's reign over the nurseries and schoolrooms of the West. As the dawn of the new era brightened his splendour grew dim ; and then at last his famous rod, instead of being constantly flourished over the heads of the young, was hung on a peg, and left hanging there unless some really grave fault called for stern punishment. Cruel people who had justified their cruelty out of the mouth of the King of Israel viewed the waning of his power with anger and alarm. But the spirit of the new age was against them. They had perforce to yield. And the great majority of parents came, by degrees, to think that the rod, if used with too much vigour, might spoil the child even more effectually than that sparing use of it recommended by Elyot and Ascham three hundred years before. From 1800 to 1860 this kindlier spirit moved faintly enough on the face of the dark waters ; but with the advance of the century the light grew stronger, until finally the old shadows melted away.

' Grown-ups,' especially those impressive potentates known as ' Papa ' and ' Mamma,' continued for a long time to stand high above the level upon which their children lived, high upon pedestals from which they seldom came down. And when they *did* descend it was more often to chastize the erring than to reward the deserving child ! The early nineteenth-century Papa was a figure of majesty and might. With his lofty stock of black satin and crackling white linen, his furry-looking top-hat, his jingling golden seals, his light-coloured trousers strapped tightly over his brilliant boots, he seemed a remote and awe-inspiring person to his small sons. Was there anything, they wondered, that Papa did not know ? Was there anything that Papa could not do—if he cared to try ? When he was not sitting in the House of Commons, or reading *The Times,* or drinking port-wine, or telling Mamma his opinion upon some deep question of the hour, Papa sometimes condescended to play with his little boys and girls.

If he were in a good humour, or had heard that the children had behaved well, he was wont to pat them solemnly on the top of the head. If he were in a grumpy mood, or were told that any child of his had misbehaved, it seemed as though the sky became overcast, and thunder, often followed by a thunderbolt, was in the air. Even those few Papas who were capable of romping as unaffectedly as Polixenes of Bohemia or Henri IV of France could be, and were, terribly strict disciplinarians when King Solomon asserted his power. Such a parent was Mr William Grant of Rothiemurchus. When the " tedious ceremony " of dinner neared its close his three eldest children, Elizabeth, William, and Jane, all " in full dress like the footmen," appeared in the dining-room, and were set on chairs in a row against the wall, there to remain, without moving a finger, until at dessert they were called to the table and given each a tiny glass of wine, some fruit, and a biscuit. When the table had been cleared there followed an hour of merry games. "Sometimes," wrote Elizabeth, " my father was an ogre . . . some-

A GENTLEMAN OF THE EARLY
VICTORIAN PERIOD
(See poem at the end of this chapter)

times he was a sleeping giant whom we besieged in his castle of chairs, could hardly waken, and yet dreaded to hear snore. We looked forward to this happy hour as to a glimpse of heaven. He was no longer the severe master ; he was the best of play-fellows." *How* severe a master Mr Grant could be we learn from his daughter's account of the rules which he laid down for the upbringing of the young Grants. During the greater part of the previous century baths had been unfashionable : to "take the warm bath " was then a memorable experience, worthy to be recorded in one's diary and seldom to be embarked upon unless by medical advice. But when the nineteenth century dawned a violent change of opinion took place, and an icy-cold morning dip became one of the day's terrors to nervous children. In winter " a large, long tub " stood in the kitchen-court of the Grants' house, a tub " the ice on the top of which had often to be broken," wrote Elizabeth, " before our horrid plunge into it. We were brought down from the very top of the house, with only a cotton cloak over our night-gowns, just to chill us completely before the dreadful shock. How I screamed, prayed, begged, and entreated to be saved ! All no use. Millar had her orders." (Millar was the nurse, and her orders had been issued by Mr Grant himself.) Breakfast in the Grant nursery consisted of cold milk and dry bread, except in the depth of winter, when there was hot porridge. It happened that all three children had a passionate, uncontrollable objection to milk : but the " best of playfellows " was not going to stand any nonsense of *that* sort. Milk was good for the young. So " the milk-rebellion was crushed." In his dressing-gown, with a whip in his hand, Mr William Grant attended nursery breakfast, and a " beseeching look " from any of his victims " was answered by a sharp cut, followed by as many more as were necessary to empty the basin."

During this time books for children had continued to multiply, queer little flat books, with queer little prim pictures, sometimes roughly printed in colours that splash beyond the outline in places. The tone of all these productions is highly improving. Even our stout-hearted friend Dick Whittington is made to exclaim :

> Then let me always watch my lips
> Lest I be struck to death and hell

So strong and so universal was this desire of the elders to ' improve ' the minds of the children that when a kindly spinster was inspired, for the first and last time in her life, to write verse these were the lines she composed, and imparted to her young nephews and nieces :

> Would you like to be told the best use for a penny ?
> I can tell you a use which is better than any ;
> Not on toys or on fruit or on sweetmeats to spend it,
> But over the seas to the heathen to send it !

Smiling looks seem to have been expected from the children thus incessantly warned and lectured and deluged with good

advice. The stern Papa in one little old story-book remarks that
he never allows a child to remain in his presence " whose company
is rather calculated to inspire gloom than cheerfulness " ; but he
does not seem to have paused to ask himself which of these two
feelings his *own* company was " calculated to inspire " in the
minds of his sons and daughters. Quite amiable people, sincerely
fond of children, always thought it necessary to bend down, as if
from an immense height, when they began to talk to them on
paper. Even a fancy so quaintly whimsical as Charles Lamb's
suddenly became stiff and heavy, as in his version of the story
of Ulysses, where the Greek heroes move so solemnly and speak
so pompously that they look and sound as though they were
wearing the double-breasted overcoats, the choking stocks, and
the tall top-hats of 1808. Mr Aikin, a worthy clergyman, thought
it necessary to assure his even more worthy sister, Mrs Barbauld,
that although she had been " censured for employing talents of so
superior a kind in the composition of books for children," such a
task is by no means " an ignoble employment." Mr Aikin himself then proceeds to compose such a book, close-packed with
useful information. " Hailstones," he assures his little readers,
" are drops of rain suddenly congealed into a hard mass, so as to
preserve their figure." The woodlark and the skylark, he tells
them, " are the only two birds which are known to sing flying.
They are considered," he adds unromantically, " very excellent
eating." It is curious to realize that this book appeared when
Shelley was a boy, and may have been given, as an edifying gift,
to the future author of " Hail to thee, blithe spirit ! "

In the early years of the nineteenth century a certain Miss
Murry published a slim volume entitled *Mentoria, Or the Young
Ladies' Instructor*, which is of interest to boys as well as to girls.
Mentoria represents herself as holding long conversations with
two high-born pupils, Lady Mary and Lady Louisa, upon such
topics as " Politeness and Gratitude," the " Use of Grammar,"
and " Elocution and Geography." On the fourth day she remarks : " Before I begin the business allotted for this morning
I shall congratulate you on your brother's arrival from Harrow,
and beg the favour of Lady Louisa to inform him I shall be
extremely glad of his company, which undoubtedly will be an
addition to your happiness." To which Lady Louisa replies :
" My dear Mentoria, I will fetch him this moment, as I know

he will rejoice to join our party." When she returns, " introducing her brother, Lord George," the polite child exclaims : " You
cannot imagine how rejoiced Lord George was to come ! " while
the even more polite Harrovian thus addresses his sisters' governess : " Madam, I shall esteem myself much obliged to you for
permitting me to partake of your instruction."

Mentoria then proceeds to pour forth a torrent of geographical
facts, interrupted now and then by questions or comments from
Lord George : " What are the chief countries of Asia, my good
Mentoria ? " " Is Africa as big as Europe, my dear Mentoria ? "
" What a number of inhabitants there must be, in the variety of
places you have mentioned ! "

This polite and inquiring Harrovian must have been a pupil of
one of the best headmasters Harrow ever had—Dr Joseph Drury.
Among his schoolfellows was a handsome, fiery-spirited boy with
a lame foot and an Aberdonian accent—George Gordon, Lord
Byron ; a boy who, though his character had been badly warped
by his foolish mother, had enough good sense and good feeling to
respond to the sympathetic interest soon shown in him by Dr
Drury. However truly Byron admired his old ' Head,' however
much he had enjoyed playing cricket (with his fag to make the
runs), or dreaming away his idle hours on the flat, lichen-tufted
tombstone in Harrow churchyard still known as " his," it is clear
from his own words that he never took kindly to his lessons.

> . . . Farewell, Horace, whom I hated so
> Not from thy faults but mine !

he wrote, years later, and he protested vehemently that he had
always loathed

> The drilled, dull lesson, forced down word by word.

Though in the opening years of the nineteenth century Harrow
was singularly fortunate in her headmaster, Eton was then as
singularly unfortunate in *hers*. Dr Keate, faithful follower of
Orbilius, Busby, and Thwackum, was a fiery morsel of a man
who used to birch his boys in batches of twenty, fifty, or even
eighty, and never wearied of wielding his great bunch of twigs.
But the very boys who quailed before him on weekdays got quite
out of hand on the Sabbath, when rats were let loose in chapel, and
a wild tumult " drowned the parson's saw."

Early rising was one of the virtues exacted from the young

by their elders in the nineteenth as well as in the fifteenth century ; but it was not a virtue which those same elders always practised themselves. At Dulwich, for example, where morning school began at six o'clock, the masters remained snugly ensconced in bed till nine. It frequently happened that half a dozen boys would gather in the bedroom of one of these scholastic

BEGINNING THE DAY AT DULWICH SCHOOL
From the painting by W. C. Horsley in the Dulwich Picture Gallery
By permission of the Governors

sluggards, and there repeat their lessons to a drowsy gentleman in a nightcap. In winter the pupils must have looked with a certain amount of envy at the cosy four-poster with its ample curtains, the warm dressing-gown of Indian shawl-stuff, which the dominie wore over his night attire, and the fuming churchwarden which he used to emphasise his remarks upon the gerund and the aorist. But in those days the boys themselves were well protected against the rigours of a winter dawn by full-skirted, leather-girdled coats, like those worn still by the scholars of Christ's College—better known as the Bluecoat School. The story of the foundation of Dulwich really belongs to the chapter on the Renaissance Boy, for it was the creation of Edward Alleyn (1566–1626) the actor, Shakespeare's contemporary, who chose that admirable way of disposing of the large fortune he had amassed less by acting than by ' running ' theatres. Alleyn's plan was for a college to consist of a master, a warden, and four Fellows, six poor brothers, six poor sisters, and twelve poor scholars. He would be surprised—and probably delighted—if he could revisit the glimpses of the moon, and learn that nine hundred boys are now on their way to becoming " Old Alleynians." Indeed it is rather a pleasant fancy, this return of the phantom-forms of pious founders to the scenes where their memory is kept green by their good deeds. Wykeham's ghost would always have been happy at Winchester, but it is doubtful whether Henry's gentle shade would have felt quite in its element at Eton under Keate.

In the same year— 1809 — that Keate's gruesome reign began at Eton a boy was born

LINCOLN'S LOG CABIN

in the State of Kentucky whose early days were passed under conditions as hard and bleak as those at the great English school, and yet who was born to a destiny as high, as tragic, and as illustrious as any boy of the century. This was Abraham Lincoln, the son of a shiftless, unenergetic carpenter and his tall, dark, intelligent Virginian wife. Their home was a cheer-less one, a wooden house on a tract of desolate, broken land from which Thomas Lincoln had the greatest difficulty in wringing a livelihood for himself, Mrs Lincoln and their children, Abraham and Sarah. The boy and girl were sent first to one humble school and then to another, their schoolmasters being Zachariah Riney and Caleb Hazel. Of Caleb it was said by one of his less famous pupils : " He perhaps could teach spelling and reading and indifferent writing, and possibly could cipher to the Rule of Three ; but he had no other qualifications of a teacher, unless we accept large size and bodily strength."

In the year after Waterloo the happy-go-lucky Thomas at last realized that he would never be any better if he remained where he was, and that the best he could do there was very far from well. Accordingly the family transferred themselves and their scanty stock of belongings to the more fertile State of Indiana and settled at a place called Pigeon Creek, where Thomas ran up a temporary shelter for them. This shelter was a shed, fourteen feet square, made of small, unhewn logs, enclosed on three sides only and devoid of floor, door, or windows. Behind and all round lay dense forests of walnut, beech, and maple, shagged with a thick undergrowth of sumach and wild grape-vine.

After a time the Lincolns moved into a more ambitious dwelling —a cabin eighteen feet square, built of hewed logs, and furnished with a table, a few stools, and a pewter dish or two. In the angle of the roof there was a tiny loft to which the boy Abraham mounted every evening by means of pegs driven between the chinks in the wall. Has any great man ever had a less joyful childhood than his, spent between a dull, unpractical father and an anxious, ailing mother in a rough hut on the fringe of a wilderness! But we have the assurance of people who remembered him in those days, that the dark, long-legged, silent Kentucky boy had his share of boyish high spirits and harmless mischief. Happier times came with the coming of Thomas Lincoln's second wife, whom he married a year after the death of the first, and who arrived at Pigeon Creek in a wagon squeaking with its load of such household stuff as little Abraham and Sarah had never seen before—such luxuries as feather beds and a bureau of polished walnut-wood! The second Mrs Lincoln was not the least bit like the stepmother of the fairy-tale. She encouraged her stepson's love of learning, and made no objection even when he seized fragments of chalk or charcoal and practised writing on the walls, the floor, and the back of the one and only shovel! Opportunities modest and few, but none the less precious, soon came for Abraham to acquire a few more crumbs of that education for which he hungered so keenly. At a log-built schoolhouse whose windows were filled with oiled paper instead of glass he continued the studies begun under Riney and Hazel in his old home. Later he attended another school, but not for long, as it was four miles' hard plodding from his home, and his father was then making a feeble and unsuccessful effort to teach him the carpenter's craft. Andrew Crawford, the master of this last school, introduced a new lesson which would have appealed more to the grave and stately Washington than it did to the awkward, overgrown Lincoln—a lesson in deportment. In the course of this lesson the boys and girls had to practise welcoming guests, presenting them to one another, showing them in and out of the room, and so forth, with as much grace as they could muster or Mr Crawford could impart. Geography and astronomy do not seem to have been included in the curriculum, but Abraham knew enough about the heavenly bodies to be able to explain to his schoolfellow Kate Roby, as they watched the moon sink behind the trees, "*We* do the sinking." Whereupon, as she afterward confessed, Kate promptly dubbed him a fool. It would, indeed, have required more than common foresight to see a future President of the United States, and one of the greatest of them, in that lank, dark lad, six feet two inches tall, with the shock of wiry hair, the deep-set, far-gazing eyes, whose usual school attire was

LINCOLN WRITING ON A SHOVEL
W. Rainey, R I

" buckskin breeches, a linsey-woolsey shirt, and a cap made of the fur of the squirrel or coon." These breeches, moreover, "were baggy and lacked of several inches meeting the tops of his shoes, thereby exposing the sharp and narrow bones of his shins."

There still exists a leaf from this uncouth scholar's school note-book, on which, beneath the tables of weights and measures, he has written :

> Abraham Lincoln,
> His hand and pen ;
> He will be good,
> But God knows when.

Unlike Napoleon, then languishing in the *petite île appartenante aux Anglais*, Lincoln excelled in penmanship. He became so famous for his skill that younger boys used to ask him to set them copies. There must have been a twinkle in his eye as he traced this couplet in a fair, flowing script :

> Good boys who to their books apply
> Will all be great men by and by.

Not *all*, perhaps ! But the seeds of true greatness were in at least *one* boy of the Kentucky backwoods, and he was born with that generous, compassionate nature that made him exclaim when, in 1831, he saw a slave-auction for the first time : " By God, boys, let's get away from this ! If ever I get a chance to hit that thing [he meant slavery], I'll hit it *hard*." Greatness of soul, pitifulness of heart, deep-rooted and inborn, made that tall, sad-eyed American shoulder a tremendous burden and take a decision of terrible significance when, thirty years later, he called a special session of Congress and proclaimed a blockade of the Southern ports,

CRADLE OF THE KING OF ROME
The one given to Marie Louise by the citizens of Paris is in Vienna, this one is at Versailles

thereby beginning that memorable war which ended Slavery in the United States for ever.

In the spring of the year 1811 the citizens of Paris gave a gorgeous birthday gift to the little son just born to the Emperor Napoleon and his rosy-cheeked Austrian Empress, Marie Louise. This gift was a cradle, wrought all of gold. Over the baby's head

a winged Victory held a laurel-wreath, from which hung silken curtains fringed with gold ; at the foot there was a golden eagle with wings outstretched, and all round were golden garlands of palms and laurels and vine-leaves. Bonfires and rockets welcomed the important and much-wished-for prince. Up in a balloon went a dauntless lady, Madame Blanchard, to scatter leaflets over lonely French villages with the joyful news. Whenever the boy, the King of the Romans, as he was called, began to walk Napoleon amused himself by clapping the famous cocked hat on the little curly head, buckling his sword over the white lace frock, and then kneeling to catch the quaint figure that would come toddling eagerly toward him. Or he would make faces in the mirror to win a laugh from his son, and scold him, though gently, if

NAPOLEON AND THE INFANT KING OF ROME
Baron Myrbach

he was frightened and cried instead. The gruff, stern Emperor was wax in those baby fingers. Even when he was holding a Council, with sentries set to guard the door, the childish voice demanding admittance and proclaiming " C'est le petit Roi ! " always made the sentry's sword dip and the guarded door fly open. Le petit Roi, as he dubbed himself, was a charming little fellow, loyal to his playmates, quick to pity any one in trouble, devoted to every one who was kind to him. He had a tiny carriage drawn by two pet lambs, and when he appeared in the Tuileries garden driving his woolly team the people of Paris gathered round, shouting with delight.

In 1812, while the Emperor was far away on the disastrous Russian campaign, Marie Louise had a portrait painted of *le petit Roi*, and sent it, across many perilous leagues of snow, to the Imperial camp. Napoleon had the picture set up outside his own tent, so that all his officers and some of his bravest men might see it. He watched unseen from behind the flap of the tent as, one by one, the scarred and grizzled veterans stepped forward, clicked heels, saluted the portrait of the child who they believed would be their Emperor some day, and then stepped smartly back again. On his return to Paris Napoleon held a great military review in the *Champ de Mars*, and insisted on taking *le petit Roi* with him on his famous white charger, Marengo, though some people thought that the boy, not yet three years old, might be frightened by the rolling drums, the nodding plumes, and the clashing weapons. Far from being frightened, he clapped his hands with glee. But all this splendour did not make him an unboyish boy. When his governess asked him what he would like best as a reward for being unusually good, he answered promptly : " To be allowed to paddle in the mud."

THE INFANT KING OF ROME
F. Gérard
Photo Alinari

After Waterloo Napoleon never again beheld the son whom he loved better than anything else on earth. For those six dreary years at St Helena he had little or no news of the boy, except that he was in the hands of the Austrians at the Court of his maternal grandfather, and his father's most relentless foe. A portrait of the King of Rome hung on the wall of the room in which Napoleon died. And far away in Austria an eleven-year-old boy was ply-ing his Austrian tutors with questions. " Is my papa in Africa ? Is he in America ? *Where* is he ? " A determined effort was made to blot out from his mind all memories of his father and of France. He was given the Austrian title of Duke of Reichstadt ; he was taught to speak German instead of French ; at the age of sixteen he received a captaincy in the White Hussars of his grandfather, the Emperor Francis I. of Austria. Soon he began to cease to speak of the things his tutors wanted him to forget ; but he was very far from forgetting. Somehow it became known in France that Napoleon's son remained steadfastly French at heart. And some one there, by a happy thought, nicknamed him *l'Aiglon*, ' the Eaglet.' The great fierce Eagle had died upon the rock of St Helena in 1821 ; but the Eaglet might yet return to the aerie. A vain dream ! Twelve years after his father's death l'Aiglon lay dead in the palace of Schonbrunn, in the very room, a stately room with arrased walls and a polished floor inlaid with rare woods, that Napoleon had occupied in 1805, after the battle of Ulm. So perished one of the most romantic, picturesque, and unfortunate of nineteenth-century boys.

In the years immediately before the battle of Waterloo there had been much anxious military preparation round the English coasts. Stout citizens had enrolled themselves in volunteer regiments, and could be seen drilling in tight, braided tunics, with the aid of dummy rifles and bewildered cart-horses, to the no small glee of all the boys for miles around. Even after the worst perils seemed to be past, and telescopes pointed from Dover cliffs no longer revealed the camp of the French forces concentrated at Boulogne for the invasion of England, the garrison towns on the south coast still hummed with activity. And in the years that came after Waterloo there still remained a heightened colour, an intenser movement, at such places as Portsmouth, Chatham, and Dover. At Chatham there lived from 1816 to 1821 a quick-eyed, observant small boy on whose baby mind such scenes as these made a vivid and lasting impression : " The gay, bright regiments always coming and going, the continual paradings and firings . . . the sham-sieges and sham-defences, the ships floating out in the Medway with their far visions of the sea." This boy was Charles Dickens. His father, John Dickens, a well-meaning, careless, feeble sort of fellow, was a clerk in the Navy Pay Office, and his duties kept him, while his eldest son was a child, in the very place which of all others would charm childish eyes. Many of the redcoats whom Charles watched drilling on the parade-ground must have fought against the terrible " Boney " not many years before ; several of the black-and-white timbered warships at anchor in the Medway may have been units in the fleet that Nelson led to triumph at Trafalgar. What a gorgeous vision for a boy with a sense of romantic colour ! But Charles was not allowed to enjoy it long. When he was between nine and ten years old his father was recalled to London, and the grimy gloom of a mean street in Camden Town suc-ceeded the cheerful glow of Chatham. Mr Dickens was soon deep in difficulties and in debt. And then Mrs Dickens made a gallant effort to mend the fallen fortunes of her family. She took a house in Gower Street, Blooms-bury, and on the front-door she fixed a large brass plate bearing the words *Mrs Dickens' Establishment*. Little Charles became useful at this point. " I left," he wrote, " at a great many other doors a great many circulars calling attention to the merits of the Establishment. Yet nobody ever came to school, nor do I recollect that anybody ever proposed to come, or that the least preparation was made to receive anybody." It was upon Charles, a " quick, eager, delicate " boy, " soon hurt, bodily or mentally," that the mis-fortunes of his family fell with the most crushing force. John Dickens exclaimed, when he was arrested for not paying his debts, " The sun has set upon me for ever ! " But he soon

NAPOLEON AT BOULOGNE
Baron Myrbach

cheered up, and was probably more comfortable in the Marshal-sea Prison, where he played skittles with his fellow-prisoners and sang songs and made speeches to them, than he had been at Camden Town. He does not seem to have felt any regret or any anxiety for his small son, who then began that dreary chapter of his life related in *David Copperfield*, working from morning till night pasting paper covers on pots of blacking in a half-ruined, rat-haunted warehouse near Hungerford Bridge. For his services he received six or seven shillings a week, most of which he spent on twopennyworths of boiled pudding and penny-worths of coffee. "No words can express," wrote Dickens many years later, "the secret agony of my soul. The deep remembrance of the sense I had of being utterly without hope now . . . of the misery it was to my young heart to believe that day by day what I had learned, and thought, and delighted in . . . would pass from me, little by little, never to be brought back any more . . . cannot be written. From Monday morning until Saturday night I had no advice, no encouragement, no consolation, no assistance, no support, of any kind, from any one, that I can call to mind as I hope to go to heaven ! "

The worst fears of this forlorn little waif were *not* to be realized. All that he had " learned and thought and delighted in " was *not* to pass from him. Time, luck, and his own vivid, eager mind rescued him from the slough of ignorance and despair into which he had sunk almost knee-deep. And he, whose own schooling had been so interrupted, so insufficient, lived to paint many memorable portraits of schoolmasters, good and bad. Seventeen or eighteen years after his ordeal at the blacking warehouse was over, when the *Pickwick Papers* and *Oliver Twist* had brought him undreamt-of fame and fortune, Dickens was collecting the in-gredients for another novel. One day he pasted into the little green notebook which was his constant companion the following advertisement, cut from a newspaper :

EDUCATION FOR LITTLE CHILDREN.—Terms, 14 to 18 guineas per annum. No extras or vacations. The system of education embraces the wide range of each useful and ornamental study suited to the tender age of the dear children. Maternal care and kindness may be relied on.

It was said, and generally believed, that scattered up and down

England, but more especially in the remoter northern counties, there were at that time mysterious schools to which people who wanted to get rid of children could send them with every confidence ; the sort of schools that Richard III might have been glad to hear of for his two nephews ; the sort of schools that might have appealed strongly to the uncle of *The Babes in the Wood*. The words " no vacations " in an advertisement were a pretty broad hint ; and such hints were acted upon by so many unscrupulous people that the advertisements soon began to grow more and more frequent. Nobody did anything about it. There was then no inspection of schools by the State. The laws against cruelty were weakly framed and weakly administered.

Dickens, whose own childish hardships had left him with a passionate fervour of pity for ill-treated children, determined that in his forthcoming book, *Nicholas Nickleby*, the whole infamous system of " no-vacation " schools should be exposed. To this determination we owe the grim picture, half-pitiful and half-comical, of Mr Wackford Squeers and Dotheboys Hall.

> Mr Squeers's appearance was not prepossessing. He had but one eye, and the popular prejudice runs in favour of two . . . a trifle below the middle size, he wore a white neckerchief with long ends, and a suit of scholastic black ; but his coat sleeves being a great deal too long, and his trousers a great deal too short, he appeared ill at ease in his clothes, and as if he were in a perpetual state of astonishment at finding himself so respectable.

This odd-looking follower of Orbilius promised that boys entrusted to his care should not only be " instructed in *all* languages, living and dead, mathematics, orthography, geometry, trigonometry, astronomy, fortification, single stick (if desired), and every *other* branch of classical literature," but also that they should have the advantage of " every beautiful principle that Mrs Squeers could instil, every wholesome luxury that Yorkshire could afford."

Mr Squeers's educational system was even more simple than that of Parson Barlow in *Sandford and Merton*. He made no attempt to enlarge the knowledge or improve the minds of *his* pupils, but went to work in this much more energetic manner :

> " Now, then, where's the first boy ? "
> " Please, sir, he's cleaning the back parlour window." . . .
> " So he is, to be sure," rejoined Squeers. " We go upon the

practical mode of teaching, Nickleby. . . . C-l-e-a-n, verb active, to make bright or scour. W-i-n, win, d-e-r, der, winder, a casement. When the boy knows this out of book, he goes and does it. It's just the same principle as the use of the globes. Where's the second boy ? "

" Please, sir, he's weeding the garden," replied a small voice.

" To be sure," said Squeers, by no means disconcerted, " So he is. B-o-t, bot, t-i-n, tin, bottin, n-e-y, ney, bottinney, noun substantive, a knowledge of plants. When he has learned that bottiney means a knowledge of plants, he goes and knows 'em. That is our system, Nickleby ; what do you think of it ? "

" It's a very useful one, at any rate," answered Nicholas.

So much for the instruction at Dotheboys Hall. As for the wholesome luxuries of Yorkshire, the only treat which the boys had was a dose of brimstone and treacle, ladled out every morning in a huge spoon which had to be emptied at one gulp. The picture drawn by Dickens was so ghastly, public opinion awoke ; new laws were made, old laws were stiffened, and the " no-vacation " school was soon a thing of the past. The story of *Nicholas Nickleby* was read and admired on the other side of the Channel, and it certainly gave the Comtesse de Segur the idea for her lively book, *Un Bon Petit Diable*, of which the hero, called Charles (perhaps as a compliment to Dickens), is sent to a terrible institution in Scotland, kept by a dominie with the promising name of Monsieur Old Nick, whose assistant master is Monsieur Boxear, and whose pupils are fed upon beans cooked in sour butter, and salad made with salt and water.

Though Creakle, the flogging pedagogue in *David Copperfield*, described himself, not without reason, as a Tartar, he was not quite such a Tartar as Squeers, and he had at least one point in common with the far kindlier schoolmaster of " The Deserted Village "—his trick of cracking jokes, at which all the boys hastened to laugh " with counterfeited glee." There is, however, another schoolmaster in *David Copperfield*, and another school. We love old rusty, dusty Dr Strong of Canterbury as cordially as we loathe Creakle and Squeers ; we are glad to pass from the clamour of Dotheboys Hall to the quietness of his school under the shadow of the great Kentish cathedral.

It was very gravely and decorously ordered, and on a sound system, with an appeal, in everything, to the honour and good faith of the boys. . . . We had noble games out of hours, and plenty of liberty ; but even then, as I remember, we were well spoken of in the town, and rarely did any disgrace, by our appearance or manner, to the reputation of Doctor Strong and Doctor Strong's boys.

Dickens's great rival, Thackeray, has left us several lively glimpses of schoolboy doings, chiefly at his own old school, the Charterhouse, which was also the old school of John Wesley and John Leech. He tells us how little Rawdon Crawley began his career at this " famous old collegiate institution." Before the first week was over a bigger boy had constituted him his " fag, shoeblack and breakfast-toaster, initiated him into the mysteries of the Latin Grammar, and thrashed him three or four times, but not severely." Young Rawdon "had plenty money, which he spent in treating his comrades royally to raspberry tarts," and on Saturdays his father—an unusually companionable Papa—

A CHARTERHOUSE BOY IN THACKERAY'S TIME

Gertrude Demain Hammond, R I.

would take him and one of his schoolfellows to the theatre, and treat them to what sounds a rather overwhelming supper of " pastry, oysters, and porter " after the play.

Here and there, one by one, these more approachable Papas began to appear as the middle of the century drew near. But there remained, set high on a pedestal for all the world to admire, a perfect and most impressive example of the old, stately type in the person of Queen Victoria's husband, Albert the Prince Consort. Both he and the Queen were anxious, and rightly anxious,

276

that their eldest son, born in 1841, should grow up to be a good, wise, and enlightened man. But they set about the task of making him into such a man in a sadly stern and unimaginative way. Round the Prince of Wales, a very diminutive blue-eyed boy much in awe of his majestic Papa, they gathered a company of grave elderly tutors who plied their task under the very eye

of the Prince Consort, and with the aid of almost daily advice from him. Greatly to Papa's astonishment and dismay, the Prince of Wales did not seem to take the slightest interest in his lessons ! We do not share that astonishment when we realize how desperately dull and dry the studies of the future King Edward VII. were made. He was allowed no story-books, not even the novels of Sir Walter Scott from which so many happier children have learnt to see the colour and romance of history. Tables of facts and columns of dates were all that the poor Prince was given to learn. Mathematics, political

EDWARD VII AS A BOY
X. F. Winterhalter
Photo Mansell

economy, geology, masses of useful and uninteresting information, were poured upon his defenceless head. It would really seem as if his tutors, Mr Gibbs and Mr Birch, were of one mind with that terrible old dame in *Dombey and Son*, Mrs Pipchin :

> " There is a great deal of nonsense—and worse—talked about young people not being pressed too hard at first, and being tempted on, and all the rest of it, Sir," said Mrs Pipchin, impatiently rubbing her hooked nose, " It never was thought of in my time, and it has no business to be thought of now. *My* opinion is ' Keep 'em at it.' "

So the hapless Prince of Wales *was* " kept at it," as sternly as even Mrs Pipchin could have desired. Papa *did* realize, however, that a certain amount of recreation was necessary. Accordingly, from time to time, one or two carefully chosen Eton boys were invited to spend an afternoon at Windsor Castle, and there, under the freezing eye of the Prince Consort, they were supposed to ' play ' with their future King. What ease or fun or spirit there can have been in their games it is difficult to imagine. One of the Etonians thus summoned to disport themselves at the Castle has recorded that the royal Papa " inspired a feeling of dread " in all of them. Still the Prince made little or no progress with his studies. It was decided, after the experiment of inviting eminent scientists to dine with him once a week had been tried without much success, that university lectures might help to expand his reluctant mind. *One* university would not satisfy Papa ; there must be at least *three*, Edinburgh, Oxford, and Cambridge. But at none was the seventeen-year-old boy to mingle with his fellow-undergraduates, or to take any part in their sports. No, he must always be surrounded by " serious men of advanced years."

The sad plight of the young Prince touched the heart of that motley-clad national philosopher, Mr Punch, in whose pages there appeared, toward the end of 1859, some verses entitled " A Prince at High Pressure." It began :

> Thou dear little Wales, sure the saddest of tales
> Is the tale of the studies with which they are cramming thee ;
> In thy tuckers and bibs handed over to Gibbs,
> Who for eight years with solid instruction was ramming thee.

Must he, cried the writer, take to " Edinburgh next his poor noddle perplexed," then to Oxford, then to Cambridge, with its

> Dynamics and statics and pure mathematics

Punch adds anxiously :

> Where next the boy may go to swell the farrago
> We haven't yet heard, but the palace they're plotting in ;
> To Berlin, Jena, Bonn, he'll no doubt be passed on,
> And drop in for a finishing touch, p'raps, at Gottingen.

And he concludes :

> 'Gainst indulging a passion for high pressure fashion
> Of Prince-training *Punch* would uplift loyal warning ;
> Locomotives we see over-stoked soon may be,
> Till the super-steamed boiler blows up one fine morning.

The danger would have been very real had " dear little Wales " yielded to the high pressure. Fortunately for himself at the time, and for his country later on, the torrents of " solid instruction " glanced as lightly off his brain as drops of water off a duck's back.

The new, breezy, good-humoured spirit voiced by *Punch* made itself felt more slowly at Windsor Castle than anywhere else in England, but by degrees its keen, cheery breath blew even the thickest and most historic cobwebs away. With this spirit came new ideas and a new sort of idealism. Its first triumph was won before Queen Victoria's accession when, in 1827, Dr Arnold became headmaster of Rugby School, and since then the triumphs have been so many that there now seem to be no fields left to conquer.

In *Tom Brown's Schooldays* there will endure for ever the bluff, brave, exhilarating atmosphere breathed by the boys who were at Rugby under Arnold. Outwardly much has changed. Tom Brown set out for school on the top of a stage-coach, to " the music of rattling harness and the ring of the horses' feet on the hard road, and the glare of the two bright lamps through the steaming hoar-frost over the leaders' ears in the darkness." Football was played in white duck trousers then, and picking

A RUGBY SCHOOLBOY OF " TOM BROWN " PERIOD

flowers was a favourite amusement on half-holidays. Yet the differences between a great English school to-day and Arnold's Rugby are few and small compared with the differences between the public-school standard as he found it in 1827 and as he left it in 1842.

The introduction of railways added a new terror to schoolboy life in the nineteenth century, for it made possible—and even easy—the more frequent presence of Papa and Mamma, he in his stove-pipe hat, she in her coal-scuttle bonnet, at speech-days. And speech-days were already, and are still, rather overwhelming occasions, when the headmaster sits looking so benign while nervous boys recite passages from Demosthenes and Cicero, or struggle through scenes from Molière, and while some distin-

SPEECH DAY

The King's School, Canterbury, holding its speech-day in the cathedral chapter-house in
Victorian times. This is the oldest public school in England , its foundation dates back
to the sixth century.

guished ' old boy ' gets up and modestly tells his successors what
an inattentive and unremarkable pupil he used to be.

Not every ' Head ' had Arnold's rare gift of inspiring both awe
and enthusiasm in the hearts of his scholars. '' We couldn't,''

280

says Tom Hughes, after describing his old headmaster as he appeared in the pulpit of the school chapel, " we couldn't enter into half that we heard—but we listened, as all boys in their better moods will listen (aye, and men, too, for the matter of that) to a man whom we felt to be with all his heart and soul and strength striving against whatever was mean and unmanly and unrighteous in our little world."

The torch which Dr Arnold held aloft has been passed from hand to hand across far lands and wide seas. The spirit of which he was the instrument lives and " fulfils itself in many ways " to-day. As the long pageant of boy-life through the ages passes before us, with its gay and sombre colours and shadows, and then narrows and recedes into the distance again, we see that the first great influence which moulded the minds of men and the lives of their sons was the love of learning. And then we see how to that love there has been added another, not less noble and not less powerful for good—the love of the open air, of sport and pluck and fair play. This is the inspiration of one of the most stirring of all school poems, " Clifton Chapel," written by Sir Henry New-bolt when his son became a scholar at his own old school. It is this that tells a boy—

> To set the cause above renown,
>   To love the game beyond the prize,
> To honour, while you strike him down,
>   The foe that comes with fearless eyes .
> To count the life of battle good,
>   And dear the land that gave you birth,
> And dearer yet the brotherhood
>   That binds the brave of all the earth.
>
> .   .   .   .
>
> To-day and here the fight's begun,
>   Of the great fellowship you're free :
> Henceforth the School and you are one,
>   And what you are the race shall be

"THE ROCKET"

A.D. 1840

WHEN I grow up, I have always said,
  Just like my Papa I'd be,
I'd have a cane with a golden head,
  A cigar as big as a tree,
A high top-hat with a little brim
  And gloves like a lemon-rind ;
I used to want to be *just* like him—
  But now I have changed my mind.

I used to think that it might be sport
  To doze when dessert was done
Over sugary fruit and a glass of port
  (Most likely more than one) ;
To fold *The Times* with a rustling swish
  And explain it all to Mamma ;
But I've changed my mind, and I do *not* wish
  To be just like my Papa

For I've seen " The Rocket "—think how it feels
  To have seen " The Rocket " go,
With her yellow sides and her yellow wheels
  And her funnel white as snow !—
And the steam and the smoke puffed silver and black,
  And the screaming whistle blew,
And she went so fast on the iron track
  She was gone before you knew.

Like a long brown streak the coaches passed ;
  In each window there was a face ;
What lucky people to go so fast,
  Puff-puffing from place to place !
While " The Rocket " is running to Liverpool
  And to Manchester back again
Two men must drive ; and when I leave school
  I'm going to be *one* of those men

When I'm grown up I will never wear
  Kid-gloves or a topper tall,
Or read *The Times*—no, I shall not care
  If I never read at all,

And have no port-wine and no sugary fruit,
    No cane and no big cigar ;
I'll be black and oily from head to foot
    As engine-drivers are.

Then *I*'ll drive " The Rocket " and make her fly
    As fast as ever she can ;
I won't be a soldier—no ; not I—
    A Judge or a clergyman,
Or a King, or a Member of Parliament ;
    In my engine I will sit,
And be oily and black to my heart's content
    And—*not like Papa one bit !*

INDEX

ÆLFRIC, Abbot, 115
Æneid, the, 82, 83
Africanus, Scipio, 74
Aidan, 97
Akhnaton, King of Egypt, 36
Albert, Prince Consort, 276 *sqq.*
Alcuin, 115, 124, 125, 126
Aldhelm, 123 *sqq.*
Alfred, King, 98, 115, 119, 128
Amen-Rā, 34, 41, 47
America, United States of, 109, 237
Androcles, 248
Anglo-Saxon boy, the, 113 *sqq.*
Anne of Denmark, Queen, 210, 216
  sqq.
Anthony's, St, School, 205
Apprentices, Statute of the, 172
Archytas of Tarentum, 57
Aristophanes, 62, 69, 70
Arne, Dr, 241
Arnold, Dr, 279 *sqq.*
Arthur, King, 173
Arthur, Prince (in Shakespeare's
  King John), 203
Ascham, Roger, 203, 237
Athelstane, King, 101 *sqq*
Augustus, the Emperor, 80

Babees' Book, The, 167 *sqq.*, 172
Basilikon Doron, the, 211 *sqq.*, 224,
  226
Becket, Thomas à, 159
Bede, The Venerable, 98, 114, 122
Berlichingen, Gotz von der, 168
  sqq.
Beverley, John of, 115, 130, 243
" Birds' Latin," 133
" Bison, The," 29
Blifil, Master, 247 *sqq.*
Bonaparte—see Napoleon
Bouflers, Ambroise de, 253
Boy-bishops, 178, 189
Brienne, 255
Britain, Celtic, 22 *sqq.*
Bronze Age, the, 17, 22, 28

Buchanan, George, 195 *sqq.*, 209,
  213
Burton, Dr, 243
Busby, Dr, 249, 250
Byron, Lord, 263

CÆSAR, JULIUS, 26, 28, 87, 161
Caligula, 87, 89, 91
Canterbury, 118, 124
Capitoline wreath, the, 84, 88
Caracalla, 89
Carey, Sir Robert, 210
Cave-boy, the, 11 *sqq.*
Celts, the, 23
Centeville, Osmond de, 139 *sqq.*
" Chapel Royal, A Child of the,"
  207
Chapel Royal, the Children of the,
  204 *sqq.*
Chariots, Egyptian, 42 *sqq* ; early
  British, 26, 27, 28 , Roman, 87 ,
  Viking, 105
Charlemagne, 96, 126, 128, 143,
  145 *sqq*
Charles I, of England, 210, 213,
  215, 216, 217, 224, 228
Charles II, of England, 224 *sqq.*
Charles the Bold, of Burgundy,
  165, 166
Charles the Simple, of France, 109,
  136, 137
Charterhouse, the, 239
Chaucer, Geoffrey, 172
Chivalry, rise of, 144
Cicero, 82, 195, 279
Circus, the Roman, 88 *sqq.*
" Clay Warriors," 71
Cock-fighting, 189
Colet, Dean, 188 *sqq*
Colloquia, of Ælfric, 115 ; of
  Erasmus, 189, 217 ; of Horman,
  181
Columbus, Christopher, 184
Constantinople, 98, 109, 128
Cook, Captain, 236

www.ingramcontent.com/pod-product-compliance
Lightning Source LLC
Chambersburg PA
CBHW031148270326
41931CB00006B/187

9 781589 637825